Zhuangzi

Thinking through the Inner Chapters

WANG Bo

Contemporary Chinese Scholarship in Daoist Studies

sponsored by

Center for Daoist Studies, Peking University
北京大学道学研究中心

Three Pines Press
PO Box 530416
St. Petersburg, FL 33747
www.threepinespress.com

Translated by Livia Kohn

Funding for this translation was provided by Mr. Kong Xiangping 孔祥平 of Yuanlianhe Real Estate. Management and interface coordination was supplied by Ms. Wang Lina 王丽娜.

9 8 7 6 5 4 3 2 1

First Edition, 2014 – Printed in the United States of America
⊗ This edition is printed on acid-free paper that meets the American National Standard Institute Z39.48 Standard.
Distributed in the United States by Three Pines Press.

Cover art: Traditional Chinese Landscape. Designed by Li Huanhuan 李欢欢.

Library of Congress Cataloging-in-Publication Data
Wang, Bo, 1967-
[Zhuangzi zhe xue. English]
Zhuangzi : thinking through the inner chapters / Bo Wang ; translated by Livia Kohn. -- First edition.
p. cm. -- (Contemporary Chinese Scholarship in Daoist Studies)
Includes bibliographical references and index.
ISBN 978-1-931483-60-5
1. Zhuangzi. Nanhua jing. I. Kohn, Livia, 1956- translator. II. Title.
BL1900.C576W3432 2014
299.5'1482--dc23

2014005900

Contents

Editors' Greetings

Chinese thought and culture have often been identified with Confucianism, and while this is certainly reasonable, it does not present an accurate understanding of the complexity of this civilization. In the pre-Qin period, the so-called hundred schools of thought flourished: various thinkers disputed an abundance of unique ideas and numerous perspectives. The Han came to power in 206 BCE. Their political leaders leaned toward Confucianism, so that other theories and thoughts slowly teetered away, including Daoism—a term then used for the combined thought of the *Daode jing* and *Zhuangzi.*

Although governments since then for the most part have not officially recognized Daoism, its authority has penetrated well into the core of Chinese life and thought. Far more than just a complement to Confucianism, it has shaped Chinese culture and influenced many renowned figures: politicians and businessmen, artists and authors, poets and musicians, healers and strategists, as well as all sorts of spiritual and cultural leaders. Its role has always been significant and indispensable, just as important as that of Confucianism for the understanding of China, where the two are not competing or opposing forces but two constructive and integrative sides of the same cultural coin.

Despite this fact, Daoism has been largely overlooked or badly misunderstood in the English-speaking world. The purpose of this translation series is to return to the genuine foundation of Chinese thought and culture by introducing major works on Daoism by leading contemporary Chinese scholars. This series is to provide English readers with access to a vast realm of knowledge about Daoism as viewed from the perspective of Chinese scholars, opening new dimensions of appreciation and mutual scholarly interaction.

—Chen Guying 陳鼓應, Beijing
—Robin R Wang 王蓉蓉, Los Angeles

Translator's Note

This work represents the translation of Wang Bo's 王博 *Zhuangzi zhexue* 莊子哲學 (The Thought of Zhuangzi), published first in 2004 at Peking University and since then reprinted several times to accommodate the over 40,000 copies sold. Rather than produce a close, literal translation, my brief was to create a free rendition easily accessible to a Western audience. To this end, I have made certain adaptations.

For one, I have integrated footnotes to textual references into the text and replaced often lengthy citations of the original *Zhuangzi*, commonly followed by rephrasing in modern Chinese, with summaries, maintaining passages from the *Zhuangzi* only when they were directly relevant to the author's commentary. Those passages I retranslated in accordance with Professor Wang's reading, using the established translations by Burton Watson, A. C. Graham, Victor Mair, and Brook Ziporyn as guidelines.

For another, matching common Western standards, I have changed reference to passages in all classical works, such as the *Lunyu* or *Mengzi* as well as the *Zhuangzi* itself, from named chapter titles to chapter numbers. In identifying exact locations of passages, the website of the Chinese Text Project (www.ctext.org) was invaluable. In addition, I have added references to Western (mostly English) translations of these works and compiled a bibliography. All Chinese titles in the bibliography are cited in Wang's book; all English titles go back to the translator.

To avoid repetition, I have furthermore integrated the original Appendix 4 into Appendix 1, and subsumed Appendix 2 into Chapter 2, so that only two appendices remain.

Other than that, I have tightened the presentation as much as feasible and on occasion substituted popular Western phrases for Chinese idioms. I hope this rendition presents Professor Wang's work at its best and stimulates much discussion on our reception and understanding of Zhuangzi's thought and ideas.

—Livia Kohn

Author's Preface

Under all the different modes of government throughout history, Chinese intellectuals have always had two fundamental choices: to participate or withdraw, to serve in office or relax in seclusion. Among ancient thinkers, the most prominent model of the former was particularly Confucius, while the foremost representative of the latter option was Zhuangzi. Not only that, he was also the first to analyze the lifestyle of withdrawal and relaxation in seclusion systematically and to propose a coherent theory. In addition, he provided clear guidance on how best to think about the interconnected relationship between life and world, in the process closely examining the overall meaning of life.

Scholars not only in China and Japan but also in Europe and America have always been well aware that Chinese philosophers or thinkers are strongly concerned with rulership as they are with life. Indeed, Chinese philosophy as a whole emerged from political concerns and discussions of various methods of government. Even the very earliest and most fundamental works—the Six Classics—are based on this. Not only philosophical classics, they are also political mainstays, choke full of ideas, ways, and models of how best to rule. Not only does this apply to the *Songs, History, Rites,* and *Music,* but also to the divinatory *Book of Changes* and the historical chronicle, *Springs and Autumns.*

Having politically relevant documents as fundamental classics has to a large extent inspired the basic character of Chinese culture, to the point even where religion and philosophy could never quite develop as independent, separate fields like they did in the West. Practical thought as found in political philosophy, ethical studies, and the like remained in a leadership role throughout, determining all the major trends of Chinese thought.

The political vision of ancient China relied heavily on the cosmological structure of Heaven, Earth, and Humanity underpinning the world of political power. The legitimization of power thus depended to a large extant on the proper interpretation of, and the right approach to, the order of Heaven and Earth. It established the baseline for all values and rules in the human world, and formed the root of people's identity and actions.

At the pinnacle of this world stood the king or emperor. As understood in the Han dynasty, the character for "king" (*wang* 王) consisted of three horizontal lines signifying Heaven, Humanity, and Earth, plus one vertical stroke, which showed the connecting link between them. That is to say, the ruler was the bridge that connected Heaven and Humanity. The key quality, moreover, that proved the efficacy of this connection was virtue (*de* 德), which most essentially indicates an attitude of venerating Heaven and protecting the people. When the emperor was at one with virtue, he had a firm grip on power; when he was separated from it, he lost all legitimacy to rule—resulting in revolution and dynastic change.

From this perspective, then, there are really only two kinds of government: with and without virtue—later described as "full of Dao" or "Dao-less." Already Confucius describes the choice faced by the learned men of his age under these differing circumstances: "If the world has Dao, come forward; if it lacks Dao, go into hiding" (*Lunyu* 8.13). Knights thus had to make clear decisions as to their behavior and lifestyle, matching rapidly changing political situations. For Confucius, these decisions were fundamentally ethical in nature. As he says about the reality of his time, an ethical person "knows something cannot be done and does it anyway" (14.38). This accurately portrays his position, always in favor of service.

Still, there was also an alternative route: to withdraw and relax in seclusion. This is the route Zhuangzi takes, thereby opening up a completely new and different set of possibilities. During his time, the world was distinctly Dao-less: rulers, warlords, and other men in power had no regard for the people whatsoever. With this attitude, they essentially released the knights from their duty to take on responsibilities in the world. Those who still got involved, like Confucius, would repeatedly sigh, "My ways are not working. I better get on a raft and float out to sea!" (*Lunyu* 5.7).

Zhuangzi, however, does more than sigh. He takes this sentiment and develops it into a systematic philosophy and quintessential way of life. For him, the ultimate meaning of life is not necessarily tied up with the world of political and ethical conduct. Going beyond this, he takes into account the world of mountains and forests, the realm of fields and gardens, as well as more amazing dimensions of life, like Not-Even-Anything Village. In other words, for him life can be found in all sorts of diverse values including, for example, freedom.

In light of this logic, Zhuangzi's philosophical work is of particular importance since it unravels these dimensions of life and world while critically questioning the sacred nature and ubiquity of politics and ethics in his time, thereby making it easier for people to separate life from government and morality. As he puts it, "He who steals a belt buckle pays with his life, while he who steals a state gets to be a feudal lord—and we all know that benevolence and righteousness are to be found at the gates of the feudal lords" (ch. 9).

Zhuangzi was also among the earliest of philosophers to reflect critically on issues of power and knowledge. Power always requires a certain kind of knowledge to be considered absolute truth, serving as an efficient tool of controlling the masses. Once we acknowledge this point, the sacred nature of this so-called absolute knowledge is destroyed, leaving only its concrete and practical value. Pursuing this kind of analysis further, the concept of "nonbeing" (*wu* 無) inevitably emerges as the center of philosophical understanding. In Zhuangzi, nonbeing is a key principle, functioning both as radical negation and to establish a new ultimacy. As principle of negation, it massively demolishes the entrenched world of politics and ethics to the point where anything that exists becomes merely a relative entity. As a principle of ultimacy, it lays the foundation of a completely new way of life.

The core of this new way of life, moreover, is life as a value in itself, combined with concepts of freedom and human rights. Nonbeing in this context destroys any attempt at establishing "being" in whatever form as top principle or in a position of highest value—so it becomes, in effect, like a continuously coiling dragon without head or tail. This, then, has the great benefit of opening a path to new concepts like liberty and equality. If nobody has the power to impose his will and concepts forcefully upon another, each individual must make his own judgments. Zhuangzi's vigorous defense of personal freedom and human rights is both radical and absolute, to the point where he completely abandons all ideas of the "masses" and completely immerses himself in his personal world. "You are not a fish. How can you know the happiness of fish?" he asks (ch. 17). With this question he points to the inherent difficulty of real, mutual communication among people and the forever-fluid nature of perception. For him, an intimate and close commonality is simply not possible.

Still, we should not be too hard on Zhuangzi's abandonment of the mass of the people, since he came from a culture that was excessive in its emphasis on them. Rather, we should understand that, within the philosophical tradition of China, Zhuangzi was among the first to establish a position of reflection on the people, making sure that the role of the whole would not be completely obliterated in favor of individual existence. Making best use of this position, we can move toward a highly beneficial transformation in thinking and living. Maybe because of this Zhuangzi was particular well received by Chinese thinkers of the Enlightenment, such as Yan Fu 嚴复 and Zhang Taiyan 章太炎.

I am not too sure how people in the English-speaking world view Zhuangzi, his life and thought. Some scholars, to be sure, have tried to relate him to certain schools in Western philosophy, such as existentialism. This is fine by me, and I think it can make a valuable contribution to the better mutual understanding between East and West. However, my priority has been, and still is, to explore Zhuangzi as part of a deeper appreciation of China and Chinese culture. As I often tell people, both Zhuangzi and Confucius are great gateways to understanding the heart and world of Chinese intellectuals, in the past as much as today. To gain deeper access to Chinese philosophy over the past 2,000 years, moreover, Zhuangzi undoubtedly represents an example of high erudition and superior eminence.

The publication of my book in this English version would not have been possible without the unfailing support and dedication of several scholars and friends. Thus, Robin Wang arranged for its inclusion in this new series on "Contemporary Chinese Scholarship in Daoist Studies," published by Three Pines Press. Livia Kohn undertook the English translation, for which I am eternally grateful. Her deep enthusiasm for Chinese thought in general and Zhuangzi in particular ensures that this rendition provides the best possible venue for introducing my ideas to the Western world.

Last but not least, a few years ago Carine Defoort of the University of Leuven in Belgium included several chapters as translated by William Crawford in the journal *Contemporary Chinese Thought* (vol. 38, 2007). I would like to take this opportunity to give public recognition of their efforts and express my gratitude to them.

It is due to the unstinting support and continued good work of these scholars that we can now open a new level of dialogue on Zhuangzi with Western thinkers, scholars, and interested readers.

—Bo Wang, Peking University

Introduction

Zhuangzi in His Time

Zhuangzi 莊子 lived in the middle of the Warring States period (479-221 BCE), during an exceptionally vibrant time in terms of philosophy and learning. Both Confucianism and Mohism were already well established, exerting considerable influence on politics, society, daily life, and thought. The tradition begun by Laozi had already developed significantly, and its schools of Huang-Lao and Yang Zhu were highly popular.

In addition, the Legalists, with their emphasis on agriculture and warfare, were so much in tune with the needs of rulers at the time that their representatives occupied leading positions in most feudal states.[1] Beyond all this, the Dialecticians, such as Huizi and Gongsun Long, flourished, exerting their analytical wisdom in disputing many concepts and pursuing key questions. During the same time, or maybe a bit later, there was also Zou Yan 鄒衍, representative of the cosmological theories of yin-yang and the five phases. All these philosophers and strands of thought interacted and disputed actively with each other, creating the potent scene known as "the hundred schools competing" in the middle of the Warring States period.

The question then arises to what degree these various thinkers and ideas influenced Zhuangzi's personal thinking or served as a backdrop for his thought. As Sima Qian 司馬遷 already points out in his *Shiji* 史記 (Record of the Historian), Zhuangzi was in touch with the full spectrum of learning during his time, but to him the schools were not equal, some more dominant and important than others (ch. 63). Just like today, society was inundated by numerous trends of thought, but only very few people truly understood and analyzed them fully. Many trends were, as the Ming philosopher Wang Yangming 王陽明 said, like "wild flowers on

---

[1] The *Shiji* says, "During this period, Qin employed Lord Shang; he enriched the state and strengthened the military. Chu and Wei employed Wu Qi; he was victorious in war and weakened their enemies. Kings Wei and Xuan of Qi employed the followers of Sun Bin and Tian Ji; they made the nobles to the east of Qi pay homage. The whole world was engaged in alliances with or against Qing, and military conquest was held in high regard" (ch. 62).

the mountainside"—blooming and wilting in solitude, remaining unseen as if they never existed. For this reason, if we are not content with a superficial discussion and want to appreciate Zhuangzi's thought in some depth, we must begin by looking at his writings and see just who and what exerted an influence on him.

The seven Inner Chapters make it clear that he paid most attention to Confucianism and Mohism.[2] The text says, "Dao is obscured by petty accomplishments; speech is obscured by vain show," particularly referring to "the rights and wrongs of the Confucians and the Mohists" (ch. 2). Taking the theories of these two schools as an illustration of disputes on right and wrong thus indicates both their pervasive influence at the time and the special place they occupied in Zhuangzi's thought.[3]

Especially the Confucians were at the center of Zhuangzi's attention and criticism. Thus, when he speaks of "a man who has wisdom enough to fill one office effectively, good conduct enough to impress one community, virtue enough to please one ruler, or talent enough to be called into service in one state" (ch. 1), he obviously portrays the typical conduct of the Confucian gentleman official. For Zhuangzi, such a one is like the little quail: "It gives a great leap and flies up, but never gets more than ten or twelve yards off the ground before it comes down fluttering among the weeds and brambles." This critter couldn't be more different from the great Peng 鵬 bird, which "mounts the wind and takes off into the sky" (ch. 1).

The parable of the sage-king Yao 堯 trying to cede the throne to his adviser Xu You 許由 (ch. 1) similarly is an attack on Confucian veneration for sage rulers. "Great benevolence is not benevolent," Zhuangzi says. "The way I see it, the rules of benevolence and righteousness and the paths of right and wrong are all hopelessly snarled and jumbled. How could I know anything about such discriminations?" (ch. 2). This is directly aimed at the central doctrines of Confucianism.

The allegory of Lao Dan's 老聃 death (ch. 3) similarly has Qin Shi 秦失 give three cries and leave, representing an attack on the Confucian system of rites and music. Other chapters make the same point,

---

[2] Sima Qian says that Zhuangzi's work "exercised criticism of the Confucians and Mohists," indicating that these two schools were his most important opponents (*Shiji* 63; Fung 1952, 1:221).

[3] This is also reflected in the last chapter of the book (ch. 33). Although not written by Zhuangzi himself, it closely matches the attitude of his followers. While criticizing all kinds of different thinkers, it dominantly targets Confucians and Mohists.

Zhuangzi featuring Confucius (Kongzi 孔子) and his most important disciple Yan Hui 顏回 directly in various tales. Hovering between truth and fiction, facetiousness and seriousness, he places words into Confucius's mouth that criticize Confucian teachings. This way of ridiculing the world is a major hallmark of Zhuangzi's grotesque and extravagant style. Any suggestion that he seriously esteemed Confucius, or even supposing that he was a Confucian himself, is not only ridiculous but also absurd and unfounded.

Sima Qian correctly states that the book *Zhuangzi* belongs among "those who discredited Confucius" (ch. 63). Some may suggest that *Zhuangzi* chapters 29 and 31, cited in the *Shiji*, as well as other sections of the Outer and Miscellaneous Chapters, reveal an attitude somewhat different from that of the Inner Chapters. In my view, if there is such discrepancy, it is merely one of style: the Outer and Miscellaneous Chapters are obvious where the Inner Chapters are subtle. What I mean by "obvious" is that they express content more directly, like prose poems in poetry; "subtle" indicates a more convoluted style, like metaphors in poetry. "Obvious" is when things are straightforward and uninhibited; "subtle" means that there are many areas containing hints and reversals.

The image of Confucius in the Inner Chapters, moreover, can be divided into two kinds: for one, he is the object of ridicule or lecturing; for another, he is the spokesman of Zhuangzi's thought. As an object of ridicule, he appears, for example, when Jie Yu 接輿, the madman of Chu, sings a song passing by Confucius's door (ch. 4) or when the master speaks with Shentu Jia 申徒嘉 who had lost a foot (ch. 5). As Zhuangzi's spokesman, Confucius is pervasive in the remainder of the text. The two roles are also distinct in their literary presentation.

When ridiculed, Confucius speaks or interacts with fictional figures, born from Zhuangzi's imagination; set up for humiliation, he suffers embarrassment and is cut down to size. When serving as Zhuangzi's spokesman, his dialogue partners are historical figures: his main disciples (especially Yan Hui) or local lords (e.g., Duke Ai of Lu). He serves as a teacher and is taken seriously but his teachings reflect Zhuangzi's ideas and are radically opposed to anything remotely Confucian. Both images yet have a few things in common: they show very little respect for the historical Confucius;[4] and they contain both fact and fiction, switching

[4] One may compare this to the relation of Plato and Socrates in ancient Greece. In Plato's works, Socrates appears commonly as a leading dialogue partner—doubtlessly a sign of respect, since Plato continued Socrates's thought.

unexpectedly between them. For example, when Confucius patiently explains the principle of mind-fasting to Yan Hui, anyone can spot Zhuangzi's smile in the background. Yet when followers of Lao Dan critically claim that Confucius can never let go of his fetters, who can say that this doesn't reflect the shadow of the historical Confucius?

Still, this disrespectful attitude and unrestrained exaggeration, even absolutization, is not aimed at Confucius as a person. Most commonly, philosophers are not thought of as people of flesh and blood but rather as representatives of certain concepts and theories. Zhuangzi's disrespect toward Confucius thus reflects their philosophical divide. This divide forms an important background of Zhuangzi's thought, as can be documented throughout his writings. Yet, this is not to say that there are not shared points among the two and, as much as they are opposed to each other, their common ground forms the best platform for uncovering their differences.

Confucius, in the *Lunyu* 論語 (Analects; trl. Lau 1979) says of himself that he "knows something cannot be done and does it anyway" (14.38). Extending this logic further, Zhuangzi is someone who "knows something cannot be done and does *not* do it." Here we have a discrepancy between the attitudes of "do" and "not do," while "knowing that it cannot be done" forms the common basis of both positions. The phrase highlights the distance between thought ideals and practical reality, a difference that any philosopher knows. From this position, then, there is a connection between the two thinkers that goes beyond the tension and conflict among philosophers, transcends their mutual attacks and recriminations. This is something deep, which only philosophers can truly apprehend. From this position, moreover, we can uncover connections and continuities among different philosophies, however much they are opposite in their outward expressions. Nevertheless, these connections are not as simple as they have been described historically—seeing Zhuangzi's thought as merely another form of Confucianism.

From Zhuangzi's perspective, the teachings of Confucius and his school are like a dream, a dream that can never come true. The text's frequent references to the intermingling of dream and reality (ch. 2) can be

---

An analogy in Warring States philosophy appears in references to Confucius in works of his own school, often introduced with "The Master said" or "Confucius said." Although some passages are more authentic than others, for the most part they are probably just attributed to him. This kind of attribution can, to a certain extent, be understood as a sign of respect. But it is obviously completely different from the way Zhuangzi uses Confucius.

seen as a way of criticizing Confucian convictions. When the madman of Chu, wanders by Confucius's gate, singing, "When the world has Dao, the sage succeeds" (ch. 4), we know that Zhuangzi is not a radical escapist or world hater. The text also says,

> Recluses in ancient times did not actually choose to hide themselves, suppress their words, or conceal their knowledge. But the times were awry. If they had been right, they could have done great deeds in the world, returned to oneness and left without a trace. But the times were against them and brought them great hardship. Therefore, they burrowed deep, rested in their own nature, and waited. In this manner they preserved their life. (ch. 16)

This shows that Zhuangzi's critique of Confucianism is not an abstract denial but the recognition that its teachings do not match the needs of the time. A world in disorder has no room for the unrealistic ideals of Confucius and his ilk. Their blind pursuit of ideals with total disregard for concrete circumstances to Zhuangzi is like "the praying mantis waving his arms about, trying to stop an approaching carriage" (ch. 3). Their valor may be highly laudable, but their failure is inevitable. Having ruin stare one in the face yet failing to retreat is *not* a smart way of doing things.

Through this comparison with the Confucians, we are starting to see Zhuangzi's detachment. A well-known metaphor suggests itself. When a neighboring house is lost to fire, should we throw a bucket of water on the hopeless heap or not? Confucius comes running with his bucket, not only in outward behavior but even in the expression of his innermost feelings. He pursues his own peace of mind, never considering the effects his actions have in reality. Zhuangzi, on the other hand, knows very well that pouring water will not help: he can keep his water for himself. Zhuangzi is detached, even cold to the point of having "no feelings" (ch. 4). Comparing the two, the Confucians are eager, heatedly involved, unable to let go, constantly pursuing the good for themselves and others.

Compared with Mozi 墨子 and the Mohists, however, Confucian ardor looks rather tepid. Confucians tend to think dominantly of themselves, making distinctions between relatives and strangers, near and far; Mohists, on the other hand, demand that we see ourselves and others with equal benevolence. The key Mohist doctrine of universal love requires goodwill toward all without distinctions, which is completely different from the Confucian teaching of graded care. "Regard another's state like you would your own; regard another's family like you would your own; regard another's body like you would your own" (*Mozi*, Universal Love I; trl. Johnston 2010). Treating another as one would oneself also means treating oneself like another. One can extend deep love to another because the other is oneself; one can also treat oneself with harshness because one is the other. The *Zhuangzi* has, "Many Mohist followers wear furs and rough cloth, walk about in wooden clogs or hemp sandals, never resting day or night, undertaking extreme self-mortification. 'If we cannot do the same,' they say, 'then we are not following the way of the Great Yu 大禹, and are unworthy to be called Mohists'" (ch. 33). Engaging in self-inflicted suffering to pursue their ideals, such as dipping into boiling water and walking over fire, they reject the value of life.

While this thinking is thus full of ardor, seen from another angle, it is also rather unfeeling. Maybe Mozi and some of his disciples could reach this high level, but how about ordinary people? As the *Zhuangzi* says, "I'm afraid they cannot be regarded as following the way of the sage. They go against common sensitivity, and the empire can barely handle them. Although Mozi may be able to handle it, how can others do likewise?" (ch. 33). For Zhuangzi, Mozi's way was thus too lofty and impractical, too extreme to be appreciated by ordinary folk. Seen from this angle, the Mohists were far more idealistic than the Confucians. The more idealistic a school of thought, moreover, and the farther removed from reality, the less its potential impact on ordinary people. It may well be for this reason that Zhuangzi only rarely takes the trouble to specifically criticize Mozi and his school.

This, on the other hand, is a job taken on enthusiastically by Yang Zhu 楊朱. The Mohist doctrine of universal love, especially when advocated to an extreme, provides an excellent historical example of "valuing things and disregarding life." Yang Zhu's position is diametrically opposite. Where Mozi proposes universal love, he emphasizes self-preservation. Thus, unlike Mozi who would risk his life for the sake of righteousness, Yang Zhu keeps himself whole at all cost. "Although he might save the world by plucking out a single hair, he would not do so" (*Mengzi* 7A26). This commonly cited trope, showing the importance of individual life, could not be more different from Mozi's expression for valiant effort: "No down left on the calves, no hair left on the shins" (*Zhuangzi* 33).

In the history of philosophy, Yang Zhu was the first to flesh out the opposition between individual life and outside things, making him Zhuangzi's forerunner. His situation was not the same as Zhuangzi's, however. Yang Zhu was a wandering knight and, like Mozi who proposed universal love, he offered "valuing oneself" as a potential policy to local rulers. Zhuangzi, on the contrary, gave up completely on any ideas of ruling a country. This most fundamental difference appears in the story of a certain Yang Ziju 陽子居 who approaches Lao Dan with questions about enlightened government (ch. 7). In texts of this period, the two characters for *yang* were interchangeable, and most scholars believe that Yang Ziju is actually Yang Zhu. In any case, the position voiced—that the enlightened king should let all develop in their own manner—is appropriate for a wandering knight. While this stance is obviously unacceptable to Zhuangzi, Yang's emphasis on valuing oneself resonates well with him. He exerted a clear influence on Zhuangzi's demand that one should free oneself from any control by outside things.

Zhuangzi's most important friend and philosophical dialogue partner was Huizi 惠子 (Hui Shi 惠施), both ridiculed without mercy and genuinely mourned in the text. While several passages in the Outer and Miscellaneous Chapters are somewhat tongue-in-cheek, the story when Zhuangzi passes Huizi's grave contains genuine emotion: "Since you died, Master Hui, I have had no material to work on. There's no one I can talk to any more" (ch. 24). This clarifies their close relationship. Some scholars think that the entire Inner Chapters were written in dialogue with Huizi. While this diminishes the unique vision and character of Zhuangzi's thought, it reminds us that Huizi's influence permeates his work.

Huizi appears in chapters 1, 2, and 5, but not in his own right. In one case, he is merely one among several figures, e.g., "Zhao Wen 昭文 played the zither; Master Kuang 師曠 waved his baton; Huizi leaned on his desk" (ch. 2). In the other two instances, he engages in a dialogue with Zhuangzi, raising an issue to incite the latter's response. This, of course, is a literary technique, used to belittle Huizi. Merely a questioner, he has no chance to express his own views and plays a rather passive role. Scholars have further pointed out that these dialogues are placed at the very end of the chapters, agreeing that this puts them in a special position, but disagreeing about what exactly this might mean. Like other dialogues in the *Zhuangzi*, they might just function as parables. Still, we should note that Huizi is the only dialogue partner of Zhuangzi in the Inner Chapters. This makes these stories different and deserving of special attention.

Huizi was an important representative of the Dialecticians or School of Names (*mingjia* 名家). The *Zhuangzi* criticizes him while acknowledging his learned nature: "Huizi was a man of many devices and his writings would fill five carriages" (ch. 33). He took great pleasure in disputation .and congregated with others fond of disputes. His main line involved fundamental concepts, such as the nature of "things," "great oneness," and "little oneness," as well as number of classical paradoxes. "The largest thing has nothing beyond it; it is called the One of largeness. The smallest thing has nothing within it; it is called the One of smallness. That which has no thickness cannot be piled up; yet it is a thousand miles high" (ch. 33).Since they fail to engage with key questions of human life, Zhuangzi criticizes them as "weak in inner virtue, strong in concern for external things" and Huizi as "chasing after the ten thousand things, never turning back" (ch. 33). A later note suggests that he was like the mythical Kuafu 夸父 who kept chasing after the sun and died of thirst. Zhuangzi's followers thus suggest that Huizi's mind was inextricably immersed in outside things. Zhuangzi is different—in his world, outside things are forever secondary while human life is primary. "Treat things as things but do not be treated as a thing by others" (ch. 20) is his central credo. This reveals the most essential difference between the two thinkers.

Still, Huizi was not always merely a passive target for Zhuangzi. Though not spelled out explicitly in the text, Zhuangzi seems to have greatly enjoyed his sparring with Huizi and made use of the disputers' particular style. Some scholars even see chapter 2 as a document of dispute, Wu Feibai 伍非白 for example placing it among the Dialecticians. While this may not be entirely unreasonable, Zhuangzi was always keenly aware of the limits of disputation. "Suppose you and I have an argument. If you beat me instead of my beating you, are you necessarily right and am I necessarily wrong? If I beat you instead of your beating me, am I necessarily right and are you necessarily wrong? Is one of us right and the other wrong? Are both of us right or are both of us wrong?" (ch. 2)

Like the ancient hermits Boyi 伯夷 and Shuqi 叔齊 criticizing King Wu's campaign against the tyrant Zhou 紂 as "fighting violence with violence," so Zhuangzi here essentially scolds the disputers for trying to "stop argument with arguments." [5] Yet if we take his position of "dispute does not provide solutions" to its logical conclusion, how can he ever put

---

[5] Shao Yaofu 邵堯夫 says, "Zhuang Zhou was a vibrant disputer, unique in over a thousand years." See *Zangyun shanfang Nanhua dayi jieji* 藏雲山房南華 大義解忌 (Yan 1972, vol. 15).

an end to disputers' desire to determine right and wrong, victory and defeat through dispute while yet using this method himself?[6]

Whether to dispute or not is actually not the most important issue here. The key question is the object or content of the dispute. For most Warring States philosophers, dispute was not a matter of enjoyment but an inevitable reality of life. Thus the *Mengzi* 孟子 (Book of Mencius; trl. Lau 1984) records a disciple saying, "The people outside of our school all speak of you as fond of disputing." To which Mencius replies, "Why would I be fond of disputing? I just can't avoid it" (3B14). There are many instances of disputes in this text, such as his discussion of inner nature, righteousness, and benevolence with Gaozi 告子 (6A) and his dispute on rulers and ministers with Xu Xing's 許行 disciple Chen Xiang 陳相 (3A). The *Xunzi* 荀子 (Book of Master Xun; trl. Knoblock 1988; 1994) similarly insists that "the gentleman must engage in disputation," then makes a distinction among the arguments of small men, gentlemen, and sages. "Small men dispute by confrontation, gentlemen dispute with benevolence. Words spoken without benevolence better remain unsaid; such a dispute had better be left alone." This is not an overall rejection of all debating, rather it is a warning against "useless disputes and irrelevant analyses" (5.11).

For Zhuangzi, the most important goal of disputes is to show that disputation tends not only to be undertaken for its own sake, but also mires people in naming and arguing, bogs them down in sounds and sights, estranges them from life, and makes them forget about reality. For this reason, while going through the motions of debating, he shows just how useless it really is, to what degree all those many words really say nothing. "Great Dao has no name; great words do not argue" (ch. 2). Zhuangzi tends to describe perfect knowledge with phrases like "not know" and "no words." For him, the perfected look at each other and laugh in tacit understanding (ch. 6), reflecting the reality of their minds—not unlike the Chan story of the Buddha holding up the flower to Kasyapa with a smile. Life goes far beyond names and words—anything that goes beyond names and disputation has the greatest potential to express the content Zhuangzi is getting at.

Another early thinker in Zhuangzi's environment is Liezi 列子. A philosopher of the state of Zheng during the early Warring States, he

---

[6] Shao Yaofu 邵堯夫 says, "Zhuang Zhou was a vibrant disputer, unique in over a thousand years." See *Zangyun shanfang Nanhua dayi jieji* 藏雲山房南華 大義解忌 (Yan 1972, vol. 15).

supposedly was a disciple of Guan Yin 關尹. His ideas were very influential throughout the three Jin states. Thus, the *Zhanguoce* 戰國策 (Warring States Strategies; trl. Crump 1970) notes that his central doctrine was "valuing rectification," which places him close to early Legalism (ch 26), while the *Lüshi chunqiu* 呂氏春秋 (Spring and Autumn Annals of Master Lü; trl. Knoblock and Riegel 2000) describes his central concept as "valuing emptiness" (ch. 99; 17/7). These two positions do not necessarily stand in contradiction, but represent the integration of different aspects of Daoist thought.[7]

In the Inner Chapters, Liezi receives limited approval: "Liezi could ride the wind and go soaring around with cool and breezy skill, but after fifteen days he came back to earth. As far as the search for good fortune went, he didn't fret and worry. He dispensed with walking, but he still had to depend on something to get around" (ch. 1). Expressions like "ride the wind" and "dispense with walking" suggest that he was getting close to the state of the immortals, providing a glimpse of a world beyond mundane life. Although Liezi pursued a life of independence and freedom, his transcendence did not reach it fully—even riding the wind he still had to depend on something. The wind here constitutes an object of dependence. While this is not the same as depending on worldly values and represents some progress, it is yet the same in that it is still a form of dependence. Zhuangzi's note that "he still had to depend on something" is at the core of his dissatisfaction with Liezi's attainment.

The other major story that features Liezi is the parable of the Gourd Master (Huzi 壺子) and the shaman (Jixian 季咸) (ch. 7). Liezi, taken in easily by the shaman's trickery, comes out looking like a little clown. Then, however, under the Gourd Master's instruction, he discovers access to true Dao and not just lesser techniques like riding on the wind. Thus, "he got rid of the carving and polishing and returned to plainness, letting his body stand alone like a clod" (ch. 7). He recovered simplicity and stood unencumbered by ordinary knowledge and emotions. This reflects a form of behavior Zhuangzi approves.

From the perspective of philosophical connection, Liezi's "valuing emptiness" may well have exerted a strong influence on Zhuangzi. In

---

[7] Sima Tan 司馬 談, in his discussion of the six schools, says that the Daoists "made emptiness and nonbeing their foundation and following and order their application" (*Shiji*, Preface). "Emptiness and nonbeing" reflects the idea of honoring emptiness, while "following and order" means a concrete application in forms and names.

ancient Daoism, already Laozi paid close attention to the question of "emptiness," recommending that one "attain utmost emptiness and maintain steadfast tranquility" (ch. 16) while lauding the sage for "emptying [the people's] hearts and filling their stomachs, weakening their ambitions and strengthening their marrow" (ch. 3). Still, this does not mean that he placed particular emphasis on emptiness.

Liezi's teacher Guan Yin, as noted in the *Lüshi chunqiu*, strongly focused on "valuing clarity," so that "valuing emptiness" may well have been a development of this. The Huang-Lao 黃老 school, too, as documented in the "Daofa" 道法 (Dao and Laws) section of the *Jingfa* 經法 (Constancy of Laws), a manuscript unearthed from Mawangdui 馬王堆, proposed similar concepts, emphasizing "emptiness and formlessness" as characteristics of Dao (1.1.1; trl. Chang and Feng 1998; Ryden 1997; Yates 1997). On this background it becomes clear that Zhuangzi's appreciation of emptiness was not his own fabrication but had substantial philosophical antecedents. Going beyond these, he extended its application to the human spirit and supplied concrete methods for its attainment, like mind-fasting and sitting in oblivion. This close philosophical connection furnishes the backdrop of Zhuangzi's limited approval of Liezi.

Another personage Zhuangzi pays attention to is Song Rongzi 宋榮子, generally understood to be Song Xing 宋鈃 (or 牼). He says, "The whole empire could praise Song, but that wouldn't make him exert himself; the whole empire could condemn Song, but that wouldn't make him mope. He drew a clear line between the internal and the external, and recognized the boundaries of true glory and disgrace. But that was all. As far as the world went, he didn't fret and worry, but there was still ground he left unturned" (ch. 1).

The text further says that Song's teachings remained "unencumbered by vulgar ways, without vain show of material things, free from bringing hardship on others, and avoiding any offense to the mob." It quotes him as saying, "The gentleman does not examine others with too harsh an eye; he does not need material things in which to dress himself" (ch. 33). This suggests that Song Rongzi was a thinker who strongly separated self and outside things and never made himself a mere instrument of outside pursuit. This is why he is said to "drawn a clear line between the internal and the external." In this respect, there seems to be some resemblance to Zhuangzi's thought. However, Song held on to distinctions between the internal and external and set himself firmly apart from the ordinary world. At the same time, he could not really leave all thoughts of self and world behind. This can be understood as a form of clinging to the self, which is far removed from Zhuangzi's vision of forgetting both self and things.

So far we have discussed various Warring States thinkers, but have not yet spoken of the one who exerted by far the greatest influence on Zhuangzi's thought: Laozi 老子. In the history of Chinese philosophy, Zhuangzi is commonly recognized as the most important successor and developer of Laozi. This understanding goes back to the early Han, when not only Sima Qian places them in the same lineage but the *Huainanzi* 淮南子 (Book of the Prince of Huainan; trl. Major et al. 2010) first speaks of both in the same sentence, showing how closely connected the two thinkers were in the minds of the time (ch. 21).

This connection is based primarily on the commonality of their thought and also, to a lesser degree, on the way Zhuangzi represents Laozi, featuring him three times in the Inner Chapters, not unlike Plato depicts Socrates—a later thinker standing in awe of the master while using him as his own spokesperson. For example, Laozi voices the following statements: "Why don't you make [Confucius] see that life and death are part of the same whole, that acceptable and unacceptable are aspects of a single reality? Then he could free himself from his fetters?" (ch. 5); "When an enlightened king rules, his achievements pervade the world but he is as if doing nothing. His transforms all things but the people do not realize this. His virtue is not praised, yet he allows all to find their enjoyment. He establishes himself beyond what can be understood and wanders the realm of nonbeing" (ch. 7).

These statements closely reflect Zhuangzi's ideas, but there is also a story that shows a different angle. It is an allegory that tells of Qin Shi who goes to mourn Lao Dan, gives a mere three cries, and leaves. Questioned about why he mourns this way, he replies that he originally thought of Lao Dan as an accomplished person but later realized he wasn't—mainly because others were weeping and wailing at his funeral. "To have gathered a group like that, he must have done something to make them talk about him," created an impact on the world that did not match the ideal way of flowing along with the times, free from all ties and emotions. "This is to go against Heaven, turn your back on the true state of affairs, and forget what you were born with. In the old days, this was called the crime of turning against Heaven" (ch. 3).

The contrast between admiration and distancing thus characterizes Zhuangzi's attitude toward Laozi. As Guo Xiang 郭象 (d. 312) says in his commentary: "I suspect that by giving priority to others and displaying goodness, he deviated from principle and thus inspired this kind of intense devotion." The pronoun "he" refers to Laozi and the tone of the passage is highly critical of him. However, already in the Tang dynasty, Cheng Xuanying 成玄英 adjusts this view. He says,

> 'Ask' means pursue. 'Others' refers to the masses. The sage's [Lao Dan's] mind was empty of personal caring and remained open to stimulation from others. He felt sympathy for those in mourning and empathy for the common people. Without deliberate effort, he spoke on their behalf. Thus, after his death, the masses came to congregate, weeping and wailing in mourning as if they had lost their mother or son. Clinging to such emotions creates attachments and leads to a false view of life and death, to gratitude for the sage's grace, and thus to a display of grief. Judging from this, we know that these are not followers of Lord Lao. (Guo 1982, 1:128)

This makes a strong distinction between the sage and ordinary people. The latter cling to emotions and are given to attachments, not at all like Laozi's followers—Daoist recluses—and vastly different from Laozi himself. Cheng Xuanying's description of Laozi as free from personal caring is quite different from Guo Xiang's understanding. This difference reflects their historical circumstances and unique perception. Guo Xiang, matching the culture of the Wei-Jin period, was focused strongly on Zhuangzi and largely disregarded Laozi. Zheng Xuanying, an ordained Daoist under the Tang who deeply venerated Laozi as Lord Lao, found it a great deal harder to criticize the sage.

The Buddhist monk and Zhuangzi exegete Hanshan Deqing 憨山德清 (1546-1623) of the late Ming offers a yet different reading, "When I first made friends [with Lao Dan], I saw him as someone who had Dao. Today, after his death, I know that he did not. . . ." On the Zhuangzi passage, "This was called the crime of going against Heaven," he says,

> "Crime" here means principle. It says that Lao Dan as a person was not able to forget his emotions while living in the world. He still harbored love and closeness to others, so people could not forget him, either. This means going against Heaven's truth, forgetting one's original being. The ancients called this a violation of Heaven's truth, which harmed inner nature. Who acts like this is not a sage.

Hanshan here borrows Zhuangzi to criticize Laozi. Considering his position as a monk in a time of Buddhist-Daoist rivalry, this becomes quite understandable. But if later readers think it to be true and take this to represent the original Zhuangzi, they are quite mistaken.

Leaving aside the parables and returning to the historical facts of the time, the philosophical connection between Laozi and Zhuangzi could not be clearer. Although we can easily list innumerable differences, they tend to be extraneous and secondary, never overshadowing their fundamental commonality. Sima Tan's description of the Daoists as "taking emptiness and nonbeing for their essence, alignment and accordance for their function" applies equally to Laozi and Zhuangzi, despite the fact that the main thrust in Laozi is the way of being a good ruler while Zhuangzi focuses primarily on how best to live in the world.

In concrete terms, during their historical time, Laozi's ideas pervaded many aspects of society—Dao, nonaction, and diminishing knowledge were as ubiquitous as his idea that "being causes it to be profitable, nonbeing makes it useful" (ch. 11) and his profound question of what is more important in life, body or reputation (ch. 44). All these are found everywhere in Zhuangzi who describes both Laozi and Guan Yin as men of encompassing enlightenment and as originally perfected.

Zhuangzi's philosophy is rich and abundant but not disorderly or confused. He is neither Laozi nor Liezi or Confucius, although they all play a role in his world. Zhuangzi is 100 percent Zhuangzi—with his unique and original approach to Dao. He is just like the creative change that, in the hot cauldron of the universe, smelts together elements of world, life, and history (ch. 6). The refined product of this great creation now presents itself in Zhuangzi's work and most potently in the seven Inner Chapters.

Chapter One

Crazy Life, Crazy Words

People generally like balance and moderation; why some might prefer to be a bit crazy is inexplicable to them. Still, there are quite a few who at times take liberties to enhance themselves, follow unconventional pursuits, and develop wild expectations, on occasion manifesting unexpected results. They would much prefer Li Bai 李白 over Du Fu 杜甫 among Tang poets. After all, he breaks into spontaneous song while relaxing with a glass of wine and chants in praise of Zhuangzi, "I am originally the madman of Chu, singing a song to make fun of Confucius." Beyond Li Bai and the Tang, this attitude is also common among poets of the Wei-Jin period—they all follow an earlier model, pattern themselves on someone more original. This is Zhuangzi.

In fact, Zhuangzi's life can hardly be characterized as "crazy." Since his lifetime precedes ours by 2,300 years, we have practically no record of its daily course. Still, there are glimpses of his lifestyle in his work. He lived in ordinary society, undisturbed by considerations of right and wrong; he was careful and prudent in his dealings, generally low-key and withdrawing; he buried himself among common folk, stayed unassuming and hid his light. How was he crazy, then? Maybe he had reasons to cover up something intentionally, but no matter what, he'd never place himself in the position of a cardboard box close to the fire. Even when in a tight spot, Zhuangzi would always reveal his unique attitude, letting us catch a glimpse how he was exceptional, "crazy" in the eyes of ordinary men. His *Shiji* biography has,

> King Wei of Chu heard that Zhuang Zhou was a wise man and sent a messenger to invite him to court, hoping to make him prime minister. Zhuang Zhou laughed and told the envoy, "A thousand pieces of gold constitute serious wealth; the position of prime minister is a position of high honor.
>
> "But have you never seen the sacrificial ox used in the suburban sacrifice? First he is fattened over several years, then decked out in embroidered finery and led to the altar. Would it not willingly

> change place with some uncared-for piglet? Be gone! Don't pollute me! I'd rather enjoy myself by floating about in the muddy stream of life than be subject to the rigors of government. I will never take office but remain free to follow my own inclination." (ch. 63; Fung 1952, 1:221)

Sima Qian only uses a few sentences to describe this extraordinary thinker, and half of them he spends on this story. He must have felt that Zhuangzi's lifestyle was sufficiently out of the ordinary to produce a record like this. "Normal" people, seriously dedicated to political power and the accumulation of wealth, must have found his attitude hard to comprehend. Here is someone who plainly rejects the freely offered income of a thousand gold pieces and the high rank of prime minister! A similar tale also appears in the *Zhuangzi*. The envoy of King Wei of Chu finds him fishing in a stream. Zhuangzi rejects the offer of employment, comparing official service to the fate of the sacred tortoise, dead for a thousand years, "wrapped in cloth and boxed, and stored in the ancestral temple." Like the tortoise that would rather be alive, he prefers to "drag his tail in the mud" (ch. 17). The *Shiji* version is more meaningful, since it not only records the rejection but also Zhuangzi's reasoning: he acts in this manner due to personal pleasure, following only his own inclination. It shows Zhuangzi as a self-indulgent man who hated being tied down in any way, even or maybe especially by the state. Do we see first traces of craziness here? Just refusing a good position is crazy enough—but for the sake of personal pleasure?

Another tale, particularly powerful due to the vivid contrast it paints, has Zhuangzi visit Huizi, then prime minister of Liang. Someone claims that Zhuangzi wants to replace him, causing him great alarm. When the two meet, Zhuangzi compares political office to a "half-rotten old rat," interesting only to ordinary owls but not to a magnificent bird like the Yuanhu 鵷雏. He "rises up from the southern sea and flies to the northern sea, rests on nothing but the cypress, eats nothing but silky fruit, and drinks only sweet spring water." He—like Zhuangzi—has no interest in the dead rat, why would he even consider going after it? (ch. 17).

The actual, living Zhuangzi has neither cypress nor silky fruit or sweet spring water: his rejection of political power means that he continues to life in destitution. Records suggest that he served at one point as Lacquer Grove Manager (*qiyuanli* 漆园吏)—a position interpreted variously. The name may indicate a particular office or department where he served as an administrator, or it might refer to an actual garden or park. Whichever, it was a rather lowly job, and Zhuangzi didn't stick with it for very long. His family lived in poverty—"in poor alleyways and cramped lanes, skimping, starving, weaving one's own sandals, with withered neck and sallow faces" (ch. 32)—not unlike Yan Hui. Maybe that's why he likes Yan Hui so much. A dedicated gentleman, Yan Hui lived in the world of Confucian virtues—Zhuangzi didn't, didn't even dream of it! While Yan Hui and the Confucians study in order to serve, Zhuangzi observes that "a study that leaves no subject untreated" limits self-awareness and consequently establishes distance to political power. For them, "to be good at learning and serve" is the proper way of living in society; Zhuangzi's attitude of "be good at learning and don't serve" is truly exceptional.

Beyond exceptional, Zhuangzi really is strange and even likes being called weird. "The singular man is strange in comparison to other men, but a companion of Heaven," he says (ch. 6). He thinks differently from ordinary people and lives an unusual, even eccentric lifestyle. This is made clear not only in his rejection of all political dominance but also in other areas such as, for example, his understanding of birth and death. In the eyes of the world, these are central events, marked by major rituals that either welcome a person's arrival or send him off after his departure from this world. Not so for Zhuangzi. Firmly rooted in his unique understanding, he has little patience for formal rites.

Thus when his wife dies, he doesn't follow the standard ritual, but "sits on the ground with legs spread wide, beating a drum and singing happily." Asked why, he explains that his wife was not alive or embodied before she took birth; she appeared as part of the universal changes of vital energy (*qi* 氣). "Now there has been yet another change, and she is dead." Since these changes are part of nature, moving along just like the four seasons, there is no point rejoicing in one state and bewailing the other. "If I went and mourned her by wailing and weeping, I figured I'd just show that I had no understanding of the underlying patterns of fate. So I stopped. (ch. 18)

Zhuangzi not only shows no respect for traditional funerary rites, but even subverts them by drumming and singing. He intentionally demonstrates something here and behaves accordingly. But the question really is not his motivation, but rather the determination with which he sticks to it and his resulting behavior. There may be quite a few people who harbor similar ideas, but they tend to hide them and go through social formalities for the sake of keeping up appearances. Zhuangzi is authentic to the bones, he's a full-blown perfected. Yes, he lives in the ordinary human world—"he did not argue right and wrong, but went along with the age and its vulgarity" (ch. 33)—but there is no way people will ever make him anything but truly himself: " I walk a crooked way—don't step on my feet" (ch. 4). His pursuit of authenticity will not be derailed, no matter what. It manifests in the way he lives his life.

Zhuangzi's determination and steady position are also evident in his attitude toward his own death. He expressly forbids his disciples to give him a sumptuous burial, instead wishing to take "Heaven and Earth for my coffin, the sun and moon for my jade discs, the stars for my pearls and beads, and the ten thousand things for my parting gifts." He wants to be exposed to nature, despite the danger of being eaten by vultures: "Above ground I'll be eaten by crows and kites, below ground I'll be eaten by mole crickets and ants. Wouldn't it be rather bigoted to deprive one group in order to supply the other?" (ch. 32).

Death to him, therefore, is nothing to be afraid of, but a mere return to Heaven and Earth, joining sun and moon, stars and planets, the ten thousand things and all existence as one integrated organism. In this understanding, the lavish grave gifts people provide at funerals have no meaning whatsoever. Once we realize that we are all part of one integrated organism, there is no point making a distinction between crows and ants. For Zhuangzi, looking at things like this is the proper perspective, a way of reaching into universal pervasion where self and all things are one. Yes, there is a certain callousness about this: the attitude tends to obliterate Confucian ardor and caring. But it also allows us to see the truth as understood by the common world in contrast to the inner world of truth, of authenticity!

This really is crazy. A society characterized by artificial distortions will always see the perfected as crazy, like Huizi criticizing Zhuangzi's drumming and singing after his wife's death. It is hard to find a unified, set meaning in Zhuangzi, but there is always the inevitable distance to ordinary views and standards. Confucius speaks from the dominant standard and says: "Since I cannot get men to pursue the proper medium, I must teach the wild and crazy! It will help the crazy to proceed apace and keep the wild from doing wrong" (*Lunyu* 13.21). "Wild" and "crazy" here are negative epithets as seen from the realm of benevolence and righteousness, the position of standard social regulations. Some people may exceed these standards, others may not quite reach them—either way, they must never get far away from ritual propriety but remain within established Confucian boundaries.

Zhuangzi's craziness goes far beyond this. He wants to turn the values of the world upside-down, uproot all standards of ordinary society, and do away with the normalcy of life. Ordinary people, he says, may roam within the boundaries of the four directions, but he goes far beyond (ch. 6). Within and beyond have nothing in common. Looking at the realm beyond from the perspective of within, those flying high naturally appear crazy. In fact, Zhuangzi places himself among madmen in several places. He never thinks of himself as merely a humble scholar in the world, where his whole life would be tied up and remain utterly without meaning, but outlines his choice by ranking figures: Confucius and Yan Hui come first, followed by Zigao 子高, Yan He 顏闔, and finally Jie Yu (ch. 4). He then places himself in a position like that of the madman, because he has an exceptional, unconventional understanding of the world and human relations.

There is no way we can avoid the world: it is everywhere between Heaven and Earth. As the madman of Chu puts it, "The future you cannot wait for; the past you cannot pursue. . . . In times like the present, we do well to escape punishment" (ch. 4). Yet despite this inescapable situation Zhuangzi never considers living in a world without joy, without Dao. As Sima Qian says, he remains a man "at play"—quite incapable of taking life seriously, unable to strive for saving the world like Yan Hui.

Playfulness, then, is a form of craziness. The madman behaves in ways that are unacceptable, even unspeakable, in the ordinary world. He couldn't care less about it, its rights and wrongs, its order and chaos, even about himself. Yet he is the most perfected among men. It is precisely because he recognizes perfection and inner authenticity that he is crazy in the eyes of the world. His innocent, muddling life is no different from a dream. Just think of Qizi 箕子, the first madman known in Chinese history. Although he only pretended to be insane, he yet exhibited all the classic symptoms. Realizing the truth about King Zhou, the last tyrant of Shang, he refused to go down with him and feigned madness. He rejected the possibility of being like someone lost to life, thus he had things he did not speak of. He feigned madness to achieve two things: to oppose the world's depravity *and* preserve himself.

Zhuangzi's case is not at all like this. He does not feign madness, yet like Qizi he opposes the dominant culture and strives to keep himself and his self-esteem intact. This is exactly why he exhibits crazy behavior time and again, laughingly going against Confucius's expectations in ways that are indistinguishable from the behavior of madmen. Anytime

Confucius is in a situation where "knows something cannot be done and does it anyway" (*Lunyu* 14.38), the madman of Chu sings his ditty:

> Phoenix, phoenix!
> How your virtue failed!
> The past, you cannot regret;
> The future, you can still pursue.
> Leave off, leave off!
> People who pursue politics today will perish. (18.5)

A state where morality and order are in decline, a world without Dao is sufficient reason to seek seclusion. Even Confucius who never seriously engages thoughts of leaving the world, sighs, "My ways are not working. I better get on a raft and float out to sea" (*Lunyu* 5.7). For him this probably was just a sentiment after realizing the futility of his efforts, but for Zhuangzi it represents the perfect lifestyle. Of course, Zhuangzi cannot actually float out to sea, nor would he leave society and live among hermits. Instead, he is "submerged on dry land, buries himself among the people, hides himself among the fields" (ch. 25), which is as paradoxical as "sit and race around" (ch. 4).

Both refer to states where the body and mind are at odds. During "sit and race around," the body is still but mind races; when "submerged on dry land," the body remains on land while the mind is submerged. That is to say, although Zhuangzi may physically live among ordinary people—his inescapable fate—his mind is as if already dead, submerged in the utmost depths of Dao. With a mind that deep, the body can go crazy. "He did not argue right and wrong, but went along with the age and its vulgarity" (ch. 33) yet he also experimented with new ways of behavior, like drumming and singing at funerals.

Besides a crazy life, the *Zhuangzi* also embraces crazy words. Guo Xiang already points out that "Zhuangzi can be said to know the origin, thus he never even started to contain his crazy words." The text is crazy in many respects, but mainly on two levels: stylistically in terms of words and phrases and meaning-wise in terms of content. Eccentric expressions, the way Zhuangzi presents his intentions in language, thus constitute a major feature of his style. Guo Xiang speaks of crazy words, but the phrase goes back to Zhuangzi himself, who describes the words of Jie Yu as "wild and wide of the mark, never coming near human affairs . . . crazy and unbelievable!" (ch. 1). That is to say, to express exceptional content, language must show some unusual characteristics. In fact, it is hard to make a firm distinction between style and content, since both form one integrated structure. To explain this more clearly, let us leave the content aside for the moment and look at the words.

Crazy words form Zhuangzi's unique literary style. This is most obvious when comparing the text with other pre-Qin documents. The *Laozi* is full of aphorisms and poetic verses, the *Lunyu* has recorded sayings and formal compilation, the *Mozi* contains standard narratives and explanatory discourses, the *Mengzi* entails discourses together with disputation, the *Xunzi* presents discussions and opinions—but they all remain in the realm of "proper discourse." The *Zhuangzi,* in contrast, is characterized most strongly by irregularity, full of twists and turns. "He believed that the world was submerged in pollution and that it was impossible to address it in straightforward language" (ch. 33). In other words, in a murky and depraved environment, Zhuangzi cannot remain level and serious. In my view, other passages where he does not specifically apply "Zhuangzi talk" have to do with thoughtful considerations, his personal reflections on language. Those passages offer a yet deeper insight into his eccentric style. They do so without requiring too much effort on our part, since Zhuangzi's followers have already pointed out the special characteristics of their master's language, providing comprehensive descriptions.

The primary chapter that describes Zhuangzi's language is chapter 27. The Qing scholar Wang Fuzhi 王夫之 (1619-1692) identifies this as the preface of the original text, while the last chapter (ch. 33) served as its postface (1985, 246). Later scholars have followed his understanding, so that many nowadays see the last chapter as a general summary and evaluation of the text, citing as it does passages from the rest of the book. It says, "He used goblet words to pour out endless changes, grave words to give a ring of truth, and lodged words to impart greater breadth" (ch. 33).

More specifically, "lodged words are like persons brought in from outside for the purpose of exposition" (ch. 27). They relate to the idea of lodging or placement. Zhuangzi is fond of this idea: it also appears in expressions like "lodge in the center," "rest in nowhere." These expressions refer to the author's alter ego, a separate entity at his back. More specifically, lodged words are "discussions outside the ledgers." "Outside" here implies that there is also an "inside," but the "inside" is latent and has not yet appeared fully, so that all we can see is the outside. This means that we cannot properly imagine mystery and emptiness. Blocked by obstacles and hindrances, we can only reflect on what is manifest in the world. The caring father cannot really offer praise for his son, because he is strongly prejudiced in his favor. His words would never hold the same trustworthiness as those of an outsider.

Because the human mind is geared toward self-protection, it has a hard time looking at things from another perspective, and anything we think about ourselves is not easily modified by new views. That is, whatever we say about ourselves is bound to be favorable; our concrete way of life, on the other hand, is easily seen by others. At this point, relying on the mouth of others to express our own ideas is a superb technique to go beyond ordinary perception. "If I were to speak [in my own words]," Zhuangzi says, "people would respond only to what agrees with their own views and reject what does not, would pronounce 'right' what agrees with their own views and 'wrong' what does not" (ch. 27).

Thus he puts his ideas into the mouths of Confucius and Yan Hui. Most people believe that this is an easy way to lend authority and attraction to the words, but I doubt that they really have this effect unless the reader is stupid and lacks discrimination. Maybe it's a trick of Zhuangzi's disciples, and we should not continue along this line of thought. Be that as it may, lodged words form a stylistic feature quite new in the *Zhuangzi*. Earlier authors, too, lodged words in the mouths of sages—the Confucians using Yao and Shun 舜, the Mohists appropriating the Great Yu, Huang-Lao thinkers working with Huangdi 皇帝, the Yellow Emperor—but the relation of personage to utterance was entirely different. These various earlier figures all said the things one would expect from them, fully appropriate to their status and perspective.

Zhuangzi's lodged words are different: his figures do not voice what they should say according to the standard tradition but often make utterances in quite the opposite direction. For example, when Confucius is amazed at Yan Hui sitting in oblivion, or when he puts the damper on Yan's ardor to save the world, this is fantastic and absurd given the actual personages. One can see this as a literary game or improvisation, where people do not play their customary roles but explore new angles. But is it just mere drama? Using these techniques, what is Zhuangzi trying to express? Is it that the world is essentially crazy so that one cannot face it directly and straight on? Or is it that his words ultimately have no meaning at all? Taking this literary style and connecting it with his philosophy, doesn't he in fact apply it to create something akin to "making all things equal," like "making all words equal"?

No matter what, the style of lodged words focuses the reader's attention on the connection between personages and philosophy and causes us to reflect on their contrast. They effectively dissolve this contrast, replacing it with "becoming one in Dao" rather than postulating that "not being the same, there can never be agreement." What emerges here is a form of craziness—how can Confucius and Zhuangzi share the same ideas? But in lodged words they do in fact merge. This reminds us to ask continuously whether whatever we think of at any given point is an actual representation of truth, whether it matches reality or is possibly contrary to it. It also allows us to go along with the opposite perspective or, alternatively, to push all the way to the deepest sense. We may even discover that there is an originally common track in the thought of Confucius and Zhuangzi, from where they unfolded into opposites. Plus, this does not apply only to Confucius and Zhuangzi, but to the distinctions and oppositions among all things. Looking at things from this angle, lodged words not only form a literary style but represent content itself, revealing the fullness of Zhuangzi's thought.

Grave words in many ways represent the opposite of lodged words. While the latter express things from the outside, these words of gravity emerge from the inner self of the author. Relying on traditional, established meanings, they borrow and double it, without even a trace of playfulness. "Grave words put an end to argument," the text says; "they are the words of the elders" (ch. 27). In traditional society, it was perfectly normal to associate wisdom with experience and old age, but that does not mean that one is wise just because one is old or experienced. There are various long-lived birds, turtles, and plants, old and wizened, with mystical power radiating from them. Traditional Daoists saw longevity as a sign of having attained Dao. The Confucians apparently weren't averse to the idea either, as Confucius says of himself, "At fifteen, I had my mind bent on learning. At thirty, I stood firm. At forty, I had no doubts. At fifty, I knew the decrees of Heaven. At sixty, my ear was an obedient organ for the reception of truth. At seventy, I could follow what my heart desired, without transgressing what was right" (*Lunyu* 2.4).

According to this, wisdom ripens with age. Maybe because of this, when speaking of grave words, Zhuangzi links them to old age (ch. 27), yet in many places the text shows figures that have old age but not necessarily wisdom. There are too many people in the world who are old for all intents and purposes but few who can really be expected to "have a grasp of the warp and woof, the roots and branches of things" or have really "understood the way of humanity. If he has not grasped the Dao of humankind, he deserves to be looked on as a mere stale remnant of the past" (ch. 27). The key point is thus not old age, but whether or not one has an understanding of Dao in old age. Zhuangzi, moreover, calls those who do not understand the Dao of humanity "people from Chen," indicating that they are influenced by Confucians or Mohists.

The third literary device Zhuangzi uses is called "goblet words," generally taken to be expressions of no-mind or a form of no-words. "With words that are no-words, you may speak all life long and you will never have said anything," Zhuangzi says (ch. 27). A goblet is a kind of drinking vessel, and after one has partaken of wine, one's language is less calculated, issuing more directly from the heart, truer and less pretentious. Without a firm director in the mind, one is less likely to drop into the sphere of right and wrong, and can express oneself more fully. These words of no-mind, these no-words, then, are like the speech of little children, not to be judged or evaluated. For this reason, they are useful to demonstrate being fully present in oneself, as the text says, "all your life" (ch. 27). For example,

> By being inwardly direct, I can be the companion of Heaven. As a companion of Heaven, I know that the emperor and I are both sons of Heaven. So, why would I use my words to try to get men to praise me, or try to get them not to praise me? A person like this is called 'child.' This is what I mean by being a companion of Heaven" (ch. 4).

"Inwardly direct" means resting fully in one's heart, unable to create extensive calculations. When people act from this place, they inevitably follow their true mind and are "companions of Heaven." All considerations of noble and humble, good and evil dissolve into oneness: people become like children and whatever they say comes out as words of no-mind. When Zhuangzi says that these "companions of Heaven" are without fault, he means that they can continue for years on end.

No matter what, when the text speaks of lodged, grave, and goblet words, it shows that Zhuangzi and his followers took the issue of language seriously, providing the foundation of this particular literary style. Zhuangzi is a complex person: he is opposed to disputation but he excels at it; he is against language but possesses complete mastery of words. At the root of this complexity may well be his disturbed relationship to the world. His choice of language, on the one hand, connects him to the world; on the other hand, it reflects his particular understanding of language. In fact, Zhuangzi holds a deep-rooted distrust of language itself:

"Words rely on vain show," he says (ch. 2). Words are always secondary to context and can never fully express meaning. "Words have something to say, but what they have to say is not fixed" (ch. 2). The object of words is always changing, never stable: how can they keep up with meaning?

The great Dao cannot be named; a great argument cannot be expressed in words. This is reminiscent of Laozi: "Beautiful words are not true; true words are not beautiful" (ch. 81); "Who knows does not speak; who speaks does not know" (ch. 56); and "The Dao that can be told is not the eternal Dao; the name that can be named is not the eternal name" (ch. 1). However, these reflections on language are not meant to imply its complete dismissal. In the end, we have to live among people and in society where speech and language form essential features of human interaction. Thus Zhuangzi opts for crazy words.

Crazy words, then, represent Zhuangzi's way of using language while also showing his urge to demolish it. In its use, he follows the common world—after all; we need language in order to live, to have fruitful exchanges, to understand each other. But ultimately, full and true understanding is reached when people get to the place of Master Sanghu and his friends who "forget each other in speech" and "never go against their minds" (ch. 6). Only by demolishing language can we find perfection. In the interchange of the application and demolition of language, Zhuangzi thus reaches the level of "words of no words" (ch. 27). Speaking from an attitude of no words, there may be language but it really is not. So he always speaks, yet never speaks. In the same way, if we hold on too tightly to no words, this becomes yet another expression of language. So even if we never say another word for the rest of our lives, we still will never be able to forget language altogether.

Looking at things from this angle, the entire book *Zhuangzi* is a truly exceptional creation. Language furnishes extreme limits to what we can do, but we must use it. We have no choice but receive it, so as we receive the *Zhuangzi*, its author strongly hopes that we can indeed hold on to its words for our own transformation. Thus in the dialogue between Nanbo Zikui 南伯子葵 and Nüyu 女瑀 (ch. 6), Aided-by-Ink, the use of texts, is a beginning dimension of the way to Dao, followed by Repeated-Recitation, i.e., the spoken word. Moving on from there in successive progress, one reaches Seeing-Brightly, possibly a way of critically examining the world, and Whispered-Agreement, which shows how we use our ears to apprehend life's inner rhythm. More subtle levels, expressed as Exclaimed-Wonder and Dark-Obscurity, may indicate finer forms of hearing, while Participation-in-Mystery stands for resting in serene tranquility, and Copy-the-Source reflects an openness, a sense of wonder, a fundamental questioning that reminds us of the "beginning of the not yet beginning" (ch. 2).

This outline of the progress toward Dao represents a gradually increase of doubt about the inner workings of the universe, the way Zhuangzi proceeds in his quest for a state beyond the ordinary. What is he trying to tell us here? Should we try to pass through language or forget it? Maybe both. In each step toward Dao, words and language—as much as our release from words and language—occupy fundamental positions. We must pass through language but also transcend it. Passing through the written word we reach speech; passing through speech, we reach vision; passing through vision, we reach hearing . . . until in the end we come to the place of the ultimate origin of all questions, a realm of pure being or nonbeing.

Maybe, when we read the *Zhuangzi*, we undergo some of this progress. We naturally understand its history, realizing that the text as described in the literary section of the *Hanshu* 漢書 (History of the Han Dynasty) consisted of 52 chapters, while Sima Qian notes that it contained over 100,000 words. The present standard edition in thirty-three chapters goes back to Guo Xiang's editorial efforts.[8] This transformation has symbolic meaning: on the one hand, it shows the enormous power of the traditional commentators who remained unmoved before the text's integrity. On the other hand, it throws open the text's original nature, revealing how there is never really a true master, how the text is always "lodged," continuously evolving into new syntheses. Whether commentator or ordinary reader, we must find where we stand with the *Zhuangzi*. We must pass through it and can never hold on to it: maybe only by working with it while continuously letting go of it can we avoid taking on the essential hardship and loneliness of Zhuangzi's work.

---

[8] The standard edition divides into three sections: Inner, Outer, and Miscellaneous, containing seven, eleven, and fifteen chapters, respectively. This division may be quite relevant in expressing the author's intention and complexity of his vision. As scholars have pointed out variously, pre-Qin works were not written by a single author but compiled over many years by lineages of disciples. Thus, the *Mozi* is the product of the Mohist school, the *Xunzi* contains sections by Xunzi himself as well as those of his followers. Generally speaking, the Inner Chapters are by Zhuangzi; the remainder of the text issued from his followers. Among contemporary scholars, especially Liu Xiaogan has provided a detailed analysis of the text's layers (1987; 1994). For more, see also ch. 9 below.

Chapter Two

The Human World

The memorial *Zhi'ance* 治安策 (Strategies for Ruling in Peace), submitted by Jia Yi 賈誼 (201-169 BCE) to Emperor Wen of the Han and recorded in the *Hanshu*, says, "There is only one reason for painful regret, but two for shedding tears, and six for heaving sighs of consternation" (ch. 24). Between these lines there is a powerful and startling appeal. Quite similarly, reading Zhuangzi's chapter on "In the Human World" (ch. 4), full of words like "futility," "inevitability," "fate," and the like, we want to let our minds absorb his meaning and explore just how the author comes to be in such a state of mind.

Generally speaking, a person's state of mind reflects his understanding of the world he lives in; it mirrors his psychological reactions and life experiences. Most certainly, the same world connects with the minds and hearts of different people, yet it produces various effects. They are determined by how spiritually sensitive the person is and also by how far the world has entered his head and forms a key element of his inner experiences. Thus, people may live in the same historical period, yet will experience different psychological reactions and life experiences. Jia Yi felt painful regret and shed tears because he perceived a major crisis his contemporaries would not see at all. While most people were rejoicing in prosperity, he remained a lone crier of alarm.

It is easy to transition from Jia Yi to Zhuangzi. His prose poem, *Funiao fu* 鵩鳥賦 (The Fu Bird), written when he was serving as Grand Tutor in Changsha, is highly reminiscent of the *Zhuangzi* and was obviously inspired by it (Dong 1994, 4:93). Jia Yi possessed a subtle sensibility toward politics and power, life and fate, Heaven and Humanity. This left him depressed when King Huai of Liang, the ruler he tutored, died after falling off his horse; it later caused him to feel remorse and die himself. The same sensitivity also led him to discover Zhuangzi, who became his spiritual solace when severely disappointed in government.

Still, he was widely divergent from Zhuangzi in many ways. Unlike the latter, Jia Yi never had any urge to leave the world and obviously had no trouble seeing through all the foibles of the human world—the main reason for his tragic life. Just as Zhuangzi says, people who work in power politics, especially in times of disorder, may escape physical punishments (manmade afflictions) and mental anguish and tension (yin-yang afflictions), yet they never really find peace and inevitably end their lives in consternation. Jia Yi's life as described in the *Hanshu*, full "self-torment for not being a proper teacher, frequent lapses into tears, followed after little more than a year by his death," is an obvious example.

The title of chapter 4 is "In the Human World," a phenomenon that means different things to different people. What exactly did it mean to Zhuangzi? No one knows for sure, but we may try to get a glimpse from his writings. I think that each part of the title has its own significance: human (*ren* 人), in between (*jian* 間), world (*shi* 世). Since human beings live in the world, how should they interact with it and with each other? Whether or not this reading is correct, the chapter provides clues how Zhuangzi thought we should best deal with living "in the human world."

Zhuangzi's meaning of "world" is clear. He had no great concern for the natural world, and questions raised by Greek philosophers, such as whether air or water is the source of material existence, most likely held no interest for him. He says, "What is beyond the six directions—the sage admits its existence but does not theorize about it; what is within the six directions—he discusses it but does not dispute it" (ch. 2). In other words, there is no point talking about what is beyond Heaven and Earth and the four cardinal directions; even what is within them can be described but should not be judged. Zhuangzi did not say exactly how "discuss" and "dispute" are different, but we may make a distinction: discussion is mere presentation of structure and patterns; dispute includes value judgments like beautiful and ugly, right and wrong.

Within the six directions, the human world is visible and tangible. It is the human world, where people are dominant—the stage on which they act and interact. Not mere individuals, they are connected in relationships on all levels. According to the usual classification as found in the "Zhongyong" 中庸 (Doctrine of the Mean) chapter of the *Liji* 禮記 (Book of Rites), these relationships include ruler and subject, father and son, husband and wife, older and younger brother, as well as friend and friend. Confucians take them very seriously; Zhuangzi pays them some heed but not to the same degree as the Confucians, who are deeply involved, even obsessed with them, focusing largely on ideals such as "family happiness." Zhuangzi, in contrast, accepts them but with reluctance and only those that he really must engage in, notably the politically defined relationship of ruler and subject. The world he speaks about thus has politics at its core, an obvious feature in this chapter

This does not mean that he dismisses the relationship of father and son; in fact, he ranks it right next to that of ruler and subject as a mainstay of the world but finds it less threatening since it tends not to entail mortal danger. In this chapter, Zhuangzi only refers to it in a secondary manner. He notes that there are "two great mainstays in the world, fate and duty. That a son should love his parents is fate—you cannot erase this from his heart. That a subject should serve his ruler is duty—there is no place he can go and be without a ruler, no place anywhere between Heaven and Earth where he can escape."

Many people think that Zhuangzi was like the stallion of Heaven charging through the skies without constraint, like the huge Peng bird soaring higher than 90,000 miles, that he cast the world off like an old slipper. They are wrong. Zhuangzi forever realized that there was no way he could put the world aside. This is what he means by "fate," echoing Duke Liu Kang's pronouncement in the *Zuozhuan* 左傳 (Zuo's Commentary; trl. Legge 1960), "All people live between Heaven and Earth, and this is called their fate" (Cheng 13).

Heaven and Earth are concretely present in ruler and parents: this is indicated by the expression "great mainstays." They can be seen as two big cangues or sets of shackles, inevitably part of human life—not installed by Humanity, but by fate or Heaven. As long as you live in this world, from the very moment you are born, you are locked in these shackles without any chance of escape. They come with birth: you cannot pick or reject them. Realizing this gives you a feeling of futility, especially if you wish to pursue freedom. However, if you look at it from a different angle, recognition of the fact that you are indeed shackled is a precondition for the pursuit of freedom. The two great mainstays with their limitations thus determine Zhuangzi's conditional acceptance of the world. Willingly or unwillingly, we all live in the human world—it is not just something out there but an essential part of your life, connected to the pulse of your very own existence.

Zhuangzi accepts the world as inevitable and thus goes beyond the escape advocated by ancient hermits like Boyi and Shuqi. They faced a moral dilemma, as expressed in Zilu's 子路 accusation of the hermit: "Wishing to maintain personal purity, you let important relationships disintegrate" (*Lunyu* 18.7). That is to say, they maintained moral integrity at the cost of defaulting on their duty to society. The dilemma continues in the tradition: Boyi is honored as a Confucian model, since, as Mencius says, he was "the purest of sages" (5B10); yet rejecting relationships can never be the precondition for any goal, because the elimination of social connections means loss of identity as a human being, a descent to the level of birds and beasts. Confucius says, "I cannot band together with birds and beasts, so if I do not join the people, who can I join?" (*Lunyu* 18.6). We must live in the human world!

Like the Confucians, Zhuangzi was very much aware that we always live among people and this awareness forms the foundation of his thought. However, what Zhuangzi means by "the world" is different. Just look at their respective lifestyles: Confucius travels from kingdom to kingdom, Mencius goes back and forth between Liang and Qi—so keen to serve in the world, hoping that some ruler would put their political ideals into practice. They may not be happy with it, but they don't shrink back from it or ever try to escape. Their discontent makes them try to change it, albeit without success.

Zhuangzi, on the other hand, has no such urge. He resists the call of the world and refuses to serve his ruler. Recognizing that he cannot escape the world, he yet does not reach the conclusion that he has to get involved in it. His way is different, somewhere between escape and involvement: be in the world but not of it. Maybe his favorite term "wandering" or "flow" (*you* 遊) describes it best—a state between joining and withdrawing, between not joining and not withdrawing. Thus Zhuangzi deals with the world. I personally think his choice has to do with two things: his personal experience of the world and his reflections on how Confucians relate to it. While his own experience is more important, his reflections are yet key to understanding his thought. In fact, the two closely connect and are hard to separate.

Theoretically, the world can be seen as having or not having Dao, being in order or disorder. Both Confucius and Laozi speak of "the world having Dao" (*Lunyu* 8.13; 16.2) and "the world being Dao-less" (*Laozi* 46). Living in dangerous times, they confronted a rather disorderly world—and so did Zhuangzi. But while they found the cause of this state in a loss of social order and political control, Zhuangzi experienced it as a direct threat to his life. Thus he begins this chapter with a dialogue between Confucius and Yan Hui, the latter expressing his desire to go to Wei, because its people need help. The Prince of Wei, he says, is "in his prime" and has an "independent and willful" disposition. "He treats his country as if worthless and refuses to see his faults. He leads his people into danger like nothing, and corpses lie all around his land like so much grass. The people do not know where to turn."

Thus the chapter begins on a rather somber note. It makes it clear that at this time the character of world depended on the whim of local rulers who exerted complete control. The Prince of Wei as described here is a brutal tyrant. And the fact that he is "in his prime" may well indicate that he is going to rule for quite a long time. The passage conveys just how pessimistic Zhuangzi feels—deeply enmeshed in impenetrable gloom, with no hope of escape. His world is a place where human life is worth little, a world that reeks of death. Other passages reinforce this: a prince at the court of Duke Ling of Wei, has "a natural disposition inclined toward killing," Jie Yu passes Confucius's gate and sings a sorrowful chant that reflects Zhuangzi's vision as he faces a world in disorder; it forms part of the deep dialogue he holds with Confucian thought. The song appears first in the *Lunyu*:

> Phoenix, phoenix!
> How your virtue failed!
> The past, you cannot regret;
> The future, you can still pursue.
> Leave off, leave off!
> People who pursue politics today will perish. (18.5)

The phoenix is a sacred bird that only appears when the world is governed by a sage: Jie Yu yearns for an orderly, harmonious world. But what about the politicians of his time? They are nothing like sages. When the world has Dao and is in order, the sage appears; and when it is Daoless, he goes into hiding. These times made seclusion a valid and reasonable choice, much better than anxiously awaiting the chance to save the world. He thus expresses his thorough disillusionment with rulers and politicians, suggesting that it is best to leave it all behind.

In the *Zhuangzi*, Jie Yu goes beyond this. Rather than simply expressing disappointment, he indicates a crisis of survival. After the initial cry of "Phoenix, phoenix," he says, "The future you cannot wait for; the past you cannot pursue." This expresses the hopelessness of the present: people have to live in it because they have no other choice, they cannot take refuge in past or future. So, what is the present like? "In times like the present, we do well to escape punishment." With corpses strewn widely, a ruler accustomed to murder, a world trapped between impossible choices—what can we do? We can but strive to survive, rather than try to save the world—a completely different situation from times when the world has Dao, when one does well to engage in civil aspirations and reach for high goals. "When the world is Dao-less, the sage merely survives." This short statement brims with hopelessness and futility: sages in this world cannot but focus on self-preservation as their principal concern.

Rather than the expression of a stubborn determination to get away from social duties, this is a cry for withdrawal in helplessness, facing extreme circumstances and with no other choice. What about ordinary people, then? They continue to wager their lives against the malevolent world. As Zhuangzi continues the song: "Good fortune is as light as a feather, but nobody knows how to hold it up. Misfortune is as heavy as the earth, but nobody knows how to stay out of its way." Thus human life is submerged in the depths of despair, close to extinction. Zhuangzi uses Jie Yu's song to cry out his despair and express his search for a place of survival. To find this, people must give up any concerns for the world: "Leave off, leave off—this teaching men virtue! Dangerous, dangerous—to mark off the ground and run!" They must learn to make their winding way down a road covered with brambles, keeping their own lives safe from harm as much as possible.

This expresses the core issue in Zhuangzi's thought: human life! Unlike other thinkers who focus mainly on political order, he is most concerned with how to live peacefully in a Dao-less world. Not entirely without concern for social order, he is yet deeply aware that he cannot address it successfully, at least not until he has found a way to live in peace. Thus, he prefers not to deal with it, at least for the time being. This choice allows him to refrain from involvement and maintain distance to the world. It not only keeps him out of immediate danger, but also ensures that he can fulfill his social responsibilities, the unavoidable mainstays of life: duty toward his ruler and obedience toward his parents.

His thinking closely reflects his world. Survival and self-preservation are natural core issues, raising questions on how best to relate to the world. They form the central focus of this chapter, and Zhuangzi offers three modes of dealing with them. Yan Hui represents the first: the urgent desire, the intellectual hope, to save the world from disorder by enthusiastically going forth to counsel a tyrant. Zigao and Yan He stand for the second: the need be involved in the world, to support the political order by fulfilling a responsible and influential position in society (as messenger and royal tutor). Jie Yu reflects the third: the tendency to keep one's distance and remain a detached bystander.

All three modes can co-exist simultaneously, running parallel on different social levels, and there are always people engaged in all of them. For Zhuangzi, however, they are not merely parallel but successive. The chapter begins with the hopeful intellectual who tries to make the world better, moves on to several people engaged in struggles with it, and ends with a mad recluse. It closely reflects Zhuangzi's way of thinking the issue through to resolution; it also echoes his dialogue with the world, his dialogue with the Confucians. In some way, Zhuangzi here explains why the Confucian position cannot be defended and why he himself decided to withdraw into seclusion.

The Confucian approach to dealing with the world in a positive, involved manner, "unless times are too Dao-less," forms a fundamental backdrop of the narratives. From the metaphor Confucius presents to Yan Hui in the beginning to Jie Yu's song uttered in front of Confucius's gate, Zhuangzi carries on a dialogue with the Confucians throughout the chapter. Both Yan Hui's plan to save the world and Jie Yu's decrying of artificial constraints and virtuous posture point directly at the Confucian position. Indeed, the intentions, attitudes, and behavior patterns listed were widespread, and not merely the product of special circumstances or coincidence.

No question: as soon as human beings appear in the world, they must function in it and maintain an active relationship with it. Zhuangzi's choice to keep his distance is the exception, not a fundamental theme of human existence. It may just be a game he plays, but I think games just provide an alternative approach without being fundamental to life. The fundamental theme is expressed in Confucianism: things like affirmation of the world, active involvement in it, participation in all sorts of relationships, and issues of responsibility and obligation. These are all ways of people to create a particular place for themselves. As a result, when disorder prevails, and there is a decline of rites and music, one must try to set things right.

Thus Yan Hui refers to his master, Confucius, who advised, "Leave the state that is well ordered and go to the state in chaos! At the doctor's gate are many sick men." In accordance with this, he wants to fulfill his obligation and confront the tyrant of Wei. His is a thoroughly Confucian attitude—maybe even one Zhuangzi held at some point. He was not born disillusioned, after all, and maybe there was a time when he, too, hoped to save the world. He certainly served as an official, however minor, so he was part of the political power structure for a while. This may well have been an expression of his desire to help the world—but can the world in fact be helped? In other words, can a single person's actions really effect change?

This, of course, is a complex question. Before even considering whether involvement can be effective, we should ask whether there is in fact a way of becoming involved. In a society under dictatorship rather than democracy, any way of becoming involved must pass through the ruler and his minions. But would the ruler approve of this involvement? Zhuangzi's favorite example, Confucius, was highly active in seeking involvement, going from state to state in the hope of activating the way of the ancient sage-kings, Yao and Shun. With what result? As his disciples point out, "Our Master was twice driven out of Lu. They wiped out his footprints in Wei, chopped down a tree on him in Song, made trouble for him in Shang and Zhou, and are besieging him between Chen and Cai" (ch. 28). He had no cooked food for seven days, and spent his days in fretful anxiety like a dog that has lost its master.

The various local rulers had little interest in Confucius's doctrines. In an attempt to surround himself with a lofty aura, he self-directed and starred in his personal version of "The Master Visits [Consort] Nanzi," an incident which drew such criticism that he was obliged to swear an oath to Heaven that he had had no improper intentions toward her (*Lunyu* 6.28). Plus, his followers had to come up with all sorts of rationales to justify his action. While the incident is rather trivial, it still shows just how intellectuals, despite all the best intentions, wind up in awkward positions.

Providing criticism of society and politics is the responsibility of the learned; intellectuals are key bearers of this responsibility. In a society under dictatorship, criticism ultimately aims at the ruler. Zhuangzi understood this well. Yan Hui, Confucius, and the Prince of Wei stand for the whole group of intellectuals and rulers. They appear a fair amount in his writing: politics continued to lurk in the background of his thinking, may in fact constitute its essential part. Whenever people enter the world, there is a sun in the sky and a ruler on the throne: this is inescapable fate.

To live in an ideal society "or at least in a society where there is hope" is certainly good fortune, but all too often people are unfortunate. And what if they happen to encounter a Prince of Wei who is young and essentially a ruthless killer? The fact that he is "in his prime" indicates that his cruel rule may continue for a long time; his "independent willfulness" reflects the tyrant's tendency to rule strictly by his own lights. You, too, may well start out as impulsive as Yan Hui, brimming over with enthusiasm, speaking out boldly, thinking that you can take your youthful ideals and transform a society in ruins, a power structure full of corruption, and a brutal tyrant. So you, too, may stride into the world of politics and approach the ruler—and just what fate awaits you? Will you reach a point of no return?

Yan Hui in the *Zhuangzi* is a young man full of impulsiveness and subject to merciless ridicule by his teacher. "Ah!" Confucius exclaims in a derisive laugh, and pronounces, "You will probably go and get yourself executed!" This sounds like a blow to the head, a slap in the face. At a time when one could avoid punishment at best and should focus on self-preservation, Yan Hui moves in the opposite direction. Zhuangzi uses Confucius to articulate a principle of central importance: "The perfect man of old made sure that he had it in himself before he tried to give it to others. When you're not even sure what you've got in yourself, how can you hope to impact some tyrant's behavior?" Just compare this with the real Confucius: "[A humane man] who wishes to establish his own character, establishes the character of others; he who wishes to reach attainment, promotes attainment in others" (*Lunyu* 6.30)!

Moving from oneself to others is central to the Confucian urge and ideal of going out to save the world. People must reach a certain level of attainment within themselves, but the key point is to promote it in others. Zhuangzi's Confucius is nothing like this. He still echoes the logic of first realizing things in oneself before spreading them to others, but the key focus is the self, giving highest priority to one's own life, with saving the world as an "also ran." Any conflict between saving oneself and saving the world can only result in one choice.

The principle of "first make sure you have it in yourself before trying to give it to others" renders concern for oneself more important than saving the world. This, of course, is only a principle and requires confirmation. You must confirm that saving the world is impossible and sacrifice is meaningless; then you can retreat with a clear conscience. For example, when faced with someone about to set out like Yan Hui, how do you talk sense to him? In the story, Confucius notes that "virtue is destroyed by fame, and wisdom comes out of wrangling; fame is something to beat people down with, and wisdom is a device for wrangling. Both are evil weapons"—however great, they just get you "to parade your own excellence" and if you do that before a mean tyrant, this may well be the end of you.

That is to say, when you think of winning others over with your great virtue and knowledge, you really think of yourself as representing the good while seeing the other as evil. You then use your goodness to cast the other's evil in bold relief, or use the other's evil to make your own good shine forth. In effect, you are just trying to smear the other, becoming a "purveyor of evil." It is like digging a pit for someone and expecting him to jump in it, but usually the person still has the option to jump or stay. In this case, however, you dig a pit right under his feet, in an area that is full of pits and sunken earth: he has no choice but to jump. It may not have been your intention, but that is not as important as what he *thinks* you tried to do. This holds particularly true for a brutal despot who is not used to think in terms of good intentions. Your virtue and knowledge just stir up his determination to fight and crush opposition. "He who hurts others will be hurt in turn. You will probably be hurt by this man"—especially if he is someone with absolute power!

Faced with this, you have the option of dying a martyr for your ideals, your virtue, and your fame. Historically Guan Longfeng 關龍逢 and Prince Bigan 比干 were killed for their troubles by the tyrants Jie 桀 and Zhou 紂, gaining everlasting fame as loyal subjects in the bargain. By the same token, they made Jie and Zhou appear even more despotic. Even Confucians, though, are not in favor of the direct approach but suggest counseling the ruler three times with care and patience, then leave. Why turn a disagreement into a matter of life and death? Moreover, as a loyal subject, how can you bear to die and thus testify to the cruelty of your ruler? As Zhuangzi would have said, death is one way of being hurt, but in the final analysis it is really rather extreme.

Fortunately, intellectuals usually know when to advance and when to withdraw. Zhuangzi paints a rather funny caricature of the intimidated counselor: "You find your eyes getting dazed, your complexion changing, your mouth working to invent excuses, your attitude becoming more and more humble, until in your mind you end by supporting him [the tyrant]. This is to pile fire on fire, to add water to water, and is called pushing to excess." Caught between the pressure of the ruler's overarching power and his own survival instinct, the counselor's once fearless confidence quickly fades into timidity. Eyes, mouth, and mind all strive to accommodate, leading to an expression that is the opposite of the original intention. Not only has the encounter left the ruler unchanged, it has fortified his position. Without intending to, the would-be savior of the world has turned into the tyrant's henchman.

Still, there may be other ways of admonishing the ruler. Thus, Yan Hui suggests that he be "serious and humble, diligent and single-minded." This would certainly help to preserve the counselor's identity; it also allows for the ruler's state of mind. For Zhuangzi, however, it is not likely to succeed with a ruler who is smug, capricious, haughty, and domineering. Alternatively he could be "of inward rectitude and outward compliance while arguing with examples of antiquity." This approach is somewhat more complex, "inner rectitude" according to Zhuangzi indicating that one is "the companion of Heaven." All people "emperor and commoner alike" are equally the "sons of Heaven," since they are all born of Heaven. There is, thus, no need to cloak one's point too carefully in the rhetoric of courtesy.

Focusing on life as bestowed by Heaven opens a state of mind that is essentially naïve, like that of an innocent child. Children are not usually held accountable for what they say. Resting in "outward compliance" is like being "the companion of people," respecting the ranks and positions of the human world. All subjects in attendance to the ruler must observe the court protocol; those to counsel the ruler must abide by it as well. "Arguing with examples of antiquity," i.e., citing works of old to make a point, means being "the companion of ancient times." The advantage of this is that even if the ruler does not like what he is told through ancient sources, he cannot easily cause embarrassment or trouble for the speaker. This rather carefully contrived approach allows the counselor to withdraw unscathed, but that is all it can do. He still won't win.

So, if he can't win in any case, are all these approaches useless? Is it better not even to try, to stay away from futile efforts? But then, unless you try, how can you know the outcome? Zhuangzi doesn't just simply let you know the result—he insists on taking you through the full thought process, on the whole futile expedition. And as if this wasn't enough, there's more futility to come.

Let us next look at the fate of the messenger. His mission is to convey a verbal message, something that is not hard among ordinary people. But what about messages between rulers? Or, even worse, between rulers of opposing states? There is the principle, "when two states are at war, their messengers will not be executed." This may provide some surety for the messenger's life, but only *pro forma*. It does not deal with all the potential causes of mortal danger to his life.

Zigao, the messenger of the king of Chu, in Zhuangzi's description, faces a dilemma as he goes on a mission to Qi. "If the mission fails, I will suffer punishments from other people; if it succeeds, I will suffer the ailments of yin and yang." That is to say, he is in a no-win situation. If his mission fails, he will be punished; if it succeeds, the anxiety, consternation, and concessions of the process will injure his health. Actually, this negative impact is inevitable, since he is stressed even before he sets out. "I get my orders in the morning, and by evening I am drinking ice water. I must be fevered within."

The strong expression "fevered within" shows the tension and worry he feels, particularly due to the clash between the demands of his mission and his life, plus the concern that he will suffer no matter what. Maybe, he should put all thoughts of life or death completely aside and thus can prevent the fever. Yet who has such disregard for his own life? Possibly there are people of high attainment who can avoid this sort of dilemma, who can act in the world while "knowing they have no other choice and in full acceptance of their fate." They may be able to avoid any harm that comes from strong emotions such as joy and anger, delight and sorrow. They may also invest in learning from past experiences, following age-old maxims like, "Convey only the straight facts, and never speak in exaggeration!" Maybe in this way they can avoid coming to harm by people. Yet the basic question remains: Why do we insist on straying into ground that is covered with brambles?

As he did in the story about Yan Hui wanting to educate the Prince of Wei, Zhuangzi paints the pitfalls of the human world in stark colors. He outlines the messenger's problems when expressing mutual esteem or anger between two parties. "Esteem gets exaggerated into flattery, and anger turns into insult; both soon become lies which cause loss of trust. Then the ability to communicate is destroyed, and the messenger suffers."

The poet Li Bai once said, "The road to Shu [Sichuan] is harder than ascension into Heaven." The challenges of nature are puny in comparison to the perils in the human world. We may avoid the travails of the road to Shu simply by not traveling at all, or maybe by going a different way. But the human world often precludes choice. As a messenger, you cannot refuse your mission. You must do your best to carry it out, yet in the process you must also care to protect yourself. Maybe you think cleverness and skill will see you through, but Zhuangzi doesn't think so. "Competitors in physical combat begin brightly, with open displays, but quickly end in darkness, with stealthy cunning. . . . Drinking rituals start out clear and orderly, but often end in boisterous confusion." Temporary good fortune cannot prevent the eventual arrival of danger. Perhaps it is best to eliminate all illusion and succumb to the inevitable, surrender to the world. Never mind whether the mission fails or succeeds, whether you live or die. This may work, but the attitude is far removed from the original ideals of men in politics.

Zhuangzi next tells the parable of Yan He, the royal tutor (*taibo* 太博). His job is essentially to instruct the prince, the future ruler, in basic knowledge and arts. A good job, no? But what is its reality? Yan He says, "Here is this young thug with a murderous temperament. If I let him run wild without constraint, he will endanger the state. If I try to restrain his impulses, he may well turn on me. He knows enough to see faults in others but can't see his own."

That is to say, when you encounter a "naturally murderous" man of some influence, you find yourself trapped, neither able to move forward nor retreat. Simple self-preservation demands that you let him do what he wants and avoid giving offense, but this means that you deny your conscience and fail in your duty. Take your pick: morality and righteousness or your life and well-being? Zhuangzi himself of course would never get into such a predicament, but he uses it as an example of the kind of danger one will sooner or later encounter in the human world.

Thus he provides advice, speaking through Qu Boyu 籧伯玉. "Be careful, be on your guard, and make sure that you yourself are in the right! In your body it is best to follow along; in your mind it is best to harmonize." In other words, be circumspect about how you react, stay calm and go along with whatever the leader does, yet make sure not to overdo it. "If in your actions you follow along to the extent of getting deeply involved, you will be corrupted, destroyed, wiped out, and brought to your knees." If closeness and accommodation turn into "active involvement," you have given in to corruption and are subject to the hatred and persecution of the world. "If in your mind you harmonize too much, you will be famous, renowned, cursed, and hurt." That is, if harmonizing with him in your mind is done excessively, things may become stormy. Either way, there will be struggle and contention, and your life suffers.

Zhuangzi further describes what he means by "going along" and "harmonizing." He says, ""If he wants to be a child, be a child with him. If he wants to follow erratic ways, follow erratic ways with him. If he wants to be reckless, be reckless with him. Understand this thoroughly, and lead him to the point where you are without fault." This is different from obeying conventions and holding on to rules. If my mind is not set on anything at all, no external change can disturb the harmony I feel within. If my mind is empty, I can absorb whatever state appears. Still, when all is said and done, going along and harmonizing are just a feint, a way of finding a protected niche so that I can remain "without fault." That's really all it is.

Then again, maybe people think such an approach beneath them; they are unwilling to accommodate and placate others, seeing this behavior as demeaning. They want to stand up to their full height, like the praying mantis that stands in the middle of the road, arms raised in an effort to stop an approaching carriage. How does he fare? He loses first his arms and then his life—the carriage rolls right over him. His intentions are good, but the impression he gives, along with the memory of his good intentions, is that he had no real self-knowledge. Zhuangzi wants us to know both ourselves and others, and to understand ourselves properly, we must understand the world. Only thus can we find our rightful role and appropriate position. Thus he says to be careful and on guard. We must not feel too strong in virtue, be convinced of our own knowledge, or take pride in ourselves, lest we suffer a fate like that of the praying mantis.

A careful and guarded attitude makes it possible to be accommodating, to go along and harmonize with the ruler. Working close to political power is like dealing with a wild tiger. A skillful trainer "doesn't dare give the tiger any living thing to eat for fear it will learn the taste of fury by killing it. He doesn't dare give it any whole thing to eat for fear it will learn the taste of fury by tearing it apart. He gauges the state of the tiger's appetite and thoroughly understands its fierce disposition." The trainer does all he can to avoid arousing the tiger's ferocity. Always maintaining an attitude of accommodation, he can coexist with the beast, but the moment he goes against the tiger's nature, he dies. The tyrant is like a wild tiger: never arouse his fury. Go along with what he wants and avoid all confrontation or criticism. You may act from loyalty, but he won't care about your good intentions.

Zhuangzi makes the same point in the parable of the horse groom, who "places the horses' manure in baskets and stores their urine in jars," taking excellent care of his charges. However, should "a mosquito or horsefly land on a horse and someone come to slap the insect, the horse will rear up, bite through its bit and injure people. In its mind, all love is gone." Although done with the best of intentions, the slap is all the horse feels. He rears up in a fit of temper, struggling and biting, attacking and potentially killing the person who cares so well for him.

"In its mind, all love is gone" is a key phrase in this story. People tend to think that love is a good thing—Confucians speak of benevolence and care, Mohists propose universal love. Whether bestowed in careful gradation [in Confucianism] or without distinction [in Mohism], the central idea is love—something actively given to a recipient, reaching from oneself to another, a recognition of the inherent sameness in two fundamentally different individuals or entities, "what makes things the same" (ch. 2). For example, Mencius says that all people's mouths share the same liking for tastes and their minds have the same inherent principle of righteousness. It signifies a general recognition of commonality, based on which we are able to match and go along with someone else's thinking or actions.

Zhuangzi, however, fundamentally does not believe in the existence of anything that "makes all things the same" nor does he think that people can really and truly know each other. He rejects the idea that love can be projected from one person to another—a logical and unavoidable conclusion. For Zhuangzi, the question is crucial: I may love a certain person, but will he be willing to accept my love? Will he even understand it? Like the horse in the parable, he may not understand the love and good intentions that cause me to slap him.

Rejecting love does not necessarily entail incurring hatred. There is no place for hatred in Zhuangzi's thought, since his involvement with the world leaves his whole being cold. I personally think that his rejection of love is merely another way of his refusal to save the world, at least in the manner of Yan Hui. This rejection brings us back to focus on ourselves rather than on others. Zhuangzi always tries to find reasons for withdrawal, but is this because he does not understand the world? Not really. On the contrary, he has deeply immersed himself in it. The *Xici* 繫辭 (Great Appendix) commentary to the *Yijing* 易經 (Book of Changes; trl. Wilhelm 1950) says, "Only through deep immersion can one understand the will of the world" (1.10). Without this depth, he could never write with such bite when he portrays what goes on in life or flesh out the deepest thoughts of so many different kinds of people. From Yan Hui and Zigao to Yan He, Zhuangzi shows us the futility of all political pursuits, how youthful determination blurs in the light of the vain conformity of the world. If this is what awaits us, why do we still want to be active?

Why, indeed? Because we have minds. As our minds are full of right and wrong, good and evil, we strive to put them all in their proper place. We relish the good and beautiful; we detest the ugly and evil. We want to turn evil into good and human decay into something marvelous. But do we have the power? Of course not. Zhuangzi is not a fool. He knows that, unless you activate the spirit of Heaven, you cannot move a mountain. And, since this spirit is indifferent and unfeeling, it won't help. So Zhuangzi chooses to give up. Once he has made this choice, he wants to make his sense of right and wrong, good and evil disappear. Even if it didn't disappear, what could he do, anyway? He could only suffer and worry more. It is at this point that the chapter speaks of mind-fasting—an important passage for both Zhuangzi and the reader. Confucius by now has rebutted several of Yan Hui's plans to save the world. Now he reveals what to do.

The core factor is the mind. All efforts to educate rulers and save the world come from the mind. You take your own standard to alter this brutal world. "Alteration" is not something Heaven does or would approve. Heaven is naturally great; it constantly responds to creative change but it does not actively alter anything. People should be like this, too. From here, Zhuangzi has Confucius present the idea of fasting—not physical abstention from "taking strong drink or eating meat or fish or pungent vegetables" (*Lunyu* 6.11), which Yan Hui associates with the term. For him, being of a poor family, this kind of fasting—necessary for certain religious observances—comes effortlessly. But Zhuangzi is after something different: mind-fasting.

Basically, mind-fasting leads to a state where the mind is empty and at rest, free from all content: "Make your will one!" He then speaks of the senses, the mind, and vital energy (*qi*) in succession. "Don't listen with your ears, listen with your mind. No, don't listen with your mind, but listen with your *qi*. Listening stops with the ears, the mind stops with recognition, but *qi* is empty and waits on all things." This moves in stages, mind superseding the senses and *qi* superseding the mind. Using *qi* is fairly advanced. Since it is empty and receptive to all, it has no desires, opinions, or emotions: it can be totally responsive, allowing us to move freely through the world without tension or conflict. Zhuangzi does not speak of the wider, more cosmological implications of *qi* as the all-pervasive, unitive force underlying all things. He just makes it clear that the senses and the mind are nowhere near its equal, since only some impressions or things are pleasing to them, while others are not.

This means that both the senses and the mind work by differentiating between things, which in turn creates strongly held views and thinking in opposites. We must supersede them and reach for a subtler level. As long as we still listen with our ears and process information with our minds, we will think of objects, have discriminating knowledge, and firmly hold on to opinions. When we start to perceive the world directly through *qi*, our minds are empty and detached. Allowing energy to function freely is the goal of mind-fasting; it makes the mind as empty and unfettered by concrete things as *qi* itself.

From here we can transform freely yet still remain in this world. As Yan Hui expresses it, "Before I heard this, I was certain that I was Hui. But now that I have heard it, there is no more Hui." This expresses the contrast between "mind" and "no-mind." The former is object-centered and creates awareness of self as distinct; it compels you to do certain things and to refrain from others. The latter is free of focus, free of self, and does not acknowledge an external world of objects. Where mind is substantial, no-mind is empty. "Have no gate, no opening, but make oneness your house and live with what cannot be avoided." This emptiness of the mind makes it possible to live in the world without being moved by fame or prestige. Achievement and reputation no longer exist. When you can speak out, have your say; when you cannot, keep silent. There is no fixed mode of coping with the world; there is no specific method to save it. All you do is adapt to the moment.

This is how you live in no-mind—though you leave traces, there really are no traces. In an earlier passage, Zhuangzi speaks of "not picking a place to settle down." This is important. For example, some people, in their desire to avoid leaving traces and escape the world, will pick a place in the wilderness and settle down. But as Zhuangzi notes, "There is no place we can go and be without a ruler, no place between Heaven and Earth where we can escape." There is, therefore, no meaning in escape. The key is not to pick a place—however far away—but to create an attitude. As the medieval poet Tao Yuanming 陶淵明 (365-427) said, "The mind withdrawn, I'm remote no matter where I am."

This reflects a deep appreciation of Zhuangzi. When the mind withdraws, whatever physical place we happen to be at becomes remote, no matter how much it may be teeming with activity. Vice versa, no matter how remote we are physically, if the mind is still engaged in the world, it will always be full of agitation. Thus, Zhuangzi does not suggest that we stop leaving traces by escaping the world. "It is easy to keep from walking; the hard thing is to walk without touching the ground." It is easy to just run away, flee to some remote spot like the mountains and become a hermit. But even there, you're still walking, leaving traces. For Zhuangzi, the important thing has nothing to do with the body—its escape is just a form of opposition and highly limited. True escape happens in the mind.

Mind-fasting is to escape in the mind: remain in the world physically but be unmoved mentally. This is not just a show but solidly based on no-mind, on "being a companion of Heaven;" it is the opposite of "minding" things, when one is "a companion of Humanity." The latter do things for show and "pretend to remain unmoved," but the former cannot. Remaining unmoved frees you from the fetters of the world, leaving you unencumbered by things and ready to transcend.

Zhuangzi calls this "flying." "You have heard of flying with wings, but you have never heard of flying without wings," he says. What he is after has nothing to do with the flight of birds: they still need wings to stay aloft. Nor is it the flight of people who still mind the world, since they are unable to overcome gravity that will continue to pull them down. What he means is soaring without wings in ecstatic flight. The mind has no wings; it can fly without relying on anything. In no-mind, it transcends the mundane world and soars into Heaven: mind-fasting makes people one with Dao.

No-mind obviously means the intentional discarding of discriminating knowledge. Confucians highly value knowledge and expertise, arguing that mental transcendence depends on them. Only by having clear knowledge of morality can we ever live in true accordance with it. Thus, the "Daxue" 大學 (Great Learning) chapter of the *Liji* admonishes us to "investigate things to reach utmost knowledge" as one of its eight steps toward proper ordering of the world. Knowledge here is like the wing of a bird in Zhuangzi, something to rely on for the mind to soar. But Zhuangzi eschews this. For him, knowledge does not even suffice to deal with this world, let alone help us fly beyond it. No matter in whom—be it Yan Hui, Zigao, or Yan He—knowledge is always like this: directed outward with a tendency to embroil and submerge you in the world. Full of knowledge, you let the mind pursue things on the outside, turning into its puppet and thus the slave of the world.

For this reason, Zhuangzi's call for the elimination of knowledge is firm and clear. Still, he does not mean to eliminate all "knowing," but makes a distinction between knowledge-based and non-knowledge-based knowing. One works through the accumulation of information and discrimination; the latter is an intuitive apperception reached through oblivion. Knowledge-based knowing, the knowledge of things, is limited; non-knowledge, the knowing of Dao, leads to transcendence.

First forget this world, then reach out to another; forget things and move toward Dao. Once things and world are gone, your mind is mere empty space, void of content, yet full of limitless illumination. Radiant with the light of true wisdom, it permeates all things and reaches to their source. It leads people away from outside things and back to Dao, guiding them to life itself. Life in pursuit of outside things can never be peaceful: even when the body sits still, the mind keeps on racing, full of schemes and concerns. Zhuangzi calls this state "to sit and race around."

To remedy this, "let your ears and eyes communicate with what is inside, and put mind and knowledge on the outside." Keeping your senses free from all pursuit of outside objects while maintaining communication with them, you can eliminate knowledge and find peace within. The mind quiets down, and so does the world.

This, then, is how Zhuangzi finds a place to keep himself safe in this turbulent world. The only way to get there is by withdrawal to seclusion. You must let go of all intentions to save the world or act deliberately, all knowledge and expertise you accumulated to that end. What do they bring you? Nothing but consternation, pain, and danger. No bargaining either: you may lose a sheep to gain an ox, but that's not the end of it. Yes, best start over and don't get involved: become completely useless.

Zhuangzi, now that he has taken us to look at the futility and pain in the human world, explores the concept of uselessness. Maybe because he served in the Lacquer Garden Office for a while, he likes trees to make his point. Thus he tells the parable of Carpenter Shi who travels to Qi and sees a serrate oak near the village shrine. It is huge, "broad enough to shelter several thousand oxen, a hundred spans around, towering above the hills, its lowest branches eighty feet from the ground—a dozen or so of them could have been made into boats." Many people admire it, but the carpenter doesn't even glance in its direction. His disciple asks him why and he explains: "It's a disintegrating tree. Make it into a boat—it sinks; make it into a coffin or chest—it rots; make it into a table—it collapses; make it into a door—it leaks sap; make it into a pillar—it's riddled with insects. This is not a timber tree. There's nothing it can be used for—that's why it reached such great age."

Later in the tale, the tree appears to the carpenter in a dream, chiding him for measuring trees by their use, which only causes them harm. "Cherry, pear, orange, grapefruit, and all those other fruit trees: as soon as their fruits are ripe, they are knocked down and thrown into the dirt. Their big limbs are broken, their small branches torn." The big tree, on the other hand, "has striven to be useless for a long time" with the clear goal of not suffering harm—"I have found this idea to be of great use to me." The one use it allowed itself was to serve as a marker of a village shrine, taking refuge in this role. "If it had not become a sacred tree, how many people would have wanted to cut it down! It keeps itself whole and values things differently from the ordinary."

Zhuangzi was well aware that his thinking ran contrary to that of most people. Ordinary people strive to be useful, to be good at learning, to gain official employment—he just hopes to be useless. In terms of productivity and practical application, the oak is useless, thus the carpenter ignores it. It doesn't bear edible fruit and can't be made into anything useful—but this is how it gets to be hundreds of years old. Zhuangzi really appreciates this point. His tree intentionally pursues being useless, having seen how others fare, being broken and cut down. "If I had been useful to someone," the tree asks, "could I have ever grown to be this large?" Zhuangzi asks us the same question, showing why he values uselessness.

In another parable along the same lines, Master Ziqi 子綦 wanders about the countryside and sees this huge tree. "It provides so much shade that it could shelter a thousand four-horse chariots from the sun." But its wood is useless in worldly terms. "Its smaller limbs were gnarled and twisted, unfit for beams or rafters. Looking down, he saw that the trunk was pitted and rotten and could not be used for coffins. He licked one of the leaves and it blistered his mouth and made it sore. He sniffed the odor and it was enough to make a man drunk for three days." Thus he understands that the tree could grow so big precisely *because* it was useless to the world.

Zhuangzi further tells of a region in Song, which is good for growing catalpas, cedars, and mulberries—all cut down and mutilated to serve people. Trees of usable wood, large or small, will always be used for human purposes; they fall under the axe before their time. Next, he speaks of animals with deformities that keep them from being sacrificed. Priests and shamans think of them as bringing misfortune, but wise men know they are really fortunate: they get to preserve their life.

At this point, Zhuangzi turns to people, with the example of Crippled Shu 支離疏, "chin stuck down in his navel, shoulders up above his head, pigtail pointing at the sky, his five organs on the top, his two thighs pressing his ribs." Despite this deformity, he does menial jobs and divinations, making a decent enough living. When the ruler raises troops or workers for public construction projects, on the other hand, he gets to stay and watch—even better, he is on welfare, benefiting from the state instead of laboring or dying for it. Just looking at Crippled Shu, people may well feel sorry for him, but Zhuangzi has nothing but admiration. While useful folk die on the battlefield or in forced labor, he supports himself and lives out his years. Such is the usefulness of the useless!

Of course, Zhuangzi does not want us all to become disabled. His point is that, physical uselessness bringing so many benefits, how much more if the mind was useless? Once our mind is infused with uselessness, even if our bodies are whole, they will be just as useless to the world—simply because we won't *want* to be useful any longer. Zhuangzi sees it as more important to have "deformed virtue" rather than suffer disabilities like Crippled Shu. He wants us to do away with all our accumulated worldly virtue and knowledge and release our minds into oblivion. He wants us to be worthless rather than full of useful talents. Thus, any thinking directed toward usefulness is eliminated and the mind imbued with uselessness.

He summarizes: "The mountain trees do themselves harm; the grease in the torch burns itself up. The cinnamon can be eaten and so it gets cut down; the lacquer tree can be used and so it gets hacked apart. All men know the use of the useful, but nobody knows the usefulness of the useless!" Reading this passage, we cannot but appreciate Zhuangzi's cool detachment, yet we may also feel a bit desolate. If it were not for men with fire and knives, would the cinnamon be cut, the lacquer tree be stripped? Cinnamon can be picked—there's no need to cut down the tree. Lacquer can be harvested—there's no need to hack it to pieces. This overkill happens because the world is without Dao. The same lack of Dao also causes inherently useful people to have no opportunity to exercise their abilities. They have no choice but to pursue wisdom on the quiet, withdrawing into seclusion and reverting to uselessness. In this way, saving the world turns into self-preservation, burning fervor changes to cool detachment, lofty feelings become a sense of futility, and the stout Confucian Yan Hui transforms into Jie Yu, the madman of Chu.

This sheds a different light on the narrative structure. In terms of protagonists, it begins with Yan Hui, moves on to Zigao and Yan He, then ends with Jie Yu. In terms of people's relationship to the world, it begins with the urge for active involvement, moves on to the discovery of difficulty and futility, and ends with the idea of keeping a distance. By the same token, the chapter moves from the active effort to be useful to the pursuit of uselessness, from ardor to detachment. It also, and more importantly, reflects Zhuangzi's life and psychological development.

As a knight, he most certainly shared the goal of his contemporaries and probably set out just as determined as Yan Hui to save the world. All learned men of the time shared this ardor. Some formed alliances with or against the state of Qin; others practiced occult arts. Some were like Xu Xing 許行, who "spoke for Shennong 神農" (Mengzi 3A4); others matched Mozi, who "rejected the way of Zhou and used the regulations of the Xia dynasty" (*Huainanzi*, ch. 21; Major et al. 2010, 864). Some echoed Yang Zhu, who "could govern the world as though it were in the palm of his hand" (*Liezi*, ch. 7); others followed Mencius who proclaimed, "[I]f you want the world to be at peace, who except me can do this in today's world" (*Mengzi* 2B22). Every single one of them went from court to court, hoping to gain a ruler's trust to have his ideas put into practice.

The fact that Shang Yang 商鞅 was executed by being torn and quartered, that Wu Qi 吳起 was killed by being cut in two, did not deter them at all. They saw their quest as clear necessity, a Heaven-given task, as Mencius says: "The scholar's taking of office is like the farmer's plowing of fields" (3A4). Still, power politics as Zhuangzi describes them through Zigao and Yan He give him pause: Is political power really worth such effort and strife? Or is there another world outside politics? In other words, is it an absolute mandate that scholar-knights serve as officials? If not, they have a choice, they can withdraw. In contrast to Confucius who "knows something cannot be done and does it anyway" (14.38), Zhuangzi chooses not even to try doing what he knows is impossible. Confucius may display admirable spirit but not great wisdom. Having an inner firmness like the stability of mountains, don't we also need subtle flexibility like the movement of water? Faced with a steep mountain nearly impossible to cross, why not just forget about it and ride a boat on a stream around it? There is more than one world: there is life beyond politics. As Li Bai says in *Xinglu nan* 行路難 (Trouble on the Road):

> Having ears, you need not wash them in the Yingchuan River.
> Having a mouth, you need not eat the wild herbs of Mt Shouyang.
> Keep your endowments hidden, value lack of fame.
> What use is lofty prominence that rivals moon and clouds?
> Since antiquity, highly accomplished men,
> Not withdrawing when their work was done, all met untimely ends:
> Wu Zixu, dead by suicide, was cast into the River Wu,
> Qu Yuan, throttled by despair, leapt into River Miluo.
> Lu Ji, strategist extraordinaire—how could he protect himself?
> Li Si, soon to retire, found his decision came too late.
> Lu never went to Huating to hear the wild crane's cry,
> Li never took his son to hunt rabbits with a falcon.
> Can you not see that the enlightened man, Zhang Han,
> Becomes homesick and returns to Yangdong at the first gust of fall?
> So, while we can enjoy the cup of wine before us while still alive,
> What use a thousand-year fame after we are gone?

Li Bai saw a world beyond ordinary reality, which he accessed through wine. This may not have been what Zhuangzi wanted—he never speaks of drink—but he certainly had access to a separate world within.

Chapter Three

Nourishing Life

Once we have given up on saving the world, our focus shifts toward questions of how best to live in it, on the process of nourishing life, which is the central topic of chapter 3. Its title, "Yangshengzhu" 養生主, has two implications: nourishing life as central or what is essential in nourishing life. The former matches Zhuangzi's overall thought more closely, the latter allows us to delve deeper into the intricacies of his thinking.

Either way, what Zhuangzi means by "nourishing life" has nothing much to do with Pengzu's 彭祖 longevity techniques, the breathing techniques or healing exercises that involve "taking in the new and expelling the old," "doing the Bear Amble and the Bird Stretch" (ch. 15). All these methods serve to extend physical life—far, far removed from Zhuangzi's key concern. Pengzu and his ilk think of the human being as a natural phenomenon, an entity that can exist without external intentions or social connections—e.g., the hermit Dan Bao 單豹 (ch. 19). Interpersonal relationships play little or no role in their thinking. Zhuangzi's focus is significantly different. His key concern is how to live within the human world, and he hones in, from beginning to end, on this aspect of life. "Nourishing life" here means how to live among other people, within society, how to find a place within the intricacies and vicissitudes of the world, among its thorns and brambles, where one can be at peace and truly oneself.

This place, then, is not a physical, concrete space to occupy, like a mountain retreat or a monastery. Rather, it is a way of life, a particular attitude toward the world. How best to understand life? How to communicate one's take on life with others? These are his most fundamental questions, central to his vision, which centers not on the body but on the mind—how to support an attitude and behavior that allows one to truly relish life. This is the theme of the chapter. It begins,

> Life has a limit, but knowledge has none. If you use what is limited to pursue what has no limit, you will be in danger. If you under-

stand this and still strive for knowledge, you will be in even more danger! If you do good, stay away from fame. If you do evil, stay away from punishments. Follow the center line for guidance, and you can maintain your body, keep your life intact, nourish your parents, and live out your years.

This makes it very clear: the core of nourishing life is to keep oneself whole and alive, to live out one's years without leaving society. The way Zhuangzi gets at this issue is also obvious: by separating life from knowledge, by delving deeply into the conflict between the physical with its various imitations and the metaphysical—the realm that reaches beyond, is free from the constraints of the world, and transcends the ten thousand things. What, then, should our attitude be when we're caught in the middle between the two?

Let us begin with a metaphor. Faced with this situation, we are as if standing on the ocean shore and looking at high waves rolling in. We have two choices: single-handedly take on the mighty ocean and try to hold it back or battle it into shape; or, alternatively, jump in and let ourselves be carried, ride out the swell to land on the sandy beach. Choosing to fight it, we may end up locked in battle, the great ocean our foe onto death, so that we either conquer or submit, live or die—and what kind of life is that? Choosing to jump in, we may well be dead scared that the waves get even higher when the tide comes in and swallow us hook, line, and sinker, or that we are so minuscule that we dissolve in the ocean's vastness. Either way, we can never fully comprehend the ocean in its fullness and, sooner or later, must come to an agreement with it.

Zhuangzi's position is clear. Pursuing knowledge to the end of one's days is a dangerous course, because it leads people into a state of never-ending dissatisfaction. Knowing just how dangerous it is and yet proceeding is an incurable disease. Just like Huizi: "Weak in inner virtue, strong in his concern for external things, he walked a road that was crooked indeed" (ch. 33).

Huizi thus used his wide learning and considerable talents in an effort to win the approval of the "learned ones." But did he reach truth? From Zhuangzi's perspective, only the perfected have true knowledge, and Huizi cannot be counted among them. The perfected are the masters of this world, not its slaves. Huizi, wanting to understand how the world works, is bound to forget about the most important thing of all: his own self. "He never found peace with this approach, tirelessly separating and analyzing all things. In the end, he was known only for his skill in exposition." This shows just how constrained he is by outside things, never getting a moment's rest, like Kuafu who keeps running after the sun. He is emaciated from hunger and thirst, running for water to save his life, yet he doesn't realize the best method for quenching thirst and finding satisfaction. Like a shadow chasing a form, like an echo following a sound—where is resolution? Where can there be resolution?

Of course, there is resolution, and it's not a tragic ending, like Kuafu running to his death. The resolution life offers is not to have form and shadow run in competition, trying to find metaphysical resolutions for physical existence or discover specific meanings for life. There must be a different level of resolution, where life expands and rises to a new level of meaning. This is what Laozi talks about when he says, "Knowledge ends but does not perish" (ch. 44). There is a limit to knowledge that is not final but offers a place where the mind desists from searching. You must find a limit of knowledge within the world while recognizing the connection between life and perfect wisdom. Knowledge must serve life—not the other way around. This way, life is forever life and not an outside entity bestowed by knowledge; it is the single object most essential to all our concerns.

This position is completely different from all other teachings of the time. Whether Confucian or Mohist, none show any care for life itself nor do they discuss ultimate concerns. As far as the Confucians go, benevolence and righteousness, rites and music, morality and order serve as their central issue. They are willing to die for benevolence, give up life for righteousness, place morality above life, and see the distinctions between good and bad, right and wrong as most important. Thus, Mencius notes that all "knowledge" is determined by the "mind of right and wrong" (6A6). As this mind is part of the inherent human endowment, its education and enhancement mean the pursuit of a life of morality, with the goal of becoming a gentleman or a sage.

When the Confucians with their emphasis on morality meet Zhuangzi with his central concern for life, conflict is inevitable. Where the core focus is on life, morality must be subordinate—a morality, moreover, that is not fixed. Confucians propose Confucian ethics; Mohists have Mohist values—but the ethics of life are singular and can be intuited by one and all. We discussed earlier how Yang Zhu, in contrast to Confucians and Mohists, proposed to "value life and disregard the body"—a teaching with yet its own morality. To benefit the world, he would "not even pluck out a single hair," a position that shows the same contempt as Zhuangzi for a morality that focuses on outside values.

The text says, "If you do good, stay away from fame. If you do evil, stay away from punishments." This still preserves the distinction between good and evil while yet beginning to dissolve it. The important part here is not what good or evil is but, applying the perspective of perfection, to follow Zhuangzi's standard (not unlike that of Confucianism): "Just because a good deed seems small, do not fail to do it; just because an evil seems minor, do not commit it." Essentially this means one should stay away from both fame and punishment, since they have a negative impact on life. Punishment represents an obvious hardship, but why would fame be any better? From here we can see morality—the distinction between good and evil—as secondary, less important than life.

All this, however, does not mean that you are now free to live an immoral life. If a moral life as based on the distinction between good and evil consists of pursuing good, then an immoral life must be its opposite, which means the destruction of good and the commitment of evil. Zhuangzi wants us to let go of both, good *and* evil, to do both right *and* wrong, so that we are free from either. Confucians might see this as an amoral life, but it most certainly is not immoral. Amoral and immoral represent a significant difference, two completely different dimensions of moral action. Zhuangzi might go even further and recommend a transmoral way of living—a going beyond of moral categories and classifications, not merely their denial.

This reminds us of Laozi who says, "When the great Dao declined, benevolence and righteousness came forth" (ch. 18), and insists, "Once Dao was lost, virtue arose; when virtue was lost, benevolence arose; when benevolence was lost, righteousness arose; and when righteousness was lost, ritual propriety arose" (ch. 38). His Dao goes far beyond any form of morality, virtue, or righteousness. Similarly, he notes that "Heaven and Earth are not benevolent" (ch. 5), nor is the sage. Zhuangzi, though in many respects different from Laozi, agrees with him on this point. Beyond that, he insists more on letting go of one's hold on anything, whether good or evil, which has no direct advantage for life. Instead, he proposes going along with, or wandering through, the world in an empty mind and recommends that we "follow the center line for guidance."

What does this mean? The key word of the phrase is "center line" (*du* 督), which signifies the central meridian running along the spine in the human body. Using this reading, Guo Xiang and other commentators have interpreted "follow the center line" as "stick to the middle path." Since it has no form in itself, this also means connecting to the empty center within. Wang Fuzhi reads the passage as follows:

> Among the eight extraordinary vessels, the Governing and Conception Vessels are the central meridians, connected to respiration. . . . The meridian that runs of the front of the body is the Conception Vessel; that running up the back is the Governing Vessel. When the latter is at rest, one does not lean to the right or left, however formless the position of the conduit. "Follow the center line" means that *qi* is clear and subtle, fine and wondrous, and moves smoothly through empty openness. It stops where it cannot pass, passes where it flows naturally, and always follows the middle path. (1985, 30-31)

This clarifies the original text. To "follow the center line" means that one never confuses right and wrong, good and evil, but goes along with the openings in the energy channels, playfully wandering or easily going along—relaxed under any and all circumstances. One may still speak of good and evil, right and wrong, but one is flexible, matching each situation.

This leads next to the famous parable of Cook Ding 庖丁, highly skilled in this kind of going along as shown in his cutting of the sacrificial ox. Zhuangzi describes his great expertise, carefully chiseling and carving yet always following the veins and arteries. As commentators have noted, the story not only follows the above introductory paragraph, but serves particularly as an explication of "follow the center line for guidance."

Cook Ding works in the kitchen of Lord Wenhui 文惠君, preparing the sacrificial ox. He cuts smoothly and with great skill, finding all the right nooks and crannies, so that his knife never gets dull. The story seems be just about a butcher doing his work, but in fact it has many levels of interpretation. So, when Lord Wenhui rounds it off with the words, "I have learned about nourishing life," it becomes clear that it is not just about butchering and understanding the carcass of the ox, but about how best to live in the world.

More specifically, the actual cutting of the ox features three visible elements: Cook Ding, the ox, and the tool he uses for cutting—his knife. In addition there are also invisible aspects, such as the cook's skill, experience, understanding, and so on. Among the three visible elements,

Zhuangzi is particularly interested in the fate of the knife. The same kind of knife, wielded by a different person and using a different technique of cutting, creates completely different results. A good cook will need to have his knife sharpened once a year; a poor one, once a month; but Cook Ding has been using his knife for nineteen years without ever taking it to the whet stone and it is still like new. This is not because there is anything special about the knife. As Xu Lishan 徐笠山 notes, "Another cook's knife, if wielded by Cook Ding, would equally last nineteen years" (Yan 1972, vol. 15). Vice versa, this also means that Cook Ding's knife, when used by another cook, would barely last a month. The key to the parable is obviously the cutting of the ox, so why this emphasis on the knife?

An ox is a huge animal, consisting of a mass of bones and tendons, joints and cartilage, with numerous complicated and difficult spots. Unless you are thoroughly familiar with its anatomy and body structure, you inevitably encounter some bones or joints the wrong way and diminish your efficiency. "A good cook has to change his knife once a year—because he cuts." That is, the knife gets blunt in the course of a year when one "cuts" rather than feels one's way through the ox. "A poor cook has to change his knife once a month—because he hacks." The knife is useless quickly when the cook uses brute force and treats the ox as so much dead matter. Cook Ding, however, says, "I go along with the natural structure, strike in the big corners, guide the knife through the main openings, and follow things as they are. So I never touch the smallest ligament or tendon, much less a main joint." He finds the right spaces, the nooks and crannies, where there is plenty of room to maneuver.

This is the first time the term "natural structure" (*tianli* 天理) occurs in the *Zhuangzi*—an important concept in the history of Chinese thought that has attracted the attention of many thinkers over the millennia. But we'll let it go for the moment. What interests us here is that Cook Ding is a master chef who sees thorough things and goes along with the natural structure of the ox, guiding his knife through the nooks and crannies. The reason why he is so good at cutting up the ox is that he starts out with an in-depth understanding of its make-up, including all its twists and turns—so tiny and minute that you need to have a fine, sharp blade to subtly insert it in the right spot and find just enough space to move. You must go along with the natural structure in just the right way to avoid the fate of becoming a cook who "cuts" or "hacks"

What, then, is the secret that allows Cook Ding to enter this world of perfect natural alignment? This is the question Lord Wenhui asks: it is also what the reader wants to know. It is, most likely, also what the good or poor cook would like to find out. From the perspective of the concrete process of cutting up the ox, the first thing that comes to mind is hands-on skill. However, underlying that, Cook Ding also has eye coordination, which is based on mental alertness, which in its turn rests on spirit pervasion (*shentong* 神通). As he says, "When I first began cutting up oxen, all I could see was the ox itself. After three years I no longer saw the whole ox. And now—now I go at it by spirit and don't look with my eyes. Sense perception and understanding have come to a stop and spirit moves where it wants." Never seeing the whole ox as a whole ox—this is eye coordination.

Cook Ding appreciates the natural structure of all the different parts, bones and tendons, joints and cartilage; he perceives the ox as an accumulation of different parts and aspects. He functions like a highly polished mirror, reflecting reality completely so that he no longer needs physical eyes to guide him. Vision now translates into hand movement with perfect coordination and ease. But not only that: beyond vision and thinking is spirit pervasion. As Cook Ding explains to Lord Wenhui, his connection to the ox depends entirely on the movement of spirit and has little to do with the senses or the intellect. "Sense perception and understanding have come to a stop and spirit moves where it wants"—spirit guides the hands, nothing else. At this stage, any outside reliance has given way to an impulse-and-response relationship, a spirit-energy flow that merges self and others. Cook Ding and the ox form one organism: when he cuts, he never moves beyond it, his work a form of art.

The transition from hands, eyes, and mind to spirit reminds us of the passage on mind-fasting (ch. 4), where the transition is from ears to mind and on to *qi*, opening up different realms of hearing. Although "listen with the ears" and "listen with the mind" are different in that the former is less advanced than the latter, they have in common that they still work with the dichotomy between self and object. Since I still perceive an object outside of myself, I do not pervade it. And how can there be perfect apperception without pervasion? How can I sufficiently appreciate the piping of Heaven that flows through all things? Using *qi* to listen or work is completely different. Now I am transformed in emptiness. This naturally does not mean that I dissolve bodily into nothing. Rather, it is a state where my mind is free and open, where my sense of self dissolves, the boundaries between me and outside things evaporate, and I become one with the world. This is how Cook Ding cuts the ox: cook, ox, and knife are one.

How, then does this ox-cutting parable connect to nourishing life? Simply put, the cook, the knife, and the ox are symbols for humanity, life, and society. Just as there are different kinds of cooks, there are various kinds of people: perfect men, spirit men, sages, gentlemen, ordinary folk, and so on. They each use different ways to deal with society, their methods matching the different quality of their blades. Some go along with social norms without any opposition; others are servants in body and indoctrinated in mind; yet others flow freely through all kinds of social settings—just like the different cooks work with the ox. For this reason, they each experience a different fate: some work hard, laboring their bodies and exhausting their minds; others get sick and die early; yet others live out their years whole and healthy. This matches the various cooks who need their knives sharpened monthly, annually, or essentially never. By presenting the story of cutting up the ox, maybe Zhuangzi wants to tell us that, however much we have to deal with a complex and difficult society, we can still find a place where we can live free from harm, in ease and freedom.

An ox is a huge animal, complacent, and useful: it stands for human society. For an inexperienced cook, as he faces the ox for the first time, its mere dimensions make him lose proper balance and get clumsy. It is a confusing and daunting object, with a natural structure far beyond your comprehension. You have to deal with it anyway; you tremble with fear. You want to avoid at all cost a blind men's chancy discovery, grabbing at one part and taking it for the whole, getting maybe one hit after a hundred misses! For this reason, you need to begin by learning the inner workings of the ox in great depth. Only after its veins and sinews, bones and joints, flesh and muscles are before you like an open book can you reach the point Cook Ding talks about: your eyes no longer see the whole ox. At this point, you are completely connected to it and can move your knife freely and naturally. In the same manner, when facing society, you must first get to know it intimately and enter it deeply: then you can understand it. Once you get to the point of "seeing through" it, you finally uncover its nooks and crannies and start flowing freely within it.

This is how we "follow the center line." As Cangyun Shanfang zhuren 藏雲山房主人 (Master of the Cangyun Studio), Ming-dynasty author of the *Nanhua dayi jiexuan canzhu* 南華大義解懸参注 (Resolution of Doubtful Passages in the Overall Meaning of the Southern Florescence) or possibly identical with Lin Yunming 林雲銘 of the Qing (Yan 2003, 574), says, "Through the story of cutting up the ox, we learn how to move [in society] like blossoms on a tree and reach the stage where we simply follow the center line for guidance" (Yan 1972, vol. 25). This is the key point of the parable. At any time, whatever object or situation we may face, there is an empty space, a nook or cranny to turn to. When you shift to face the full spaces, it is like butting against the ox's joints and bones, muscles and flesh. There's no way to avoid a collision. You would be just like the good or poor cooks who cut and hack—unable to avoid a fate of suffering and death. Do you want to be like that? Of course not! Zhuangzi's intent is clear: "Stay in one piece, keep yourself alive, look after your parents, and live out your years."

As noted earlier, unlike the kind of nourishing life envisioned by Pengzu, Zhuangzi focuses on how best to live in relation to human society and his key focus is on managing this relationship. He expresses this concretely as skills of living in the world, which are just like cutting up the ox—they depend to a large degree on proper understanding. "I go along with the heavenly structure, strike in the big corners, guide the knife through the main openings, and go along with things as they are." First you need to know how the heavenly structure of the ox works and what it is like on the surface. Then you can follow it, depend on it, and work with it in your actions. Anything in the world, any social pattern has aspects one can follow easily, and people can learn what they are. At this point understanding (of the object) and behavior (toward the object) merge: this merging is skill.

This brings us to the role of knowledge. Knowledge in itself is not a negative thing—the crux is the relationship it has to life. Is life in service of the pursuit of knowledge, or vice versa? As long as knowledge of external things and situations can help us reach a better life or attain control over them, it is helpful and merits approval. On the other hand, if the only meaning and purpose of one's life is the pursuit of knowledge, if chasing after outside things constitutes the whole of one's life, this is "using what is limited to pursue what has no limit"—it constitutes danger.

Now let us look at skill. Lord Wenhui marvels at his cook's skill and exclaims: "Imagine skill reaching such heights!" This level of skill is truly a form of art. "At every touch of his hand, every heave of his shoulder, every move of his feet, every thrust of his knee—zip! zoop! He slithered the knife along with a zing, and all was in perfect rhythm, as though he were performing the dance of the Mulberry Grove or keeping time to Jingshou music." This, however, is already beyond mere technical skill, reaching into the transcendent realm of Dao. Technical skill alone leads to the production of man-made objects, which in turn creates set mindframes and limitations. Dao, in contrast, is at one with the natural flow. Thus Zhuangzi speaks of the natural flow of creation, the "heavenly craftsman"—a level that people's skill never quite reaches. Thus he says, "When the sun and moon have already come out and the torches are yet burning—isn't it futile to compare their light?" (ch. 1).

Similarly someone with three years experience may be able to manage a certain skill, but it is futile for him to imitate a true master craftsman. Both have a certain level of expertise, but only when it is fully pervaded by Heaven and Earth can it manifest fully on the human plane. So, when Lord Wenhui praises Cook Ding for his "skill reaching such heights," he answers, "What I care about is Dao, which is not skill," referring to the unsurpassable realm of natural flow. The difference between Dao and skill is thus the same as between Heaven and Humanity (mind and no-mind) as well as between *qi* and ears, spirit and eyes: "I go at it by spirit and don't look with my eyes."

Zhuangzi himself is thus an outstanding craftsman who uses the parable of the butcher to explain how best to live. He uses the process of butchering to reveal deep-seated aesthetics and artistic spirit. The process of butchering, made almost divine allows people to forget about the concrete facts of the job and instead float off in an atmosphere saturated with art. Yet it may also indicate just to what degree the human world is nothing but a big slaughter-house—where we are not only not holding the knife but are hiding in fear from those brandishing it. We cannot seriously expect those who hold the knife to put it down and become suddenly enlightened—but we certainly can cower and hide.

Unlike in chapter 4, "In the Human World," which repeatedly emphasizes that fate is unavoidable, and unlike the helpless cry "avoid yin, avoid yang, there's nothing I can do," here we see aspects of personal autonomy and initiative. Facing society as it is, we are not completely helpless, forced to listen and obey. Rather, we can seek out the nooks and crannies in the fabric of society and flow through them, pursuing our very own life in the narrow cracks. Make no mistake: Zhuangzi has strong respect for the unavoidable and supports "resting in fate." But at the same time he also supports asserting one's autonomy and taking charge of one's own fate within the reigning circumstances.

In other words, the forces of fate are just a structural backdrop to life: they are by no means all of it. Beyond fate there is also the development of people's knowledge of their own limitations and their growth on the stage of skill. In this personal development, freedom emerges. Thus Cook Ding's knife moves smoothly through the carcass and he proudly enjoys his accomplishments. Yet together with the freedom of the action there is also the need for care and caution. "Whenever I come to a complicated place, I size up the difficulties, tell myself to watch out and be careful, keep my eyes on what I'm doing, work very slowly, and move the knife with the greatest subtlety, until—flop!—the whole thing comes apart like a clod of earth crumbling to the ground." Thus, in complicated situations in life, one cannot be careful enough.

However much care you take, there still may be times when you suffer harm. You can only nourish life so far—there are areas where it is simply not possible. Also, you can mainly nourish the mind, but not the body, which is beyond control: what kind of body you are born with, whether you are whole and limber or deformed and crooked, strong or weak, tall or short. Nor can we choose our parents, who are given to us by Heaven. Even the things that happen to the body in this world are largely beyond our control: accidental injuries, infections, punishments by branding or amputation.

Zhuangzi tells the story of Gongwen Xuan 公文軒 who sees a man with only one foot and asks how this came about. "It was Heaven, not Humanity," is the answer, something the person was born with. "People's appearance is a given," Zhuangzi says, and adds, "Heaven gave him human form—why not call him a person?" (ch. 5). This "body" or "form," moreover, is not limited to just the genetically determined physical body but also includes its transformations in the course of life and its encounters in the world. As he says, "If you play around in front of Archer Yi's 羿 target, you're right in the way of the arrows, and if you don't get hit, it's a matter of fate" (ch. 5). If you do get hit, it's a matter of fate, too. Similarly, in Zhuangzi's world, whether you meet with punishment or not has nothing specifically to do with yourself or your actions.

This, on the other hand, does not mean one cannot nourish life or that one should not do so. It just means that knowing that life and death are determined by fate, you can relax about what you do within that framework. As Mencius says, knowing fate means one will never stand on a steep cliff ready to jump to one's death (7A2). Knowing fate means that we acknowledge the inevitable and realize that there are things we cannot do, but it also means knowing what we in fact *can* do. With regard to the physical body, it means exhausting our human efforts while listening for Heaven's commands. But how about the mind? It most certainly is an area where people can exert serious influence, be autonomous, and create extensive nourishing.

From Zhuangzi's perspective, the essential part of things is not what we can see in the world, made from metal and wood, but what is bestowed by Heaven. What gets hurt in the physical world is merely the bodily form, but what faces the wrath of Heaven is the mind. While any hurt or destruction of the body may be due to fate, any distortion of the mind is entirely the responsibility of the individual. You may have no control over the body, but you most certainly are in charge of your mind.

This means that, however much the body may suffer or be harmed, as long as your mind is whole, you are still a complete person. By the same token, your body may be whole and healthy, but if your mind is hurt or twisted, you are no longer truly yourself. As Zhuangzi says, "Blindness and deafness are not confined to the body alone—the mind has them, too" (ch. 2). That is to say, being physically blind or deaf cannot block the radiance or perception of your mind—but what if your mind is blind or deaf? Then, however physically strong and whole you may be, you are not a complete person. Seeing from this angle, nourishing life is obviously not about keeping the body intact; it is all about fostering and preserving the mind. The most important aspect, then, is to have a naturally flowing, autonomous mind! You do not want it in a cage of any shape: "The swamp pheasant has to walk ten paces for one peck and a hundred paces for one drink, but it doesn't want to be kept in a cage. Though you treat it like a king, its spirit won't be content."

The little bird has a hard life getting its nourishment, but it would never give it up in favor of captivity, however well endowed. It values its freedom above all else. So, where is your freedom? Whenever your body reaches a state of full satisfaction, you let go of your mind. But the fact is: your body never quite reaches full satisfaction—it remains a vaguely hoped-for state. At the same time, the moment you allow yourself to hope for full satisfaction even a tiny bit, your body has already lost its full freedom and your mind is already submerged in material longings. Hope for satisfaction, however minute, means the loss of true authenticity: you give up true life for things you can only try to call your own.

Thus Zhuangzi says, "If you do good, stay away from fame." Already Laozi—with his call for "no fame" and his question, "What means more to you, you or your renown?" (ch. 44)—raised the inherent conflict between life and fame. What do we live for as human beings? For vain glory and fame? Or for something more important? Birds in a cage may well be glorious—if not, why would someone keep them? The master described above may be rightfully famous for his exceptional skill, but he is held captive because of it. He occupies a high position, has a great reputation, and receives a good salary from his lord. Like a bird in a cage he is very well treated, much admired by the people around him. But isn't this state of fame and fortune also a form of punishment?

Of course it is. Let us just reconsider the cases of Zigao and Yan He (ch. 4). In the eyes of the world, they are both famous people, but looking at them all anxious and confined after they receive their orders, aren't they rather like ants on a hot plate? They run hither and thither, with no way to escape. At this point, they may even regret their choice to enter the cage of official service. Submitting to the cangue in body and mind and suffering torments and anxiety, they are ever farther removed from the chance of happiness.

From here all they can do is admire the drifting clouds and wild cranes, free birds like the little swamp pheasant. They may even envy Zhuangzi, because he is just like such a little bird. He made the decision to let himself out of the cage, rejecting whatever position the king of Chu offered. His life in poverty—wearing ragged clothes, with withered neck and sallow face, trading chestnuts with the local lord—is much like that of the swamp pheasant, "walking ten paces for one peck and a hundred paces for one drink." Still, being free has its own reward: happy like a tortoise dragging its tail in the mud, he joyfully moves through the world. Having let go of all concerns for the body, he enjoys authenticity of mind.

Unlike human-inflicted hardships, those meted out by Heaven are both harsher and harder to overcome. Punishments in the outside world are visible: locks and chains, axes and hammers, physical pain and disability. Heaven's hardships are formless, but they reach deeper, far into the mind. Still, they can also be dealt with—and this is the core of "nourishing life."

In this context, Zhuangzi tells the story of Qin Shi who went to mourn Lao Dan, giving a mere three cries and leaving the room. When asked why he mourns in such a perfunctory manner, he explains that he originally thought Lao Dan a deeply authentic person, but seeing how people mourned for him—crying and wailing as if for a mother or son—he realized that he wasn't. "To have gathered a group like that, he must have done something to make them talk about him, though he didn't ask them to talk, or make them weep for him, though he didn't ask them to weep. This is to hide from Heaven, turn your back on the true state of affairs, and forget what you were born with. In the old days, this was called the crime of hiding from Heaven."

Right in the middle of the discussion on nourishing life, Zhuangzi brings up death. It is almost as if he reverses Confucius's question, "Unless you know life, how can you know death?" (11.12), changing it into, "Unless you know death, how can you know life?" Life and death determine each other and can only be understood in conjunction. They essentially form a single organism, constituting different phases of the same process, like arrival and departure during an on-going journey. Can we possibly ride them like the wind? No, we can't, nobody can. They move all on their own. How, then, should we deal with things we cannot ride or control? Zhuangzi says, "Know what you can't do anything about and be content with it as fate" (ch. 4). "If you are content with the time and willing to follow along, then grief and joy have no way to enter" (ch. 3).

This, then, is what it means to be free from strong emotional reactions. This, of course does not mean to have no emotions whatsoever—they are, after all, a vital part of life. Rather, it means letting go of emotional reactions after deeply understanding the structure of things. In terms of death, this means seeing it as part of life and understanding that neither life nor death are truly in our possession. There is no real need to get all happy and excited when a person arrives in this life; nor should you go into deep mourning when one departs from it.

Emotions like these are "weeping as though for a son" or "for a mother," reactions to what are, in Zhuangzi's view, Heaven-given hardships. Not accepting these for Zhuangzi is as if "hiding from Heaven, turning one's back on the true state of affairs, and forgetting what you were born with." People with extreme reactions show just how deeply oriented toward the human world they are. They move farther and farther away from Heaven until they get to the stage where they think people are really Heaven. This is a highly distorted perspective, taking a mere thing to be the center of all. This mere thing, moreover, is the human being—not his body but his mind. The mind's distortion, then, causes a screwed view of reality, which in turn necessitates "being divinely freed from all bonds."

"Being divinely freed from all bonds" means freeing people from distorted vision. But the word "bonds" (*xuan* 懸) also means "hang" or "suspend," indicating the upside-down nature of the vision. When a person is hung upside-down, he will urgently fight for liberation. But what if that happens to the mind? Maybe he'll fight, maybe not. If you are aware of having an upside-down perspective from the very beginning, with a clear sense of upright versus reversed, you experience a strong desire for liberation. But this desire, as in Zhuangzi, is not primarily directed toward liberating the world; it is more focused on freeing oneself as a first priority. Zhuangzi needs to get himself into a position where his head is upright, toward the blue sky, and his feet stand on solid ground—not the other way round. "Feet on solid ground" means that he never leaves the human world; "head toward the blue sky" means that his spirit is as free as a soaring bird. This is the right way to live. The other way, with feet up and head down, is being thoroughly submerged in the affairs of life.

This chapter speaks of freeing (*jie* 解) in different ways: when Cook Ding cuts up the ox, he frees a thing; when Zhuangzi speaks of divine release, he frees the mind. In all cases freeing is the release of something knotted or confined. For Cook Ding, it means that he cuts open the ox, an entity full of knots and twists, by passing his knife through tendons and joints, using the crannies between skin and muscles to create a free space or openness. But how about freeing the mind? This, too, means removing excessive knots and twists. Mental knots, however, are made by things and people, creating lasting perceptions that fill it and produce the "fixed mind." Originally death is part of the natural process; there is no need to exhibit great grief. Still, when Lao Dan dies, "old men weep for him as though for a son; young men weep for him as though for a mother." This is a clear manifestation of mental knots and heart blockages. They need to be opened up, set free. The best way to do so is through a thorough understanding of the functioning of things, a way of being that is firmly grounded in reality and goes along with all.

This again is a form of opening things rather than the mind, and it all goes back to "following the center line for guidance." This phrase most certainly is the nub of this chapter. The ultimate truth of nourishing life is this: find an open space in the complicated and intricate human world, then go along to wander freely in it while living out your Heaven-given years. But in order to find the nooks and crannies, first of all your mind has to be empty. You can't fill it with aspirations for accomplishments, fame, profit, or position. Face the world with an empty mind, and it will open its spaces for you, allowing you to live with ease and freedom.

This does not mean that you pursue eternal life. Zhuangzi had no interest in permanence or eternity, knowing full well that the only eternal thing is universal change and transformation, certainly not any individual life. Where there is life, there must be death, and death is yet another form of life. Thus the chapter ends with the words, "Though the grease burns out of the torch, the fire passes on, and no one knows where it ends." Xu Lishan comments, "The chapter begins with the statement that 'life has a limit, but knowledge has none,' indicating that all is connected but not stable. It ends by turning the beginning around. Noting that the torch holds fire, Zhuangzi asserts that 'knowledge has a limit, but life has none'" (Yan 1972, vol. 15).

Zhuangzi's writing often contains marvelous twists like that. In this case, the counter position of "limit - no limit" matches that of "burning out - passing on," which in turn echoes "northern darkness - southern darkness" (ch. 1) and "southern sea - northern sea" (ch. 7). However, we are really more interested in what lies behind the writing. The torch in the image indicates something that has a limit, while the fire passes on without end. The metaphor must have something to offer our understanding of life, such as human fate being limited while universal transformations continue forever.

From beginning to end, Zhuangzi seeks to expose what is unlimited within the world, connecting to the vastness of life. He is also concerned with showing that that human life is only a tiny speck in the great transformations of the universe, like "a deer passing a crack." From this position, two things emerge: compassion and detachment. Although he takes life very seriously, he never gets into any kind of life extension program like the immortality seekers. Rather, he focuses exclusively on how to live freely in mind and unharmed in body.

This is truly the perspective of authenticity, allowing us to go beyond the physical body, beyond human morality, and even beyond life and death. The best way to nourish life is to enter fully in the creative change of the universe, where life and death, existence and perishing are part of the same interconnected organism.

Chapter Four

Full in Virtue

To live successfully, skill is certainly essential but even more important is the basic understanding of life itself. This understanding inevitably involves an appreciation of the world, a connection to all the different creatures and things it contains. It can manifest in people's minds to a different degree and take them to different realms. If it reaches a high degree or vast realm, we speak of "virtue" (*de* 德). Designating a very important concept, the term is ubiquitous in Chinese thought and particularly in Daoism, which is described as the "school of Dao and virtue" (*Shiji*, Pref.). All its core philosophical texts contain the term, including the *Laozi* and *Zhuangzi*, particularly chapter 5, "Dechongfu" 德充符.

The words after *de* in the title demarcate a difference in emphasis: *chong* (full) indicates the inside; *fu* (tally) points to the outside or the matching of inside and outside. That is to say, whenever someone's mind is full on the inside, what kind of person does that make him? This is probably the most important aspect of this title. One way to answer the question is represented in the *Laozi*: "He who contains the fullness of virtue is like an infant" (ch. 55). But this is not what Zhuangzi is talking about.

Zhuangzi takes great pleasure in describing cripples and amputees as being full in virtue. He relishes these figures, from Wang Tai 王駘 and Shentu Jia who had each lost a foot through Shushan No Toes 叔山無趾 to Mr. Lame-Hunchback-No-Lips 闉跂支离无無脤 and Pitcher-Sized-Wen 瓮口大癭—all greatly impaired in their bodies. Maybe he wanted to demonstrate how, despite physical handicaps, the virtue inside can still be whole and complete. All these characters in the text, however disfigured, are exceptional and charismatic individuals—exuding an attraction or charisma that has nothing to do with the physical body but instead rests in their virtue, the powerful radiance that oozes from the fullness of their hearts. The contrast between virtue and the physical body, then, is the central thread of the chapter.

Virtue is always something closely related to the heart or mind, a fact that is obvious by merely looking at the character. The old form of the character consists of *zhen* 真, "perfected" or "authentic," plus *xin* 心, "heart" or "mind." However, its meaning is understood differently and often hotly contended, not only among Daoists but also among Confucians. Confucius says, "Keep your will on Dao, hold on to virtue, rely on benevolence, and go along with art" (*Lunyu* 7.6); and "govern always with virtue" (2.1). The "virtue" he talks about is quite different from what Zhuangzi intends: focused more on an inner attitude of benevolence that finds expression in the outside behavior of ritual propriety. For Zhuangzi, too, virtue involves benevolence and propriety, but for him the mind should be empty, as in the section on mind-fasting (ch. 4). But empty does not mean that there is nothing there at all. As in the expression "an empty room brings forth whiteness," so an empty mind brings forth a world of bright radiance, a world that is of the spirit rather than of material forms. The chapter begins by describing Wang Tai, a teacher in Lu who only had one foot. Despite this handicap, he had as many followers as Confucius. When Chang Ji 常季 asks about his popularity, Confucius describes him as a sage, insisting that we "should all become his followers!"

Zhuangzi here consciously features a figure with a physical disability. Although handicapped, Wang Tai attracts as many followers as the renowned Confucius. Why is that? It's not *what* he does. As Chang Ji says, "He doesn't stand up and teach, he doesn't sit down and discuss." Still, his followers "go to him empty and return full." It is as if he has abandoned all speech and created a direct communication from the heart, completely different from the Confucian method of transmission in words while teaching in body. But is this really possible? As Chang Ji asks, "Does he really have some wordless teaching, some formless way of bringing the mind to completion?"

Zhuangzi's goal here is to point to the mind behind the words, to the formless background of all shaped, material things. He wants to go beyond the physical and direct people's attention to the inner mind and depth of virtue. The two phrases, "go empty and return full," and "bring the mind to completion" closely echo the chapter title. Confucius in the story firmly believes that Wang Tai is authentic and exerts his unique attraction, even expects to become his disciple and expresses regret that he hasn't yet done so. Not only should he himself go and learn from him, but he thinks "we should all become his followers."

Wang Tai's charisma has nothing to do with his physical looks or behavior; it resides entirely in his virtue. As can be seen from the words of Chang Ji, virtue here is the way he "uses his mind." Wang Tai is unique: he does not bow to conventional modes, and the more he develops the farther away he moves from the ordinary. This remove is contained in another aspect of the word *de*, the character *sheng* 升, "ascent." The Han dictionary *Shuowen jiezi zhu* 說文解字注 (Annotated Explanation of Characters and Interpretation of Phrases) says, "Virtue: that is ascent." Ascent is a form of transcendence, a going beyond of the ordinary world—precisely where for Zhuangzi the pursuit of Dao comes into its own. This makes it clear that virtue is not only connected to the mind, but also to Dao. Just as Laozi says, "Great virtue flows from Dao alone" (ch. 21). In this sense, Zhuangzi's idea of virtue can be easily connected to the attitude of "flowing the mind in Dao," the unique and exceptional way Wang Tai relates to the world. This world, moreover, when seen from the perspective of "flowing in Dao," is itself unique and exceptional, and so is the relationship you develop with it.

As Confucius says in the chapter: "Life and death are great affairs, and yet they are no change to him. Though Heaven and Earth flop over and fall down, it is no loss to him. He sees into what has no falsehood and does not shift with things. He takes it as fate that things should change, and he holds fast to the source." The world changes incessantly, just as people pass continuously through different stages of life and death, just as Heaven and Earth keep on changing as they cover and support all existence. But these are physical changes, and our mind cannot easily keep up with them, nor do we have any control over them.

However, we do have one choice: we can choose not to move along with them. To do so, we hold on to the ancestor of all things: pure Dao. This is the one and only entity in this world of incessant change that remains firm, as Laozi says, it "stands alone and never changes" (ch. 25). Hold on to this and you can go beyond the world of change. On the other hand, you can never reach it as long as you stay fenced in by ordinary things and stick to being in the world. You may dispute the distinction of liver and gall bladder, of Chu and Yue, and thereby stay among restricted things.

But when your mind comes to flow with Dao, you discover that all things are in fact mutually pervasive and are all one at the source: there is neither liver nor gall bladder, neither Chu nor Yue. All form-based distinctions vanish. You no longer have to make an effort for your ears to let go of hearing different sounds, your eyes to relinquish seeing different sights, your mind to merge with the differences and changes in thoughts and ideas. Instead, you just transform once to become fully serene, tranquil, and at peace. Here you realize that all things are but one integrated and eternal organism free from gain and loss, life and death.

What, then, is Zhuangzi saying here? "He lost a foot and is still superior to the Master." Wang Tai cannot intentionally grow himself another foot; he has no impact whatsoever on the physical changes taking place in his body. He lives in the form-based world yet has already gone beyond it. His mind as it flows with Dao has fully transcended knowledge and ordinary thinking, reached the level of the "constant mind"—a mind that no longer changes under the impact of things outside. The constant mind, moreover, is nothing special: it is just mind in a state of emptiness and stillness—the only mind that can produce stillness in the world. "Only what is still in itself can create stillness in others."

The Buddhist thinker Sengzhao 僧肇 (374-414) says in his *Wu buqian lun* 物不遷論 (On the Immutability of Things; trl. Liebenthal 1948, 46-55): "The raging storm which uproots the mountains is in fact still; the rushing streams that pour through all do not flow" (II.3). Although Sengzhao is worlds away from Zhuangzi in historical period and world-view, their expressions are close. There will always be a blowing gale, there will always be a swift current, but from the perspective of oneness they are fixed and stable. Zhuangzi here does not claim that the world itself is empty or that nothing really exists (as the Buddhists would), but that all phenomena return to serenity if one is in a state of true inner stillness. For Zhuangzi, the world is the world—crowded, confused, noisy—but as I grow empty and still in my mind, it too becomes empty and still.

Stillness and emptiness, moreover, are not natural to the mind. They have to be pursued, practiced, and attained. "In the way he goes about it, he uses his knowledge to get at his mind, and uses his mind to get at the constant mind," Chang Ji says about Wang Tai. This indicates the path of attainment: work through yourself, not through others; close the doors of the senses that connect you to the outside world and put it completely out of your mind. The text says "use," but we really should read "stop": stop knowledge and stop the mind, then you can attain the constant mind, when you can remain unmoved no matter how confused and troublesome the world may be.

The constant mind is the outward expression of strong inner virtue, where Wang Tai's charisma really resides. An obvious example is the pine tree: it stands tall among other plants, unmoved and unchanging throughout the seasons; it is always green, always erect, beyond the vicissitudes of weather and climate. It manifests in the sage rulers Yao and Shun, who maintain uprightness no matter what the masses demand. It also shows up in brave soldiers, valiant explorers who enter uninhabited wilderness. "How much more, then, can this state be possible for a man who governs Heaven and Earth, stores up the ten thousand things, lets the six parts of his body be only a dwelling, makes ornaments of his ears and eyes, unifies the knowledge of what he knows, and in his mind never tastes death?" This is what it means to attain Dao. In this state, how can the changes of the world have any impact? They obviously cannot. And thus it is that the unmoved mind is also the most natural state possible.

Wang Tai is a prime example of someone with an unmoved mind. He is never carried away by outside things, but always strives to maintain the prime nature of his heart, making it possible to transcend the form-based world. Shentu Jia is another example. Both have lost a foot, and both, like Zichan 子產, are students of Bohun Wuren 伯昏無人, the Nonhuman Uncle Haze, a name that in itself points to just how unlike ordinary people these figures are. In the story, Zichan is a man of some standing who takes both himself and his body very seriously. He is ashamed to be studying together with a footless man and wishes to distance himself from him, saying to Shentu Jia: "If I go out first, you stay behind; if you go out first, I'll stay behind." Not only limited by his perception of the importance of physical shapes, he goes yet another step further and pulls rank: "Now I will go out. Are you going to stay behind or aren't you? When you see a prime minister, you don't even get out of the way—do you think you're the equal of a prime minister?"

Those involved in political power will always focus on distinctions of rank and social standing. Dependent on divisions of class, office, fame, and the like, they pigeon-hole anyone and everyone. From their perspective, that's it: people are their position, their social role, without any other distinguishing marks. Zhuangzi obviously cannot stomach this kind of attitude. Unlike Zichan and his kind, he sees inner authenticity as the key factor in everyone and places all else—social rank, fame, and position—far beyond. When he has Shentu Jia say, "You take delight in being a prime minister and pushing people behind you," he shows his deep understanding of how the world works. Political rank and high office have nothing to do with human authenticity—they are won or lost without any real connection to the person, due to the vagaries of fate.

Shentu Jia has lost a foot: that's just another vagary of fate. He says:

> To know what you cannot do anything about, and to be content with it as you would with fate—only a man of virtue can do that. If you play around in front of Archer Yi's target, you are right in the way of the arrows, and if you don't get hit, it's a matter of fate. There are lots of men with two feet who laugh at me for having only one. It makes me boil with rage, but I come here to the Master's place and I feel calmed down again and go home. . . . The Master and I have been friends for nineteen years and he's never once let on that he's aware I'm missing a foot.

For our appreciation of virtue, this means that the most important consideration is our attitude to fate. We must acknowledge fate as a major factor in life and realize that anything to do with the physical body—whether you have two feet or one, are born noble or humble—depends on fate and cannot be helped. Then we need to acquiesce to this, rest in the fated circumstances and remain free from all joy and anger. To speak with Shentu Jia, we are all in some way or another "in front of Archer Yi's target," facing a shooter so skilled that his arrows never go astray. Should one miss the mark, that's not due to incompetence but to an act of fate.

In fact Shentu Jia here says, "I was punished by losing a foot and you weren't, and now you're in a position of power and I'm not. But that doesn't make you a better person or me a lesser man: it's all part of the vagaries of fate. Once you realize that it's fate, well, better forget about it. Don't waste your time fretting or complaining." People's authenticity manifests in how they relate to things, how they use their mind. To illustrate this Zhuangzi uses aspects of the self and emphasizes the contrast between body and mind. The body includes our relationship to outside things and circumstances—they depend entirely on fate. The mind involves personal thinking and attitude—they are of our own making, where authenticity takes root.

But it's not any kind of mind that can be authentic and relax into flow, certainly not one that is deeply engaged with outside things. "If the mirror is bright, no dust settles on it; if dust settles, it isn't really bright." The mirror here stands for the mind—an image that occurs variously in Daoist texts. Thus Laozi speaks of "the mysterious mirror being cleansed" (ch. 10) and Guan Yin describes the perfected as one "whose movement is like that of water and whose stillness is like that of a mirror" (*Zhuangzi* 33). Likewise the mind has to be empty to be clear, and when it is full of outside things, when it evaluates the world in terms of good or high or lofty, it cannot shine forth or flow with Dao. Worse, the moment it strives to reach this flow and makes Dao a conscious and contrived value, it will quickly drown. This is the case with Confucius who holds on tightly to concepts such as learning and names and can never let them go. His mind is completely tied up in them, focused on nothing but "teaching men virtue," yet he rejects Shushan No Toes when he comes to study with him: "You weren't careful enough! Since you've already broken the law and gotten yourself into trouble, what do you expect to gain by coming to me now?"

Shushan feels deeply disappointed. He thought that Confucius "would be like Heaven and Earth," kind and impartial, but now has to realize that he is just as narrow-minded and form-focused as everyone else. Shushan goes to Confucius not because he hopes to get his foot made whole by some kind of reconstructive surgery, but because he has "something that is worth more than a foot," reaching far beyond the question of physical wholeness. The parable is particularly remarkable because it makes clear is that "valuing a foot" has nothing to do with wholeness. This is the central point of virtue for Zhuangzi, this is what being "full in virtue" looks like.

Confucius may similarly be quite aware of just how vulgar his behavior is, but his mind has been tied up in dense conceptualizations for so long that he cannot be set free in one fell swoop. He still sees Shushan as someone who "is striving to learn so he can make up for the evil of his former conduct" and is thus unable to forget about his physical reality. He has no clue that, as far as Shushan is concerned, the physical body is long forgotten. Nor does Shushan have any more concepts of "learning" or "evil." Learning for what? Making up for what evil? Do good for what? To become famous? Dao is immensely far beyond any form of learning, beyond any kind of good and evil. Thus, these concepts have nothing to do with Shushan and his pursuit.

In that, he closely matches Daoist thought. Already Laozi says, "Learning means to increase day by day, practicing Dao means to diminish day by day" (ch. 48), showing that Dao and learning are activities that lead in opposite directions. In order to learn, one must cultivate knowledge and the conscious mind, but to practice Dao one must put them on hold. "Without going out the door, know the world; without looking through the window, see the Dao of Heaven. The farther you travel, the less you know," Laozi notes (ch. 47). Zhuangzi essentially says the same thing, making it a natural feature for Laozi to appear as his spokesperson.

In fact, the parable of Shushan No Toes is the second place where Lao Dan appears in the text—although his death is mourned in the previous chapter, he shows up quite alive here, in direct contact with Confucius. Quite possibly this picks up on the semi-historical anecdote of Confucius seeking instruction from him as described in the *Shiji* (chs. 47; 63), although to characterize Laozi as Confucius's teacher is a bit strong. Here, appealing to Shushan's sense of compassion, he expresses the hope that Confucius can still be made to see "that life and death are the same story, that acceptable and unacceptable form a single string," thus shedding the fetters that have tied up his heart for so long. These fetters, moreover, are a punishment from Heaven, not from Humanity—which could be escaped far more easily.

What, then, exactly is meant by "punishment from Heaven"? Does it indicate the fact that Confucius cannot cure himself of his condition? Or does it represent Zhuangzi's appreciation of the irreconcilable differences between his thinking and that of Confucius and his school? Or, again, is it an acknowledgment of the overarching influence of that kind of thinking? Maybe all of the above. Zhuangzi is no dogmatist, he does not accept a single, uniform understanding of anything, a single "best" attitude toward life or one philosophy that fits all. He establishes his unique position by arguing different sides and providing evidence for a certain way of life. But he never thinks of anything as universal or denies potential alternatives. He obviously thinks Confucius's teachings are faulty, but only within the confines of opinions. He would never denigrate the hundred schools and present only himself as worthy of mention. He knows he doesn't have that right nor can he take it from anyone else, and thus he is free from excessive expectations.

More importantly, "punishment from Heaven" involves a particular appreciation of the mind. Punishments meted out by humanity are limited to the physical body, like the amputation of a foot or the cutting off of toes. But Heaven's inflictions fetter the heart and are so much more fearful for it, crippling the spirit and destroying virtue. They go far beyond the pain and constraint one can put upon the body. Is Confucius with his particular punishment ready for some kind of "liberation"? People cannot provide this liberation; it can only be effected by Heaven, by creative change—the one underlying constant in Zhuangzi's world. There is nothing that does not change, except something that underlies it.

The story continues with Confucius telling of his travels to Chu, where he sees a litter of piglets nursing at the body of their dead mother. "After a while, they gave a start and all ran away and left her, because they could no longer see their likeness in her; she was not the same as she had been before. In loving their mother, they loved not her body but the thing that moved her body." Placing these words into Confucius's mouth, it is almost as if he "is striving to learn so he can make up for the evil of his former conduct," gradually changing into a representative of Zhuangzi's thought. Using the example of the animals, he fleshes out the tension between the physical body and "the thing that moves" it. From the position of the physical body, the dead sow is no different from when it was alive. Still, the piglets are startled and run away because they "no longer see their likeness in her" and recognize that "she was not the same as before." Despite the fact that the body is still physically present, what made the sow a sow has gone. "The thing that moved her body" is lost, the body is no longer whole, the "mother" has disappeared. What "moved her body" is that which made the mother a mother.

What, then, is this "thing that moved her body"? It is virtue, inner power, the active functioning of the mind. Similarly, Ai Taituo 哀駘它, without the noble position of a lord that might enable him to save people from death, without a major fortune that might enable him to give others food, exerts charisma. "When men were around him, they thought only of him and couldn't break away, and when women saw him, they ran begging to their fathers and mothers, saying, 'I'd rather be this gentleman's concubine than another man's wife!' There were more than ten such cases and it hasn't stopped yet." Attraction such as this is entirely due to virtue, to the active functioning of the mind. What kind of functioning, though? Zhuangzi speaks of being "whole in natural ability" and "formless in virtue."

Being whole, then, means being impervious to "life and death, preservation and loss, success and failure, poverty and riches, favor and disgrace, reputation and slander, hunger and thirst, cold and heat—the ongoing patterns of the world, the vagaries of fate." They keep on changing and are beyond our control: "They should not be enough to destroy your harmony; they should not be allowed to enter the inner core of your spirit," which should remain harmonious and joyful.

In contrast to being punished by Heaven, with one's natural ability stymied, crippled, or lost, being whole in natural ability means to be protected and guarded by Heaven. In the former case, one is like Confucius, eager to help Heaven; in the latter, one radiates naturally as its part. In fact, the very word "ability" (*cai* 才) echoes the word for "Heaven" (*tian* 天); it is often used as a synonym for "inner nature" (*xing* 性) As Mencius says, "Right and wrong form part of natural ability," i.e., one's Heaven-given endowment, the character one is naturally born with. "Whole in natural ability" thus means that whatever gifts and nature one is endowed with by Heaven are complete and ready to be fully developed.

One must take great care not to let other people and worldly conceptions destroy this wholeness, fully understanding the divide between the heavenly and the human. The heavenly, then, is part of fate, the vagaries of life we can do nothing about. The mind has to learn to leave them alone, put them beyond the sphere of its thinking and measuring, never allowing them to disturb its inner emptiness, stillness, and deep-rooted peace. When it comes to fate, other than finding peace with it, there is nothing I can do.

Zhuangzi specifically singles out emotional reactions and sensory impressions as the key factors that create distinctions and divisions in the world: the eyes see different colors, the ears distinguish various sounds. If the mind always remains joyful no matter what the senses and emotions produce, it prevents them from becoming its master. But the mind also provides analytical understanding of reality, classifying things into patterns such as the four seasons, day and night, and other natural phenomena. With regard to this, it should be open and pervasive, unattached and unrestricted by distinctions, instead maintaining its unmoved stance however much reality may change or the world be in turmoil. This, then, is harmony or perfect happiness. Under any kind of circumstances, the mind is full of life and vitality, it has "joint spring with everything." Free and light, it never drowns in the world's morass.

One's natural ability whole, the mind unmoved in face of the world, one's inner nature is complete. There is no need to run after fame and gain, no chance of destroying one's inner security and peace. The mind is even and level: "Among level things, water at rest is the most perfect, and therefore it can serve as a standard. It guards what is inside and shows no movement outside. Virtue is the establishment of perfect harmony. Though it takes no form, things cannot break away from it." Virtue being formless connects to other statements about harmony: "In your mind it is best to harmonize with him;" and "Though you harmonize, you don't want to be drawn out too far" (ch. 4). The body has a tendency to be drawn into outside things, notably into sights and sounds, a fact that makes it impossible for the mind not to move. Keeping inner nature formless, then, means not to use it for show, as a tool of self-adornment. Zhuangzi here brings in the metaphor of water: when still, it is completely even and level. Similarly, the mind can be in harmony as long as it remains in stillness. A mind in harmony, moreover, can remain within the body and not exceed its range.

That is to say, wholeness of natural ability and formlessness of virtue indicate a state of mind that ranges from being unmoved to complete inner peace, based on the understanding of the workings of fate and the interaction of the heavenly and the human. A person in this state will not pursue others or the world with unwearied effort—Ai Taituo's inner calm and acceptance being one example. He doesn't say anything, yet wins people's trust. He doesn't do anything, yet gets close to others. The same hold true for Wang Tai who has lost a foot. Although he never speaks, his virtue fills other people's heart. "Though virtue takes no form, things cannot break away from it"—that expresses it perfectly! The attraction exerted by this kind of virtue makes people forget how ugly or deformed the person is physically, because they are so radiant and whole from within.

Other cases include Lame-Hunchback-No-Lips and Pitcher-Sized-Wen, frequently in conversation with ruling dukes. Their inner virtue, personal charisma, and mental acumen render their physical appearance irrelevant. "Duke Ling was so pleased with No-Lips that when he looked at ordinary people he thought their necks looked too lean and skinny." The very names in this passage show what kind of deformity these people exhibit, yet the dukes forget their physical misshapes. Not only that, the deformed body is completely filled with virtue and allows it to radiate freely to the point that, once you've gotten used to seeing this kind of misshapen form, hale and healthy bodies will seem lacking. "If virtue is preeminent, one is oblivious of the body." The contrast is massive: virtue is vastly more important than physical appearance.

This is also where he introduces the essential concept of forgetting or oblivion: the intentional act of discarding things, of actively expelling them from the mind. Like what? The body, for example. It must be eliminated from the mind because it is part of fate and anything connected to fate must go. Do you have any control over your body's transformations? Life cannot be ruled, death cannot be stopped; beauty cannot be created, ugliness cannot be prevented. None of these have anything to do with the individual's actions, thus they have to be sent into oblivion. As you do so, you take your mind and remove it from the body, liberate it from the form-based world and enter into the realm of formlessness. At this point you find yourself flowing about with ease, like fish in water. Your life unfolds in a world of emptiness and openness, purity and spirituality, without any obstruction. This is truly the world of Dao and virtue: oblivion of the body and transcendence of all physical form. That's why Zhuangzi says to "forget what you cannot change." The mind should be able to be part of the body and also be full of virtue, but from the perspective of the latter, the former must be given up.

Zhuangzi strongly pushes virtue, because it makes a person fully human. The body is part of fate and, while essential to being human, really has nothing to do with the inherent quality of humanity. It provides shape, a human look, the same we all have. Moved by an external force, changing beyond control, it forces us to live in society and work hard to keep it fed and safe. But Zhuangzi is not content to live like everybody else, merely in search of physical welfare. He seeks to separate body from mind: while he cannot but live physically in society, he can use his mind to ascend into a realm beyond the form-based world. He says,

> The sage wanders everywhere at ease. For him, knowledge is an offshoot, contracts are glue, favors are a patching up, and craft is a peddler. The sage hatches no schemes, so what use has he for knowledge? He does no carving, so what use has he for glue? He suffers no loss, so what use has he for favors? He hawks no goods, so what use has he for peddling?

Both the sage and the ordinary person have bodies, an unchangeable reality given by nature. The big difference is virtue, the way their mind functions. The sage does not have the feelings of ordinary people. Yes, he has a body, but he has none of the ordinary person's attachments to it. Thus he can wander freely, flow through life. Flowing or wandering means to live without obstructions, going along with whatever environment one is in: no need for knowledge, contracts, favors, and craft. Knowledge means planning and scheming; contracts means fixing and gluing relationships; favors means using and connecting to other people; and craft means engaging in buying and selling. For people living in the ordinary form-based world, all these are essential. But the sage, like the people of Yue who cut their hair short and have no need for ceremonial hats, has no use for them: he knows that anything these social skills might affect depends entirely on the natural transformations of things, the vagaries of fate, and is decided by Heaven. Thus the text says, "These four are called heavenly gruel. heavenly gruel is the food of Heaven," i.e., something beyond human reach. And since they are beyond, can their back-breaking, brain-draining pursuit be anything but ridiculous?

They are just like the frog in the well or the River God, whose worlds are limited by the reach of their bodies and for whom anything beyond is merely a laugh (ch. 17). Don't most people live just like that? They only know the human part, never even dreaming of seeing the heavenly, the source of creative change. They often think that human beings are all powerful, that they can participate in the creation of Heaven and Earth, make an equal third partner. But the fact is: people are not of the same stature as the source of creative change, they just form a small part of Heaven.

From the perspective of the ongoing creation of the universe, any form of feeling or emotion is petty—joy, anger, sadness, happiness. When you are happy that you're alive, don't you realize that you're already dying? Looking at it like this, what meaning do happiness and sadness, joy and anger really have? Maybe it's best to get rid of them altogether. This, of course, does not mean having no feelings at all, which would render the person to be like a stone or piece of wood. No, what Zhuangzi means by being "without feelings" (*wuqing* 無情) is a form of transcendence.

As he says in a dialogue with Huizi, "When I talk about having no feelings, I mean that a man doesn't allow likes or dislikes to get in and do him harm. He just lets things be the way they are and doesn't try to help life along." Being without feelings thus means moving along with the flow of the mind. Likes and dislikes are obviously feelings but it is possible to have them without letting them injure oneself—then they become no feelings and are just functions of the mind. Using the mind like this means that one does not allow the human part to destroy the heavenly, nor will one ever try to alter the natural course of events. In other words, we can nourish life, but we cannot change or increase it. Nourishing life means living out our Heaven-given years; increasing life means going beyond the natural sphere. Already determined by Heaven, how can it be changed or increased?

"Having no feelings" thus means being free from human feelings, but full of heavenly emotions. Zhuangzi has no way of eliminating the joy and anger, sadness and happiness issuing naturally from Heaven, and he doesn't want to do so—what he rejects are human-imposed extremes. Thus, when his wife dies, he feels grief and sadness at first. But as soon as he realizes the inevitability of death as part of the natural transformations of life, he lets go. Should he hold on to his grief beyond this point, he would "hide from Heaven and turn his back on the essential" (ch. 2). Being without feelings thus means practicing proper recognition and respect for Heaven, going along with its changes in a relaxed state of mind and easy attitude to life. It means not letting feelings grow so strong as to harm one's person or life. More than "suffering from yin and yang" (ch. 4), for Zhuangzi this means being pushed around and controlled by these feelings, becoming completely dependent on outside things and turning into their victim—a mere thing among things.

The close connection between no feelings, virtue, and life becomes obvious here. All of Zhuangzi's tales and arguments focus on this issue. His strong emphasis on virtue ultimately serves to show a better way of living in the world, releasing body and mind from endless, unspeakable toil. Huizi in this context stands symbolic for all those who labor their bodies and exert their minds. In constant pursuit of outside things: "Heaven picked out a body for you and you use it to gibber about 'hard' and 'white'!" He pays attention only to what is same or different, big or small, completely forgetting the essence and spirit of life within, "treating his spirit like an outsider and wearing out his vital essence."

This is reminiscent of the *Laozi*: "He who contains the fullness of virtue is like an infant . . . Unaware of sexual congress, his member is erect—the height of vital essence. All day long he cries without getting a sore throat—the height of inner harmony" (ch. 55). Vital essence and inner harmony here are manifestations of *qi* which in turn stands symbolic for the fullness of virtue. Huizi moves in the opposite direction, his life full of toil and trouble: "Leaning on a tree and moaning, slumping at his desk and dozing." Ordinary people might find a bit of rest and relaxation, but their minds will not be at peace and they continue to depend on outside things to lean on or slump against. Their life is in decline, their virtue in decay; they are mere moving piles of flesh, walking corpses with as little radiance of virtue as the mother sow.

From beginning to end, this chapter sings the praise of virtue. "Puny and small, he sticks with the rest of men; massive and great, he perfects his heavenly nature alone." What makes him stick with people is his physical body which necessitates living among others, in society, but this is just "puny and small." What allows him to go beyond people is his virtue which makes him fully realize his heavenly mind, and this is "massive and great." The body is puny; virtue is massive. People are tiny; Heaven is great. The same contrast also appears in Mencius, who speaks of big body and small body, the former being the mind, the latter being the senses and the physical form. "Follow the big body and become a big man; follow the small body and become a small man," he says (6A15). For both thinkers, it represents a choice we all have to make while yet containing a preference that is a foregone conclusion. It really is a choice of no choice. To use Mencius's famous passage, when given the choice between fish and bear paws, "I reject fish and pick bear paws" (6A10).

In this chapter, Zhuangzi outlines the choice for virtue while rejecting or obliterating the body—symbolized most poignantly by the various deformed figures. But, then, why is it necessary to be deformed, why not have a hale and healthy body? Zhuangzi's answer would be that, yes, of course one can have a healthy body, but then the likelihood is that virtue would be stymied. Body and virtue cannot both be whole, just as the heavenly and the human cannot both be joined. This holds particularly true in a Dao-less society, such as the one of Zhuangzi's time. His presentation of cripples indicates that punishments were everywhere, an inescapable fate. At this period in history, it was not possible to live without encountering outside infringements, cruelty, and punishments.

From here we can delve yet deeper into Zhuangzi's thought. So many cripples and amputees cannot possibly have been a happy sight or joyful presence, yet the radiance of virtue would spread through them like a hidden shadow, oozing from their bodies. One cannot always live purely in the mind; one must live in the physical body. The moment you open your eyes, your attention is drawn to it. At this point, can your mind issue vibes of peace and tranquility? The body may be puny, but without it we have no life in this world. Thus, discarding the body means giving up on a part of life, but one that is not all that important. Losing a foot obviously is not something we'd inflict on ourselves, but the way Zhuangzi speaks of it so joyfully, it involves being successful at letting go.

There is yet a further symbolism in the loss of a foot, I think: it is in itself a parable. Being short a foot means that one cannot walk properly, a metaphor for people's inability to live properly in the human world. Indeed, a world full of unavoidable hardships is an impossible place for the body to develop freely. As noted earlier, physical and social life must be approached the right way, we must find the nooks and crannies, from there to follow the twists and turns in our pursuit of wholeness. Even without having lost a foot, is your body really whole? Never able to grow properly, you are forever tied up in chains, forever deformed. Like the praying mantis you get up to an act of bravery, expand yourself for once, but then what? Then you return to serenity and stillness. This way you can avoid the fate of the praying mantis and make an active choice of your particular deformity.

This conscious choice of deformity, as an act of self-mutilation or self-inflicted pain, is a key point in Zhuangzi. To live skillfully in the Dao-less society of his time, self-mutilation of some sort was inevitable. In order to prevent others from harming your body, you had to harm yourself first. But these are two different kinds of harm. Other people's harm would most likely impact your physical body, your flesh and bones; self-inflicted harm might well go beyond this and involve your standing in the world, your social self, what the Confucian thinker Han Feizi 韓非子 calls "natural dynamics" versus "manmade circumstances," maybe best described as your "manmade body" (3.3).

In other words, it involves the expression of yourself in society and among other people: how you lift your hands, step your feet, your speech and facial expressions, your personal style and behavior. Independent of how much you may discard the world in your mind, on the physical level you still value its esteem. As Zhuangzi says, "Lifting up the tablet, kneeling, bowing, crouching down—everybody does it, how dare I not?" (ch. 4). In your mind you may be free from ideas of noble and humble, but you still have to bow your head before the local nobility, lest you forfeit your life. At the very least, as Zhuangzi says, you "cannot give up on right and wrong while still living in the world" (ch. 33).

Seen from this angle, being whole in virtue and mutilating oneself are two sides of the same coin. As we develop an unmoved mind, we don't see it as a mysterious or enlightened level of being, but realize that it involves a new attitude toward the form-based world, a learned indifference toward our body. Since it isn't really part of us, we can be radical toward it and discard it. It may create unpleasant circumstances, like the loss of a foot, the growth of a tumor, or the mutation into a hunchback. When this occurs, we just let it happen because, as our virtue tells us, these changes cannot really impact us as spirit, as part of Heaven. From here we can live with a clear conscience, facing whatever twists the body or the world get up to. What else can we do? The most important thing is to stay alive, to escape death, however twisted the life we have to lead.

This reminds us of Zihuazi 子華子, a later follower of Yang Zhu, who said, "a life in wholeness is best, a life in goodness is second, death is third, a life in fear is worst" (*Lüshi chunqiu*, ch. 7; 2/2). What he means by "life in wholeness" is quite different from Zhuangzi—not just keeping oneself alive and whole but a state when "the six [sensory] desires are satisfied." A life in goodness means that the senses are at least somewhat pleased, next best after being fully satisfied. Death is obviously not as good, since there are no senses to pleasure any longer. But the worst is "a life in fear"—a state when one is physically able to satisfy one's desires but cannot do so due to circumstances. Living in perpetual pain Zihuazi him is worse than death. How would Zhuangzi see this contrast? He would prefer life, to be sure, but free from pain. There may be physical pain but one can persuade the mind to discard its impact, not to suffer from it. In fact, if one has no feelings left toward body and world, how can they ever cause him suffering? Suffering is produced by the mind—and Zhuangzi's mind remains unmoved.

This unmoved mind is essentially indifferent, free from hate and also free from love—quite unlike Confucius or Mozi. Those two are involved and enthusiastic, easily agitated by what happens around them—but what are they agitated about? Their world is not this world, it is merely the "chaff and dregs" of the past. Confucius tends to labor his mind, unlike a mind like dead ashes, like sunk energy, from where one "no longer walks the road but rides a raft to float out to sea." Zhuangzi lets go of his mind and thus can avoid agitating it. He chooses to close it off and make it indifferent, unmoved, without feelings; yet it is a place where virtue shines forth brightly. This kind of mind, then, is a protective shield: all indifference toward self and world is essentially a form of self-protection. Underneath the outward appearance of coldness, there is strong layer of warmth radiated by virtue. "He doesn't have the feelings of a man, thus right and wrong cannot get at him": life has no power to destroy his depths. And isn't this is the most authentic way of living?

Self-mutilation or self-inflicted harm thus don't really reach the deepest level of self. The idea is close to Zhuangzi's take on uselessness (ch. 4). Anything useful tends to come to grief: useful trees are cut down, useful animals are sacrificed, useful people continue to suffer from the "afflictions of others" or those of "yin and yang." Then, why not become useless? This kind of uselessness is not at all like that of people who are born dull or those who are just puppets of others. Rather, it is an active choice to "relegate it all to the constant" (ch. 2) while one still has the potential of being useful. Being useless while still able to have use, looking stupid while being full of wisdom, appearing clumsy while having great skill—all these are ways to hide from the world and thus forms of self-mutilation. It is a choice to make: not forced by pain and suffering, but a positive step toward self-preservation.

Still, it is not easy for a competent person to let go of all usefulness. To accept this release calmly is even harder. Some people may get there after they repeatedly bang their heads against a wall and draw blood in their struggle to serve. In that case, it may well be just a release in body while the mind is still full of anger and agitation. How is this any different from being harmed by life? You may get to the point where you're immune to the afflictions of others but you're still vulnerable to those of yin and yang. Your inner heat still chafes, and you cannot live in peace. Maybe you end up like Qu Yuan 屈原 (340-278), drowning yourself in the river, or like Jia Yi, dying from depression. In other words, letting go of the body is not as important as releasing all holding in the mind. This is where Zhuangzi speaks of virtue, the power within to keep the mind at peace, to make the body cooperate with the world and go on changing as it pleases. A radical form of self-mutilation, it yet provides inner peace and stillness. Virtue is massive and inescapable. Zhuangzi says, "To understand what you can do nothing about and to be content with it as with fate—this is the perfection of virtue." We must remember this. People cannot control or change the world, but they can control and change their minds.

Chapter Five

Equalizing Things

The title of the second chapter is "Discussion on Equalizing Things" (Qiwulun 齊物論), indicating that it presents more discussion than stories. The chapter notes that "the sage recognizes what is beyond the six realms but does not discuss it; he discusses what is within the six realms but does not judge it," yet it seems that the author does not bind himself to his own rule. This is similar to Laozi noting that "those who know do not speak, those who speak do not know" (ch. 56) and promptly composing a text of 5,000 words. Perhaps it was to compensate for this defect that later generations created the narrative of the border guard Guan Yin forcing Laozi to write his book (*Shiji* 63): Laozi didn't really want to put his ideas into writing, but he had no other choice.

Discussion entails dispute, thus the chapter reads much like a dispute, with Zhuangzi on one side and the Confucians and Mohists on the other. It makes Zhuangzi appear more like a skilled orator than the recluse we commonly think he is. But if you really think of Zhuangzi as an orator, that is a big mistake. Just as some thinkers use language to clarify how unreliable it is, he uses dispute only to show how pointless it is. Stopping dispute with dispute is like using the military to get rid of the military— however sound the principle may be, the intention is obvious.

Grammatically the chapter title can be understood in two ways: "Discussion on Equalizing Things" or "Equalizing the Discussion of Things." Both are somewhat justified in the text, but the preferred choice is the former, since Zhuangzi's key issue is the nature of things rather than the quality of discussion. Disputes over things can be avoided but things cannot: any issues relating to them must be resolved. This resolution is not concrete or practical, since that would entail physical changes in things, such as expansion, contraction, or even destruction. Zhuangzi has no such power, and neither does anyone else. You might be able to change one, several, or a certain number of things, but you can never change all things in this way.

Nor is the resolution psychological, although it has a lot to do with states of mind. Some mental states focus your attention or distract you from things, but they mainly represent mood changes or psychological activities and have nothing to do with deliberation or logic. Zhuangzi's resolution, then, is philosophical, a solution in terms of meaning. He discusses and analyzes meaning, explicates a certain understanding of things, and eventually arrives at some relationship between things and the mind, reaching a point where things no longer burden the mind and where the mind no longer dominates or controls them.

This is what he means when he speaks of "equalizing" things, hoping to accomplish something that common sense tells us is impossible. Mencius says, "The inequality of things is in their nature" (3A4). How are we ever to equalize them? Maybe with Xunzi's "equality of inequalities"? Maybe with Huizi's "universal love of all things in the unity of Heaven and Earth" (*Zhuangzi* 33)? Maybe as part of the relativity of all created things as proposed by the contemporaneous thinkers Peng Meng 彭蒙, Tian Pian 田駢, and Shen Dao 慎到? The way things look in this chapter, it is none of the above. Equalization of things does not happen in things themselves, but only in the mind. Things are not equal, but if my mind is not fixed on that inequality, then what significance does it have?

Thus, the core focus of the chapter is on the mind. It begins with the parable of Master Ziqi going into trance, described as "the body like a withered tree, the mind like dead ashes," a state where "I have lost myself." The key figure here is associated with the south, the direction which in the first chapter, where the big Peng bird flies south from the northern darkness, symbolizing movement toward the realm of spirit. Being part of this realm, his mind is like dead ashes: all its activity has ceased, outside things no longer impact it. The mind is still there, but it is as if it wasn't: it is in a state of no-mind, a state of no-self, no personal identity.

Some may think that "I have lost myself" is just a word game, since "I" and "myself" are one and the same. If "I" represents a complete person, then "myself" seems to be only a part of that person. Just what is it, then? Clearly, it is not a physical entity, since without a bodily form "I" would not exist, to say nothing of "myself." Does it maybe refer to the mind? No, not that either. Therefore, it must be a state of mind, something like an attitude. The mind should be empty, like a mirror, so that any object in the world can appear in it without leaving traces. But an attitude clings to things: it evaluates according to likes and dislikes, produces judgments of right and wrong, divides the world into self and others, accepts some things and rejects others. "Myself" emerges from the cluster of attitudes, immediately giving rise to "you" and "he." This leads immediately to relationships and oppositions, stress and conflict. "Myself," then, is the consciousness, the subjective awareness of being or having a self, a way of thinking that divides self and world while dividing all into categories according to its own standards. In other words, "myself" is a mental state that clings to a personal self. "I have lost myself" is a way of saying "no-self" (ch. 1).

Why, then, should I want to lose myself? Why should I want to be without a self? Of course, we can simply say that you need to do so in order to equalize all things. Yet why would you need to do that? The "I" must be eliminated because it inevitably brings harm to self and world. What does it mean for there to be an "I"? Its existence means that we divide the world conceptually to relate to this "I." It means that there will be a "you" and a "he," and the "you" will also have its own "I," and so will the "he." There will be multiple different "I's" contending, clashing, and fretting in close connection with each other.

Zhuangzi here distinguishes great and small knowledge, the former being "effortless and expansive," the latter "picky and discriminating." This is because those who really know are not insistent about speaking out and do not hunt up divisions while those who deal with petty things are intent on careful calculation. The relaxed and insipid quality of great knowledge is due to its being free of self. Without an "I," there can be no differentiation between self and world: the mind remains unoccupied, free and open. Small knowledge, on the other hand, is busy and self-centered: it works with right and wrong, beautiful and ugly, creating opposition and contention. Life is submerged in unending rounds of to and fro, back and forth, always calculating and planning, clashing and worrying. "In sleep, people's spirits wander off; in waking hours, their bodies hustle. With everything they meet they become entangled. Day after day, they use their minds in strife, sometimes grandiose, sometimes sly, sometimes petty." The mind engaged in furious activity, it never comes to rest but is mired more and more deeply in set attitudes and fixed opinions. This is the death of the true mind.

A world determined by fixed minds, run by multiple different "I's," divided by numerous different attitudes and opinions, is a world of false appearances where true reality is hidden. People are intoxicated by the piping of Humanity, such as tunes played on instruments, until they no longer remember their original source. The piping of Humanity, moreover, comes from the piping of Earth, just as human tunes go back to the air. Aren't the songs of the *Shijing* 詩經 (Book of Songs; trl. Pound 1954) called "airs"? Yet for Zhuangzi piping is less a matter of air than of the human heart, ideally still simple and pure. This is the piping of Humanity, and no matter how good it becomes, he doesn't really like it: it still contains a potential "I."

He thus speak more of the piping of Earth, called the "Great Clod," which brings forth wind, blowing through myriads of hollows and making different sounds.

> In the mountain forests that lash and sway, there are huge trees a hundred spans around with hollows and openings like noses, like mouths, like ears, like jugs, like cups, like mortars, like rifts, like ruts. They roar like waves, whistle like arrows, screech, gasp, cry, wail, moan, and howl, those in the lead calling out *yeee*, those behind calling out *yuuu*! In a gentle breeze they answer faintly, but in a full gale the chorus is gigantic.

In antiquity, officials measured the *qi* of Earth with the help of pitch pipes, listening to their sound to differentiate the winds of the eight directions by listening. Even ordinary people could hear wind blowing on things to make different sounds. If, like Zhuangzi, you happen to be in a mountain forest with multiple hollows when the wind blows, you can hear all sorts of sounds, changing with the wind's strength and direction. Then, when the wind stops, there is quiet, "all the hollows are empty again." What did this make him realize? No one—not wind, hollows, or anything else—commands sounds to be produced: it just happens naturally. And since the particular shape of a given hollow determines the quality of sound, it has no choice but to produce that sound and none other.

At its root, then, is the piping of Heaven, completely free from the deliberate mind. It is not a concrete thing or a particular phenomenon beyond the piping of Humanity or Earth, but pure openness to cosmic wandering in a state of no-mind. Like the piping of Earth it has no conscious mind or deliberate intention: there is no "I" anywhere in the process. Does each hollow have its "I"? No. Is there an "I" in the wind? No. If there is no "I," then there is no mind either. Similarly, Zhuangzi's three literary devices include goblet words, spoken after drinking wine and flowing spontaneously rather than deliberately, matching the state of no-mind. This being so, goblet words correspond to the piping of Heaven.

"Great words are clear and limpid; little words are shrill and quarrelsome."

Most language, though, never makes it to the level of goblet words and has nothing to do with the piping of Heaven. It is not plainly irrelevant, though: "Words are not just wind." The piping of Humanity and Earth are not the same. Words issue from the mouth, but the mouth is only a tool for articulation. They really come from the mind: "Words are the voice of the mind." When a sound comes forth that expresses the mind, people attach significance to it. If the word corresponds to a certain thing, it inevitably describes, evaluates, or expresses some view concerning that thing. That view, however, only belongs to a certain mind or a certain "I;" other minds or "I's" may well come up with entirely different descriptions or evaluations. A thing is just what it is and nothing more, yet it appears differently to the consciousness of different people—and not because it changes like a chameleon and eludes firm understanding. No, it is entirely due to the differences in people's minds, the various "I's" that correspond to these minds.

A good example is the division between Confucians and Mohists. Confucians believe in fate; Mohists argue against it. Confucians respect ghosts and spirits but keep their distance from them; Mohists support and enhance belief in them. Confucians take music seriously; Mohists downplay its importance. Confucians model themselves after Kings Wen and Wu; Mohists emulate the Great Yu. One single world—yet how many different, opposing viewpoints? And each of them is sure that "I" am correct while "he" is mistaken. "I" am right, while "he" is wrong. They each use their particular idea of right and wrong to criticize someone else's idea of right and wrong, which means that each considers wrong what the other deems right, and considers right what the other believes wrong. This leads to the question of whether right and wrong do in fact exist. And if they do, whose version is right?

The world is what it is, and all things are as they are: originally there is no differentiation of right and wrong. Each thing may well have its particular characteristics and use—roosters sounding the dawn, dogs guarding the yard, carts ferrying goods, and boats crossing water. But the moment the special characteristics of a thing become its strong points, they also become its limitations. Boats can cross water: they can't move on land; dogs guard the yard: they don't sound the dawn. So how are you supposed to treat them? Does being a boat negate something else being a cart, or does liking dogs mean that you have to hate roosters? Perhaps Zhuangzi had it right when he said, "Each thing has its own way of being and its own potential; nothing is without its way of being and its particular potential."

Seen in its own right, each and every thing has its unique way of being and its particular potential; seen in alien terms, judging it by an extraneous set of criteria, nothing is right or has potential. Seeing this thing in terms of that means to deny this while upholding that. Seeing that in terms of this, this has potential while that does not. In the world of things, all are related in terms of this and that: "Everything has its 'that,' everything has its 'this.' From the point of view of 'that,' you cannot see it, you only know what is 'this' to you." Viewing the world from its own standpoint, each thing considers itself "this" and others "that." So does each and every thing. Seen from his meta-perspective, just what does the difference between this and that mean? If things can be either this or that to each other, yet insist on maintaining a this-that distinction, a situation arises like that in the parable of the monkey keeper and his monkeys. With their ration of peanuts fixed at seven a day, the monkeys become angry if they get three in the morning and four at night, but are thrilled if offered four in the morning and three at night. The monkeys can only see the difference and miss the commonality. Does that apply to people, too?

People obviously are not monkeys, but if we believe Darwin's theory of evolution, then maybe there are some that have not quite outgrown their primate ancestors. Yes, people may easily see that three in the morning plus four at night and four in the morning plus three at night are the same thing, but the universal principle of "that" being produced by a matching "this," and vice versa, may not be so obvious. The world is not in fact divided into this and that, and any division creates a pattern where everything is both this and that, depending on perspective. Then, what do these distinctions mean? They reveal the law of mutual interdependence. As Zhuangzi puts it,

> Where there is birth there must be death; where there is death there must be birth. Where there is acceptance there must be refusal; where there is refusal there must be acceptance. Where there is recognition of right there must be recognition of wrong; where there is recognition of wrong there must be recognition of right. Therefore the sage does not proceed in such a way, but illuminates all in the light of Heaven.

What does this mean? Is there really birth or death? Is something ultimately acceptable or not? Mired in the material world, immersed in the thinking of material things, we can never reach a firm conclusion but are doomed to endless struggle. But if we look at it differently, from a wider, detached perspective by "using the light of Heaven," is there still a radical opposition of life and death, acceptance and refusal? Perhaps birth is also death, and acceptance is also refusal. Perhaps life and death, acceptance and refusal do not really exist. In the bright light of Heaven, oppositions disappear, leaving behind it a world free from distinctions.

"Heaven" here appears both in "the piping of Heaven" and the "light of Heaven," indicating a state of no-mind that is quite the same as perception from a position of no-self—accessible by transcending the "I." Someone without a fixed "I" looking at the world will not let his perception be colored by particular attitudes or ideas. To him, the world appears just as it is, without distinctions of this and that or right and wrong. Ducks will fly, fish will swim, flowers will be red, willows will be green—all things of this world, abundant as they are, exist without distinctions. This and that or right and wrong are concepts produced by humans: they reflect the fixed mind. To establish right and wrong before views are formed in the mind is like saying "set out for Yue today and arrive there yesterday." It is turning what is not into what is. Even the Great Yu with his spiritual insight would not know how to do that.

How, then, can I? A fixed mind is precisely what can turn something that does not exist into something that does, such as when right and wrong are imposed on a world that does not really contain them. "Setting out for Yue today and arriving there yesterday" is a paradox of Huizi (ch. 33). Zhuangzi seems ready at almost any time to aim a satirical barb at his old friend. In Zhuangzi's view, you may want to play thought games at the level of language, but in real life, this is impossible—as impossible as having right and wrong without first developing a mind.

A fixed mind entails the presence of an "I," and a person without an "I" is no longer a person, but a flowing entity at one with Heaven. Only the body is human; it in resides the heavenly mind, which is no-mind. No-mind means that this and that are no longer paired in one's thinking. Each entity is now its own unique being, without a match, a partner, a complement, an opposite—like Master Ziqi who lost himself. He probably would not feel bereft or alone: with no awareness of this or that, no sense of right and wrong, what is there to miss? All distinctions disappear as the fixed mind dissolves, and the whole world is seamless and undifferentiated. At this point, all you feel is a sense of fulfillment, based on the idea that "Heaven and Earth were born with me, and all things are one with me."

This fulfillment may appear free and released. The oneness of all things Zhuangzi intends here is different from Mencius's statement that "all things are complete within me" (7A4), reached not by merging things into oneself but by abandoning all. Things may or may not exist—I remain unconcerned with all, be it beautiful or ugly, right or wrong, long or short, big or small. If Confucians or Mohists have particular ideas of right and wrong, so be it. I stay away from arguments, pursuing a third point of view that places me above dispute, in a position of transcendence. "Where there is recognition of right there must be recognition of wrong; where there is recognition of wrong there must be recognition of right." This being so, I need not enter into the dispute. I maintain an attitude of detachment, of indifference toward the issue of right and wrong, going beyond both. Right and wrong keep rotating in an endless cycle, and Zhuangzi wants to place himself in its very center. No matter how frantic the rotation becomes, things are quiet and peaceful in the eye of the storm.

This is where Dao comes into play. Laozi defines Dao as the universal source, the mother of all things. Zhuangzi follows this and similarly sees Dao as the source of the world, the root of all things, the repository of true forms. Things themselves cannot provide clear understanding, which is only found by returning to the source, the origin, where they reveal their true form. At this point Zhuangzi outlines a series of four stages of development from the source: 1) perfect knowledge, a state that is entirely unaware of things, the level of perfect nonbeing; 2) the perception that things exist but with no recognition of boundaries between them; 3) the perception of limitations, boundaries, and categories; and 4) the judgment of right and wrong. "When right and wrong appeared, Dao was destroyed, and once Dao was destroyed, love became complete."

All these stages flow from Dao, which is beyond material things, limiting distinctions, and the judgment of right and wrong. Strictly speaking, it can only be described as something prior to things, because Dao is nothing other than nonbeing, or even non-nonbeing. Admittedly, Dao may be described in terms of non-distinction or no right and no wrong, but such descriptions do not do it full justice. Even the term "nonbeing" is not really adequate. Zhuangzi pursues this by tracing the beginning of the not-yet beginning of the not-yet beginning, the nonbeing before nonbeing before being, and so on, *ad infinitum*. "There is a not yet beginning to be a not yet beginning to be nonbeing. Suddenly there is nonbeing. But I do not know, when it comes to nonbeing, which is really being and which is nonbeing."

If we say that Dao represents the beginning, was there a beginning to this, and did the beginning to the beginning also have a beginning? If we say that Dao is nonbeing, was there a time when there was not even a nonbeing, or a time when the nonbeing before nonbeing did not even exist? This line of questioning raises people's awareness of the issue of beginnings; it also points to a way of understanding the logical structure of classical abstract concepts, taking them to absurdity. While not physically leading into nothingness, this inquiry will never come to an end. It will never transcend the limitations of the physical world. The beginning of all things, their origin, has to be something other than a thing itself. Describing Dao as nonbeing is only a stop-gap, an expedient way of coming to grips with the situation. But what happens if you start thinking of nonbeing as a thing? Then nonbeing becomes something, and so you need to create a new abstraction, like not nonbeing or maybe not not nonbeing." Zhuangzi uses these absurd logical chains to show that Dao is fundamentally different from things which exist as something—no matter what shape they take. Dao has no such existence.

What, then, does nonbeing mean? Nonbeing indicates that the world, with all its abundant variety, essentially goes back to a single source. Things may look and behave differently, but in their core substance, they are all one. The slender stem and the great column, the ugly Li and the beautiful Xi Shi, are quite at odds when seen from the perspective of things. Seen from Dao, however, they are all one. "Things ribald and shady, grotesque and strange: Dao pervades them all in oneness." This means that the many differences that distinguish and separate one thing from another are swept aside when seen through Dao. Things have no unity among them, they collide and clash with each other. But nonbeing and being can become one.

Nonbeing will never be at odds with any form of material existence, because it has nothing material; instead, it pervades all without resistance. From its perspective, all boundaries and limitations are relative—there is no point hanging on to them. To you, Mount Tai may be large and an autumn hair small, but I say, "There is nothing in the world bigger than the tip of an autumn hair, and Mount Tai is tiny." You may think that Pengzu lived for a long time and a sick child died prematurely, but I counter, "No one has lived longer than a dead child, and Pengzu died young."These statements do not reflect a dispute about large and small, old and young; they point to the ultimate absurdity of all distinctions.

This, then, is the equalization of things. It never alters the way of the world, however "ribald and shady or grotesque and strange" it may be, in favor of bland uniformity. Dao pervades all, but it does not make them the same. The ten thousand things remain as they are and retain their differences in appearance and action. However, when you trace them back to their source, "the beginning, the point where Dao gives birth to them," you find that there are no boundaries, distinctions, or separate things. There is only nonbeing, and perhaps not even that. Here, even the word "ten thousand" is gone, leaving behind only "one" in nonbeing. When you get to this point in your mind, will you still make distinctions such as a stem versus pillar, the ugly Li versus the beautiful Xi Shi?

Of course not. As long as you still classify and distinguish things, you have no real appreciation of Dao. Someone may object that people really are not Dao, so while Dao may be able to equalize all things, how could people do so? True enough. People are not Dao, but they can make their minds soar into Dao—open to all, it never turns anyone away. Sometimes Dao may be hidden. People with fixed minds, caught up in distinctions of right and wrong, cannot possibly see it. They live surrounded by boundaries and limitations that artificially restrict their minds, never even peeking beyond the horizon. It is that kind of fixed mind that drove Gongsun Long to hang on to tight distinctions, such as those between a horse and a white horse and engage in sophistry. "There is no object which is not a finger, yet a finger is not a finger" (*Gongsun Longzi* 公孫龍子, ch. 1). Perhaps this sort of thing won him fame and honor, so that even Confucius's descendant, Kong Chuan 孔穿, acknowledged him as teacher. But he kept on getting farther away from Dao. "Dao is hidden by petty accomplishments—they obscure Dao." People preoccupied with nitpicky calculations have forgotten the most fundamental factor of all.

Rather than worry about nitpicky calculations and technical distinctions between a horse and a white horse or between a finger and other things, Zhuangzi admonishes us to focus on the core difference between life and world. He follows Laozi: "Which means more to you, you or your renown? Which is more to you, you or what you own?" (*Laozi* 44). This is completely different from Gongsun Long who, like Huizi, has immersed himself in the world of things to the point of no return. He may have an excellent understanding of rocks or horses, but not of life.

Where, then, does life come in? It really doesn't. Zhuangzi describes people like him as just about being alive, hanging on to their bodies while waiting for the end. "Sweating and laboring to the end of his days and never seeing his accomplishment, utterly exhausting himself and never knowing where to look for rest." Zhuangzi has nothing but pity for such people, who are confused and forever at odds with life. Tragic figures, their minds and bodies are the slaves of things. They may be physically alive but their minds are already dead—and they don't even realize that! Awareness would be the first step of awakening, a ray of hope for rebirth. But without it, they are beyond redemption.

Other, similar figures are Zhao Wen the zither player, Shi Kuang the music master, and Hui Shi the orator. Although different in skill and specialization, they all lost their minds in the world of things. Manipulating the material world, even with consummate expertise, is nothing more than a minor technical skill: far removed from Dao. This is quite different from Cook Ding, who too had extraordinary skill in butchery and was very good at manipulating the carcass of an ox. But he worked through the mind, and his mind was pervaded by Dao—he saw with spirit rather than with his eyes. When his overlord expressed incredulity at his skill level, he said, "What I care about is Dao; it goes beyond skill!" While skill thus remains restricted by things, Dao transcends the physical world and returns to life itself.

To attain this return, the mind must lead. It alone can extricate itself from the world of things and liberate itself from slavery. The mind must find its true home, its point of ultimate return. This is not a concrete space or material object—they only provide temporary lodging. The true home of the mind is the universal source, where all things and people originate: Dao. Only within Dao can the mind find itself and recover authentic living, where things no longer constrain it, where, like Dao, is pervades all in oneness. It no longer sees distinctions such as horse versus white horse, finger versus thing. Rather, in this state Heaven and Earth are but a single finger, all things are but one horse, and the person himself is an ox or a stone. It does not matter. The mind roaming in the calm of Dao, there is no room for any sort of distinctions.

This is obviously not an epistemological discussion. From the epistemological point of view, even Zhuangzi would have to acknowledge that Mount Tai is large, autumn hairs are small, Xi Shi is beautiful, and Ms. Li is ugly. Equalizing things has nothing to do with concrete knowledge, but only with life, the state of mind necessary for survival. Zhuangzi has no urge to get involved with the human world, although he lives in it and knows he cannot escape it. Getting involved means achieving something, having "wisdom enough to fill an office effectively, good conduct enough to impress one community, virtue enough to please one ruler, or talent enough to be called into service" (ch. 1).

With changing context, however, achievement may turn into liability: reputation may detract from moral integrity, and one person's gain may be another's loss. Zhao Wen's zither playing provides an example. He plucked *gong*, and there was no *shang*; he plucked *zheng*, and there was no *yu*. When he didn't play, he had neither gain nor loss. Should he play or not, then? Well, it's what he does, so he does it. But what about Zhuangzi? He might sit and drum, but he would certainly not play the zither and in all cases would never let minor achievements detract from life. To him, worldly achievements are mere "confusions and doubts that dazzle people": the sage does away with them.

Fame and glory dazzle people; they also create confusion. Zhuangzi wants nothing to do with them; he'd rather be an ordinary person. Still, his mind is anything but ordinary. He has talent and wisdom, so much so that when King Wei of Chu heard of him, he offered him an appointment as prime minister. But Zhuangzi refused, having no desire to use his talent and wisdom, because it might cause him to lose his way or even his life. He preferred to appear useless, with no dazzling qualities, although this is not at all what he really was.

Because of this, he "abides in ordinariness"—a state of being common, mediocre, insipid, and devoid of dazzling qualities. He does so intentionally. As Laozi said, "The sage dons coarse cloth but bears jade within" (ch. 70). A gifted individual who yet pretends to be ordinary may be like Laozi's "great wisdom seeming foolish"(ch. 27). But Laozi here refers to the art of rulership, while Zhuangzi hopes to survive by keeping a low profile. Remaining in ordinariness, you live without attracting attention. You may not have or use any dazzling qualities, but you stay out of danger. Thus you "bury yourself among the people and hide yourself in the fields" (*Zhuangzi* 25). Zhuangzi consciously chose this way of life and elected to rest in uselessness—a concept closely connected to the idea of abiding in ordinariness.

Uselessness is not the same as being of no use—the latter indicating that one has no chance of serving the world, while being useless means that one can very well serve but chooses not to. Confucians speak of excellence in learning so one can serve in office, but in Zhuangzi one excels and does *not* become an official. You may play the lute but there is no need to become a Zhao Wen; you may have perfect pitch but there is no urge to stand out like Shi Kuang. For Zhuangzi, uselessness has the greatest use of all: ordinariness is useful, what is useful is open, and openness reaches to Dao.

Ordinariness being useful does not mean that the two are identical; rather ordinariness is a function of a particular use, namely openness or liberation (*jie* 解). Being ordinary means letting go of fame and visible accomplishments, releasing the self. Then what is there left to care about? Life itself, nothing else. This, in turn, leads to the hope that outside things will do you no harm, that you can maintain a neutral relationship with them. That is openness: no gaps, no boundaries among things, no break between you and all there is. Any existing boundaries are blurred; they vanish and melt into oneness.

This is what it feels like when you have attained Dao: it's like soaring through the greater universe. When your mind is caught up with worldly things, you are busy making distinctions of right and wrong. When your mind roams in Dao, boundaries disappear. Then you realize just how meaningless pronouncements of right or wrong really are and how absurd it is to hold tenaciously on to fixed views. Dao and speech are mutually exclusive: choose Dao and give up speech. "Since I am already one with Heaven, how can I say anything? But I have just said that we are one, so how can I not be saying something? The one and what I said about it make two, and two and the original one make three. If we go on this way, then even the cleverest mathematician can't tell where we'll end, much less an ordinary person."

"One" is a word that can be spoken, but once uttered, it adds to the original one, so that there are two total. Add myself into the mix, and that makes three, and so it goes on, *ad infinitum*. Thereby you sink more and more deeply into the world of things, until you can't extricate yourself anymore. "Great Dao does not speak": Dao has no limiting boundaries, while words will always have limits. The futility of attempting to use a limited medium to speak of limitless Dao is obvious. Distinctions and differentiations appear where there are no boundaries originally. Then people stubbornly cling to a certain concept or its opposite, such as righteousness or duty, making subtle distinctions and contending with each other.

Then what happens? Confucians have one concept of right and wrong, Mohists have another. Is either one right? Are all? Or neither? For Zhuangzi, there is no such thing as universal right and wrong. When human beings sleep in marshes, they get back aches, but do eels? People get scared climbing high into trees, but do monkeys? Is there any agreement among these three species about where best to live? Certainly not. Nor is there any agreement among any and all beings in the world as about any norms, be it appearance, flavor, or anything else. Human beings think Xi Shi is gorgeous, but fish see her and dive for cover, birds scatter into the sky, and deer dash off in fear. People eat things that mice detest; deer like food that crows scorn. There is no single universal standard to create categories for the things of this world. Without a universal standard, there cannot be a single set of right norms. Why worry or dispute about them?

Zhuangzi must have been tired of all those disputes around him. His argument thoroughly destroys their foundations and he has a clear reason for stopping them: the relativity of all things. The chapter mentions twice that "it is best to use clarity": shining a bright light mainly on "this" and "that" and illuminating their relativity, thereby saving people from sinking into the depths of dispute. Any "that" has its own right and wrong: eels like moist hollows (right for them) and dislike dry places (wrong for them). Any "this" has its own right and wrong: monkeys like to live in trees (right) and detest being in water (wrong). Such is the reality of the world, and understanding this is clarity. On the other hand, if you criticize the eel's watery depth on the basis of the monkey's tree, or criticize the monkey's tree based on the eel's watery depth, you are judging one in terms of what is right for another, forcing a particular standard on them. This is what philosophers and disputers do. A world where this is common naturally sinks into disorder.

Zhuangzi has yet another reason for why people should stop debating. Disputes can never be won because, however much we argue, we can never be sure whether "we are both right or both wrong. If you and I don't know the answer, then other people are bound to be even more in the dark. Whom shall we get to decide what is right?" Neither you nor I or anyone can reach an agreement or make a final decision, which means that there can never be real understanding. Different "I's" lead parallel existences, each steadfastly clinging to his or her particular point. This being so, not only disputes, but any speech based on conscious distinctions has ultimately no meaning.

This is yet another way of pointing to the relative nature of all life. You, I, and others are just like human beings, monkeys, and eels—we are like different species with nothing in common, however much we each have a rationale for our particular views and preferences. Apart from this "I," there are many other "I's" whose existence you must acknowledge. Having so many "I's" means that there really is no ultimate "I," since none has the prerogative to make others their own, to change them into a "you" or a "he."

Even the emperor cannot do this. "Long, long ago, Yao said to Shun, "I want to attack [the three barbarian states of] Zong, Kuai, and Xuao. Although I face south on the throne, this thought troubles me. Why is this?"Maybe he felt that, since he possessed such great virtue, all under Heaven should submit to his moral authority. But then there were these three outside states. His "I" could not accept them as different, so he thought of attacking them. Yet, while thinking about it, he possibly considered the rights of other "I's." This might raise doubts about his attack, possibly freeing his mind from these thoughts.

"Shun replied, 'These three states are merely tiny specks among weeds and brambles. Why do they nag your thoughts? In the old days, ten suns rose at once and all things were lit up together. How much better are multiple virtues than these suns?'" Shun here clarifies the issue by reminding Yao of the myth of the ten suns—much brighter than just one, they illuminate all corners of the world. But they also must acknowledge each other and allow for their existence. There is not just one that resides in Heaven or a single one that shines on Earth. With this dialogue, Zhuangzi suggests that sagely virtue must not be narrow like just one of those suns, but should be multiple and inclusive, like ten suns or even more.

When Yao wanted to attack the small states, his intentions were not evil—he may even have been driven by the positive desire to rescue their inhabitants from dire straits. Yao being an ideal sage-king of the Confucians, Zhuangzi uses him to engage in dialogue with them. The Confucian virtue of benevolence rests on the principle of loving others, characterized by "establishing one's own character by supporting that of others, reaching high attainment by promoting it in others" (*Lunyu* 6.30). This approach of projecting one's own ideas onto others reveals the warm and caring, enthusiastic dimension of Confucianism. For Zhuangzi, however, such ardor can also burn. Just how do you know that what you need is also what others need? If so, then everyone is happy. If not, then you are forcing your will on others and causing them to suffer. Confucians believe in universality shared by all humanity. As Mencius says "There are flavors for mouths that all men relish, there are sounds for the ears that all men enjoy, and sights for the eyes that all find beautiful. As for men's minds, can they alone have no shared inclinations? What is that toward which minds incline? It is principle and righteousness" (5A7).

This assumption of universality justifies projecting one's ideas onto others. But Zhuangzi denies this categorically. Beginning with the idea that there is "no shared rightness" all the way to "you and I and the other cannot know what is in each other's minds" (ch. 33), the book presents ample proof. Zhuangzi thus does not accept benevolence as a valid standard, because it excuses the projection of one person's ideas onto others. "Great benevolence is not benevolent" (ch. 2): this is not an empty statement, but embodies Zhuangzi's deep understanding of the world. Dao and benevolence (or love) are mutually exclusive: "What causes Dao to erode is what causes love to be realized." This is reminiscent of Laozi's statement, "When great Dao declined, benevolence and righteousness came forth" (ch. 18). Benevolence or love comes from the "I," and takes the "I" as its premise. Being not benevolent means to look on all things with equal benevolence, letting go of one's "I." This is when equalization of things happens.

Equalizing things is at odds with all forms of differentiation and dispute, but connects to the idea of closeness. Differentiation, analyzing things to pieces, is the way of life of ordinary people; closeness, merging things into oneness, is the way of the sage. Thus ordinary people "see an egg and immediately hear a rooster crow, see a crossbow and immediately expect a dove roasting." The sage, on the other hand, "matches sun and moon, scoops up time and space, and merges all things into harmonious oneness. . . . He blends all differentiations of ten thousand harvests into pure seamless oneness." The former position shows detailed calculations and premature expectations; the latter represents closeness to the universe, direct communication with Heaven and Earth, unity with all things. It involves complete disregard for all confused contentions about right and wrong, lofty and humble, noble and common. The two attitudes match life according to ordinary differentiation and sagely closeness, one leading to a lifetime of diligent toil without escape, the other allowing all differences to disappear while the mind returns to clarity and simplicity. In this state, all things enfold all others, there are no boundaries, one is free from opposition and contradiction.

Zhuangzi calls this "resting in the boundless," the realm of nonbeing and non-differentiation, the true home of the mind, the right attitude to maintain. How do we get there? By "matching the innate balance of Heaven," i. e., "forgetting all distinctions." More specifically, we should realize that anything we call "right" or "such" is also "not right" or "not such" for someone else. "If anything right were really and always right, it would be so obviously different from not right that there would never be an issue." The innate balance of Heaven embraces all boundaries and distinctions of nature, but not anything manmade. Right and not right, such and not such can never be determined through dispute since if there was an absolute standard, there would be no need to argue. Some distinctions, such as between species and their habitat, form part of the innate balance of Heaven; others are artificial, set up by people with fixed minds.

Zhuangzi here points to people's relation to Heaven, applying it to eliminate disputes and end argumentation, with the goal of ultimate harmony along the lines of Laozi's concept of "mysterious merging," a way of "harmonizing one's light and merging with obscurity" (ch. 56). This is different from "blending into mud," which means acting as a third party to adjudicate a dispute or struggle, maintaining a neutral position to effect an accommodation between the parties. Harmonizing one's light has nothing to do with brokering agreement among opposing parties, but involves the seamless integration of all right and wrong, an attitude within and toward one's self. Doing so, sharpness dulls, tangles open, and there is nothing but clear responsiveness—no more I or you or other, just the subtle process of creative change (*zaohua* 造化) that underlies all yet remains forever beyond our grasp.

Does creative change have boundaries? Certainly not. You may try to pinpoint some, but the moment you do so, they are already gone. Now it is day; soon there is night. Now there is birth; soon there is death. The creative process moves on and on, with no regard for years or morality: the long-lived Pengzu and a dying child, universal love and self-centeredness are all part of the whole, merged in the furnace of creative change, melted into oneness without distinctions.

This gets us to Zhuangzi's real point of equalizing: it frees people from the world of things, allowing their minds to be aware of them without being controlled by them. Awareness means mastery; being driven is a form of slavery. We cannot physically leave this world, but we can release it mentally by leaving all concerns behind. Thus our minds are liberated and become free. You may have a particular idea of right and wrong, and so does he. Everyone is welcome to it, but why should any of it concern me? I do not get involved as a dispute partner or even as a third-party referee. I simply remain detached and unconcerned.

Zhuangzi calls this twofold motion—stillness in activity. Motion involves walking: people walk on different paths and pursue different things, but I don't. Instead, I stand still in the center, amid the jostling crowd, my mind at rest like the surface of standing water. Zhuangzi's awareness is eminently clear, which is precisely why he feels such immense aloneness. He is right there in the world, among the masses, yet also as far removed from them as the shores of Heaven. It's as if he lives in a dream, in an unreal world, yet he is also acutely awake. He knows it is not he who is dreaming, but other people: they keep pursuing illusory things and have forgotten what is real. They love and cling to life, hating death and never realizing that it may well be the return to our true home while life is merely a temporary lodging on the way.

They are just like Lady Li, kidnapped by foreign soldiers. "She wept until her tears drenched the collar of her robe. But later, when she went to live in the palace of the ruler, shared his couch with him, and ate the delicious meats of his table, she wondered why she had ever wept." This is the true tragedy of life: we weep when we should be happy and laugh when we should be weeping. People think that they have found their true home or perfect happiness in this world, but ultimate satisfaction remains elusive.

Dreaming and waking are massively different. "Some may dream of wine and song, but weep when they wake up; others may dream of worry and sadness, but merrily go off hunting in the morning. While we dream, we don't know we are dreaming; we may even try to interpret our dreams in our dreams." In a dream, everything seems to be so real. Ordinary dreams all end; we wake up and understand that it was just a dream. But when life itself becomes a dream, who wakes the dreamer? Death? That's a bit late. Maybe an awake person will call out to startle people out of their dreams. But then what happens? The dreamers think they are already perfectly awake and see the caller as a madman who is disturbing their peace: they get rid of him and dream on.

This is not the worst of it. In Zhuangzi's view, the worst is when the caller is himself a dreamer and the distinction blurs. How can we ever be sure whether we are dreaming or awake? When I say that you are dreaming, might I not also be dreaming and talking in my sleep? This is an absurd question: Zhuangzi calls it bizarre, utterly impossible to resolve. Maybe once in ten thousand generations, a great sage appears who might provide a resolution. How would he do that? I think he would just let it all be. The true significance of Zhuangzi's absurd question is to admonish those who are awake to leave off clinging to the distinction between dreaming and waking: any clinging represents but another form of dreaming.

There can be no dreaming without waking. Once you know you are dreaming, you are actually awake. Zhuangzi, being fully awake, likes to talk about dreams, especially his own.

> Once Zhuang Zhou dreamt he was a butterfly, flitting and fluttering about like butterflies do. He had a wonderful sense of pleasure and felt greatly alive. He had no idea that he was Zhou. Suddenly he woke up and could clearly sense that he was Zhou. But he did not know whether he was Zhou who had just dreamed that he was a butterfly or whether he was in reality a butterfly who was now dreaming that it was Zhou."

Well, maybe he was both. This, however, is not the real issue of the parable. The real issue is that, while there is obviously a distinction between Zhuang Zhou and the butterfly, that distinction is gone in the dream. If you can be me, I can be you, and either of us can become he or she, are there any true distinctions? None at all. Everything is joined into one through creative change, a concept that Zhuangzi calls "the transformation of things." Non-transformation is static and without flow, but transformation moves continuously. In this flow, this free wandering, boundaries between things disappear: a big fish can turn into a huge bird, a man can be a butterfly, and all things can merge into oneness.

It is quite significant that the chapter ends with this beautiful dream. It illustrates the transformation of things, but does it not also transmit a feeling of futility? Zhuangzi may well realize that people who cling tenaciously to distinctions between this and that as much as those passionately engaged in disputes about right and wrong are dreamers—but maybe even those like himself who advocate equalizing things may well be merely having a dream. Perhaps equalizing things is an ideal only to be realized in dreams. While awake, you have no choice but to confront all sorts of distinctions and become immersed in them. This, then, is truly bizarre. Human beings stand undecided between dreaming and waking, linger between caring and indifference.

Since the chapter is presented in a discussion format, its true theme is often misunderstood or overlooked. Some even see it as a document of the Dialecticians or otherwise claim that it was not by Zhuangzi. Actually it shows just as much concern for human life as the other Inner Chapters, focuses throughout on the meaning of life in a world of things, on the relation of mind and external reality. Right from the beginning, it states "I have lost myself." This shows its key issue: how to let go of the fixed mind and attain a state of pervasion, where one is completely unconstrained and rests carefree in Dao.

Equalizing things will get you there; it creates an attitude of detachment and mental openness that lets go of all things. Then differences among things disperse like smoke, and all comes together in oneness. Things no longer burden the mind or encumber life. Someone who has reached this state is a perfect man.

> Matching pure spirit, he is impervious to the heat of great swamps burning, to the cold of mighty rivers freezing. He is not scared, even if violent lightning shatters the mountains or howling gales churn up the ocean. He mounts on clouds and mist, rides on sun and moon, roams beyond the four seas. Life and death have no effect on him—how much less any thought of gain and loss?

Some may think this description rather exaggerated and even unbelievable. Zhuangzi, of course, does not claim that the perfect man really does not get burned or chilled. He uses this extreme imagery to show the degree to which such a person is detached from the world and impervious to outside things. Having reached this state, he or she remains light at heart, unaffected by any changes in the world, and lives beyond the realm of concrete things. They can soar into Heaven with ease, float among clouds and mist, and wander beyond the four seas.

But there is more, notably with regard to the physical body. If equalizing things means that "in your mind it is best to harmonize," does this not also imply "in your body it is best to follow along"? In fact, in a state of "following along" or "moving with" the world, what meaning would distinctions still have? None, I'm sure. Here equalizing things becomes a necessary lifestyle choice, a direct reflection of the intense futility Zhuangzi feels. The chapter thus conveys a particular lifestyle and attitude rather than information or knowledge.

Chapter Six

The Great Ancestor and Master

The overall mistrust of the human and its correlate, the strong reliance on Heaven and Dao, has been a central aspect of Daoist thought ever since Laozi, who already says, "The grandest forms of virtue come from Dao as their only source;" (ch. 21) and, "Humanity patterns itself on Earth; Earth patterns itself on Heaven; Heaven patterns itself on Dao. Dao patterns itself on the self-so" (ch. 25). The Huang-Lao school expresses the same idea with "Dao gives rise to law" (*Jingfa* 1.1.1) meaning that law cannot properly issue from humanity but must come from something outside it. The *Jingfa* has,

> Life means harm, brought about by strong desires and not knowing when it is enough. Life also means movement, and once there is movement, there is harm, brought about by untimely events and seasonal disarray. Movement, moreover, creates affairs, and they too produce harm, brought about by going against the flow, lack of balance, and ignorance of how to use things. Affairs in turn involve speech, which creates more harm, brought about by falsehood, disrespect, deceit, vanity, exaggeration, and empty bragging. (1.1.3)

All these kinds of harm issue from humanity, and the only way to get out of them is by following Dao. This understanding does not quite match Zhuangzi, but it helps to put his vision into perspective.

The sixth chapter is called "The Great Ancestor and Master" (Dazongshi 大宗師). This is its theme throughout, but it has nothing much to do with ordinary ancestors or masters. The superiors here are not people, like the Confucian sage rulers Yao and Shun who established civil and military culture (*Liji*, "Zhongyong"), the Great Yu venerated by the Mohists (*Zhuangzi* 33), or even the Daoist saints Laozi and the Yellow Emperor. For people living in the human world, always faced with inescapable futility, Zhuangzi's masters are immeasurably huge and far beyond intentional reach while yet also constantly present and involved in the world. To move beyond this world of futility, we must tread not a small and narrow path, but follow a wide thoroughfare. As Zhuangzi praises the "master,"

> He passes judgment on all things but does not think himself righteous, who is gracious to myriads of generations yet does not think himself benevolent. Older than highest antiquity, he does not consider himself long-lived; covering Heaven and supporting Earth, he makes innumerable forms, yet does not consider himself skilled.

This amazing master cannot be anything but Dao itself! What else could reach out to all things, extend through time, be connected to everything, and shape life? For this reason, this chapter in Zhuangzi has most instances of the word "Dao"—it is one big song of praise.

The chapter describes Dao as having essential reality and manifestations but being free of action and form. This echoes Laozi: "Profound it is, dark and obscure; it contains an essence. This essence is utterly perfect; it contains ultimate truth" (ch. 21). Nonaction and formlessness—that is how later Daoists speak of Dao: "Original stem, original root: it has always existed since antiquity. Wondrous spirit, amazing deity: it gives rise to Heaven and Earth." Laozi himself says, "It precedes Heaven and Earth; it comes before all rulers" (ch. 25). Compared with these passages, Zhuangzi adds something: rich in imagination and creativity, he never lets his reader despair, but always focuses on the practical relationship of Dao and humanity: "You can hand it down but you cannot receive it; you can get it but you cannot see it." As long as there is no intentional blockage, no obstruction toward Dao, it can be transmitted and held on to. But this transmission or holding is not at all like that of ordinary objects, like something you can hand over and take hold of.

Dao is beyond creation: it existed before all things, brought forth the universe, and imbued the gods with power. "Present beyond the highest height, one cannot call it lofty; spread beneath the lowest depth, one cannot call it deep." Dao was there before anything else, yet it is not long-lived; it was earlier than anything, yet it is not old. Different divine and sagely figures of antiquity obtained it and reached their unique fulfillment in the world. Able to hold on to Dao without relying on anything else, theirs is truly a subtle art, not unlike the unstructured, nonegotistical connection between father and son. Such Dao-holders rely on their own strength. Attaining Dao is thus an entirely personal experience, which cannot be shared with others; in its expression and practical application, it differs from person to person.

That's why Zhuangzi lists a number of different figures. He wants to flesh out what exactly the nature is of these "masters" of Dao. After all, a master's position and standing depend on the existence of disciples as testimonial, and since Dao is formless and infinite, its disciples cannot possibly be bigoted in any respect. Like the Yellow Emperor, they can ascend into Heaven; like the Queen Mother of the West (Xiwangmu 西王母), they can be anywhere, small or wide. Like the river god Feng Yi 馮夷, they can float along on waterways; like the sage ruler Zhuan Xu 顓頊, they can live in mysterious palaces. Like the politician Fu Yue 傅說, they may apply Dao to governing the country; like the long-lived Pengzu, they may use it to extend life. Dao is massive and mysterious—everyone can find in it what he or she needs most. So what does Zhuangzi want from Dao?

That's easy: he wants to live authentically! Bowed under the dead weight of social vanity and artificiality, he desperately wants to find true ease, to live like the perfected. What, then, is a perfected?

> The perfected of old did not resent being humble, take pride in accomplishments, or plot affairs. They could be without regret if things went wrong and remain free from self-congratulations when they went right. Thus they could climb high places without getting scared, dive into water without getting soaked, and pass through fire without getting hot. Their understanding was such that they could rise and join Dao at all times.

Asking for a definition, Zhuangzi yet gives a rather non-definitive answer. Point by small point, he elucidates the image of the perfected as people who stay beyond things, detached from outcomes and at ease in all kinds of different situations. But behind these disjointed tidbits, there is a constructive strand that readers discern gradually. It can be understood in two ways. For one, being a perfected emerges as a mode of life that reaches out to Dao as creator, to the realm of the Way by working with "knowledge ascending to Dao." This happens from the inside: we have to grasp Dao's truth internally to live fully. For another, it represents a life in the perfection of Heaven. This is an approach from the outside: we can see and describe Heaven's workings. According to Zhuangzi, the perfected live without conscious planning, in a state of no-mind. They go along with Heaven, with the natural flow of life. Ordinary people may plot for the eventuality of gain and loss, success and failure, and behave in various ways as required by their goals, but the perfected won't and can't do so—because their life has nothing to do with gain and loss, success and failure.

Zhuangzi says: "In sleep, men's spirits go visiting; in waking hours, their bodies hustle" (ch. 2). The perfected of old did none of that; instead, they "slept without dreaming and woke without concerns, eating plain food and breathing deeply." They breathed so deeply: in fact, that their breath reached all way to the heels and not just to the chest like in ordinary people, who are "bent over and submissive, croaking out words as if they were retching," with only a thin connection to Heaven. Unlike worldly people, "these perfected had no clue about loving life and hating death, coming to life without celebration and leaving it without messiness." Always connected to their origin, they felt secure and never inquired about where they would end. "Whatever came their way they enjoyed; whatever went its way, they just let go."

In other words, the perfected are a great deal more relaxed than ordinary people. While the latter hustle in their souls and bustle in their bodies, the perfected remain at ease no matter what happens—representing a radically different way of life. Souls hustle and bodies bustle: that's because their owners keep running after outside things with a fixed mind. One can be free from dreams and remain without concerns because one goes along with the changes in a state of no-mind. In this description of the perfected we see no trace of desire for fancy meals or other extraneous things—all they are after is to live fully and consistently in alignment with the workings of Heaven.

Their connection to Heaven is deep: it reaches all the way to their heels, while in ordinary people it stops at the chest, the rest of the body being choke-full of superficial outward-oriented desires. The perfected know that life and death are part of a natural sequence like the succession of the four seasons, thus they neither particularly yearn for life nor detest death. They just emerge when they emerge, leave when they leave, go when they go, come when they come. They match the natural flow of life to the utmost, exerting not even a trace of human effort.

This, moreover, is not because they are unable to make human effort, or that there is no space for it in Zhuangzi's ideal life. Effort is valuable but it has its place: at the onset of their knowledge, in their clear analysis of circumstances, as the basis of true accordance. First you need to know what is due to Heaven and what is due to Humanity, then you realize what you can accomplish as an individual. This is perfect knowledge, authentic awareness. No other form of knowledge can match it! Thus, "he who knows what Heaven does and what human beings do has reached the peak." This way the perfected rest with Heaven yet use their knowledge to expand it further while living out their years. Zhuangzi calls this "perfect knowledge" (*zhizhi* 至知).

Perfect knowledge is nothing less than a full understanding of life itself unlike analytical knowledge (as in biology or medicine), which elucidates the concrete structures of human existence. What Zhuangzi is after is the true process of life, which is at the same time its innermost core. Once this becomes clear, we can really work with Heaven. The key phrase here is, "know what Heaven does and what human beings do." It points to the mystery of life, to the fact that people emerge from Dao and are brought forth by Heaven. Originally emerging from Heaven, people are in fact Heaven, Heaven's direct heirs. That means, Heaven is in fact their true ancestor. Here the "ancestor" in the chapter title becomes clear: the word originally refers to Heaven in distinction to Dao, the true "master." "Regard Heaven as a father and love it within yourself"—this puts Heaven squarely in the position of ancestor. Zhuangzi accordingly defines his ideal humans in terms of Heaven: "Who does not depart from the ancestor is a heavenly man; who does not depart from purity is a spirit man; who does not depart from perfection is a perfect man." In addition, the sage is one who "makes Heaven his source, virtue his root, and Dao his gate" (ch. 33).

All these definitions refer to Heaven in some way. Taking Heaven as one's true ancestor, then, means that one finds something in life to rely on that goes beyond the human world, and thereby one becomes a person who honors a power beyond. People recovering the connection to Heaven are as if returning home; patterning themselves on Heaven, they recover the root. Living like this is the only truly authentic way of being, the manifestation of perfect human effort. For Zhuangzi, perfection always connects to Heaven. "Model yourself on Heaven and value perfection" (ch. 31)—this phrase from beyond the Inner Chapters expresses it perfectly. The perfected are thus just like the various heavenly men (ch. 33), another kind of person who never parts from the ancestor.

How, then do these people act? Would they go after outside things like success, fame, wealth, and honor? Get entangled with worldly virtues and argue about value judgments? Certainly not. Created by people's fixed minds, these are all manifestations of the workings of the common mind. Authentic living means to rest in the workings of Heaven: it is completely free from these manifestations. Thus Zhuangzi expresses his deep reverence for the ultimate in living: nothing to be known rationally, nothing to do with good and evil, right and wrong, or any outside entity, nothing even with any form of perfect knowledge.

Perfect knowledge is closely linked to Heaven and life; it appears in the perfected as true knowing. "Knowing what human beings do, the perfected use the knowledge of what they know to expand the knowledge of what they do not know, thereby living out the years Heaven gave them—this is the perfection of knowledge." Our core activity in this world should be to live out our Heaven-given years rather than trying to analyze Heaven or Dao. Knowledge should be focused on a single point: life! Plus, living out our years is not just hanging around for a long time, but to serve life in all our actions. The years we have in this world are tied to Heaven and they may be linked to ourselves individually person, but ultimately they have nothing to do with the human level—thus the text calls them "Heaven-given."

The expression points to the intricate relationship between the heavenly and the human. In fact, where Confucians such as Mencius speak about virtues—benevolence, righteousness, propriety, wisdom, etc.—as part of human nature, they understand them and the value system they represent as part of Heaven. Heaven in this sense is something we have firmly within us; not something that comes to us from the outside. Mencius says, "He who has exhausted his mind, knows his inner nature; he who has exhausted hi parts inner nature, knows Heaven. To preserve one's mind and nourish one's inner nature is the way to serve Heaven" (7A1). Practicing the Confucian virtues and exhausting one's mind thus means to preserve one's mind to match and serve Heaven.

Zhuangzi sees things differently. For him, the perfected never "use the mind to reject Dao or the human part to help out Heaven" —which is exactly what Mencius proposes. According to Zhuangzi, we can get close to Dao and match ourselves to Heaven only when the mind is empty—as is made clear in the passage on mind-fasting (ch. 4). Mencius, in contrast, wants to reach to the heavenly by enhancing the human mind, filling it to overflowing. The two are thus quite opposite—empty versus full, oblivion versus knowledge—representing two major approaches to the heavenly in this world.

But which of them really gets you to Heaven? This is hard to judge. Just as Zhuangzi says, "How can I know that what I call Heaven is not really human, and what I call human is not really Heaven?" It's not easy to get a clear sense of which is which, especially with an intellectual analysis that is opposite to subtle inner workings. Practically speaking, one may be able to discern what forms part of Heaven and what is an aspect of Humanity, but then there's still the gray area where they intermingle. The only way is to let go of all analytical distinctions. Not only Zhuangzi, the Confucians, too, desire some distinction. Isn't Mencius's distinction between inner nature and fate as well as between heavenly structures and human desires a form of analytical division? Still, what he describes is different, and what he calls the heavenly Zhuangzi would ascribe to the human part, and vice versa. For Mencius, all ethical values and moral norms are part of our Heaven-given nature; for Zhuangzi, they mean "using the mind to reject Dao, using the human part to help out Heaven," harmful to inherent perfection.

In this context, Zhuangzi further uses the two words "brand" and "mutilate," taken from the world of criminal justice, to show just how bad he thinks virtues are for people. Yi'erzi 意而子 comes to seek advice from Xu You about wandering freely in Dao, but he has already received instructions from the sage-king Yao to "practice benevolence and righteousness and speak particularly about right and wrong." Since Yi'erzi is thus "branded" by these values, Xu You wonders how he "expects to go wandering on any far-off, carefree, as-you-like-it paths?" To him, Yi'erzi is like a blind man with regard to Dao, mutilated by the virtues. Still, he hopes for redemption: "Wu Zhuang 無庄 forgot her beauty, Ju Liang 据梁 forgot his strength, and the Yellow Emperor forgot his wisdom—they were content to be recast and remolded. How do you know that creative change will not wipe away my brand, stick my nose back on again, and let me ride on the process of completion and follow after you?"

The parable places words into the mouth of the sage-king Yao, shown as a model of Confucianism, the product of benevolence and righteousness. The names Yi'erzi and Xu You, too, evoke the reader's imagination. *Yi* 意, lit. "intention," always has to do with the mind and creativity; *you* 由, literally "to follow," indicates moving along with things in no-mind. From the perspective of Xu You, the virtues and value judgments Yao taught to Yi'erzi are just like branding and mutilation, seals forcefully stamped upon the mind. Once stamped like this, the mind is as if blinded: it cannot go along with creative change. For this reason, we need to let go of all distinctions and remove all differences, stop the mind being fraught with concerns of benevolence and righteousness, right and wrong, this and that—only then can we ever find peace.

Zhuangzi speaks of "going wandering in any far-off, carefree, as-you-like-it paths." On the one hand, this means developing a spiritual and mysterious esteem for the workings of creative change; on the other hand, it is being at ease in freely going along with the changes. Anyone holding on tightly to virtues and norms cannot possibly do so. Living in the midst of regulations that prevent the emergence of one's real, Heaven-given nature, the earth becomes a prison and life is nothing but a bundle of fetters. There is no way one can enjoy its fullness and beauty, richness and abundance. People like this are like blind and deaf, but while ordinary blindness and deafness is limited to eyes and ears, theirs is one of the mind—and that much worse for it.

It is important, though, to understand that, while Zhuangzi denies that the Confucian virtues are part of our heavenly nature, he does not reject moral sentiments or ethical values in general. Rather, his thinking reflects Laozi who says, "Heaven and Earth are not benevolent but take the ten thousand things as mere straw dogs. The sage is not benevolent but takes the hundred families as mere straw dogs" (ch. 5). He also insists that "when great Dao declined, benevolence and righteousness came forth; wisdom and shrewdness appeared, and great hypocrisy ensued. When the six relationships fell out of harmony, filial piety and elder care manifested. When the states and clans fell into disorder, there were loyal ministers" (ch. 18). To remedy this, one should "let go of benevolence, get rid of righteousness, and the people will benefit a hundredfold. Leave off sageliness, discard wisdom, and the people will recover true obedience and caring love. Leave off skill, get rid of profit! There will be no more thieves and robbers" (ch. 19).

This is to say, there are true forms of loyalty and trust, filial piety and caring. Both Laozi and Zhuangzi favor the authentic and dismiss the artificial—Laozi calls it pure, the "uncarved block;" for Zhuangzi, it is Heaven. Heaven is genuine, perfect, authentic: it has its match in each human being, the "truly human." Perfection, then, means that the heavenly and the human parts merge smoothly in one organism. On this basis, Zhuangzi develops several new defining points of the ideal person.

> He who delights in bringing success to others is not a sage; one who has affections is not benevolent. He who looks for the right time is not a worthy man; he who cannot encompass both profit and loss is not a gentleman. He who thinks of conduct and fame and misleads himself is not a man of breeding; he who destroys himself and is without truth is not a user of men.

This critical definition of sages and worthies targets the Confucians. The Confucian sage directs his mental attention toward others and gets a feeling of joy that connects above and below, Heaven and Earth. As Mencius says, "The ten thousand things are complete in me. Reflection on oneself and being sincere—there is no greater happiness than this" (7A4). For Zhuangzi, on the contrary, this kind of happiness still depends on having an ego and making divisive considerations. Instead, the sage should be one whose "mind forgets, face is calm, forehead is broad. He is chilly like autumn, balmy like spring, and his joy and anger prevail through the four seasons. He matches what is right for others and no one knows his limit." Going along with all in no-mind, he may be detached, but he can also be soothing; he may be joyful, but he can also be angry. All kinds of human emotions and feelings move through his mind, and he wanders about naturally once he receives an impulse. "One is not a sage unless one's happiness connects to others." Similarly, benevolence should not happen merely in the context of affections, a gentleman should not be beyond benefit and harm, a man of breeding should not give up his true identity for fame and reputation, and a user of men should not be beyond keeping himself whole and maintaining inner perfection. For Zhuangzi, the Confucians have lost their authentic self in the jungle of virtues and values; they behave like people no longer true to themselves. Whether called sage, worthy, or whatever, they all mutilated themselves for the sake of so-called righteousness, forfeiting their lives. "They all slaved in the service of other men, took joy in bringing other men joy, but could not find joy in any joy of their own." None of them lived purely for themselves; they sacrificed their truth for some artificial, imaginary fame. Thus their bodies and selves became mere tools for reaching some extraneous goal, their authentic life submerged in the quest for fame in the realm of virtues and values.

People living in the ordinary world are always constricted by boundaries, imprisoned in a cangue of some sort that typically consists of hopes, profit, or virtues. Those who work for profit may despise those who merely pursue hope; those who dedicate themselves to virtues may despise profit seekers. But what have any of them to do with Dao? People living in Dao are free from all manner of pursuit. They only think of resting in no-mind and going along with creative change in spontaneity and freedom, living in deep inner peace. They never think of virtues or pass judgments, remain free from benevolence and righteousness, right and wrong. Not interested in praising the sage-king Yao or condemning the tyrant Jie, they have no desire to be involved with people and things and thus never get submerged in the currents of life. Given the choice, they would rather "forget all in the flow of rivers and lakes."

All those imprisoned in the cangue, on the other hand, can they find release from their constrictions? Of course they can. Creative change is marvelous. Just as Yi'erzi says, "How do I know that creative change will not wipe away my brand and stick my nose back on again?" By the same token, why should I not eliminate all thoughts of virtues and values? I certainly can, but this is not a convenient, easy process. It requires some smelting and hammering. Under it impact, everything extraneous must be radically discarded, leaving behind only one's unique nature and perfected mind. The discarding process, moreover, is what Zhuangzi calls "oblivion," presented in the famous dialogue between Yan Hui and Confucius. The former is pleased to report that he has left benevolence and righteousness behind, but Confucius encourages him to go further. Next, he can let go of rites and music. This is still not enough. Eventually, he can sit in full oblivion: "I let my limbs and physical structure fall away, do away with perception and intellect, separate myself from body-form and let go of all knowledge, thus joining great pervasion."

The parable uses Confucian characters to denigrate Confucian values, not unlike the tales discussed earlier. At the core is the concept of *wang* 忘, literally "forgetting," which indicates leaving things behind and becoming intentionally oblivious. By eliminating various Confucian values and concrete, social realities, Yan Hui moves gradually to the complete oblivion of self, body and mind, where "the body is like dried wood, the mind is like dead ashes." Why go so far? What does all this mean? Simply put, oblivion is the complete abolition of all bodily imposed limitations, a return to a state of true inner perfection that allows one to go along freely with creative change. Benevolence and righteousness in any form are limitations; rites and music in any shape constitute fetters. Only by being free from them can you truly be yourself.

But then you still need to eliminate any idea of self, eradicate the very root of all limitations and fetters. At this point, not only are all values lost, but the self is also gone; all structures and frameworks, anything that can create boundaries, is no longer there. Then you reach the stage of "joining great pervasion." Great pervasion (*datong* 大通) is none other than the unlimited, infinite flow of creative change, none other than Dao. As the text has, "Whether a little stalk or a great pillar, a leper or the beautiful Xi Shi, things ribald and shady, grotesque and strange: Dao pervades them all in oneness" (ch. 2). In this state of great pervasion, there is no more like or dislike, no more right or wrong. Everything in constant flux, there is no more solid world—just as in Zhuang Zhou's butterfly dream, one wanders about matching the changes in no-mind.

Pervasion itself requires two factors: one is emptiness—as long as there is solidity or fullness, pervasion is impossible. "Solidity" means a firm presence in space, that is, something which easily turns into a blockage. "Fullness" means harboring content in one's mind, such as right and wrong, likes and dislike. Echoing this, the *Daoyuan* 道原 (On Dao the Fundamental), a manuscript found at Mawangdui, says that only after reaching "great emptiness" can one "pervade the essence of Heaven and Earth" (4.1.5). The *Guanzi* 管子 (Book of Master Guan; trl. Rickett 1985; 1998) similarly emphasizes that "the Dao of Heaven is empty and formless: empty, it does not bend; formless, it does not stand. Thus it flows through all things without change" (ch. 36).

All these passages point to the close connection of pervasion and emptiness. Responding to the world from a position of emptiness, one can be just like Cook Ding who "inserts what has no thickness" into the nooks and crannies between the joints, having plenty of room to maneuver his knife. The other major factor in pervasion is transformation. As the *Xici* commentary to the *Yijing* says, "Where there is change, there is pervasion" (1.2). Pervasion thus means continuous transformation—there is nothing solid or permanent anywhere. It is also reminiscent of the summary in chapter 33,

> Blank, boundless, and without form; transforming, changing, never constant: are we dead? Are we alive? Do we stand side by side with Heaven and Earth? Do we move in the company of spiritual brightness? Absent-minded, where are we going? Oblivious, where are we headed? Things range all around us—not one of them is worthy to be singled out as our destination.

"Blank, boundless, and without form"—that's emptiness; "changing, never constant"—that's transformation. "Are we dead, are we alive"—all that follows is a description of just what constant change means. Whoever penned this passage, he was certainly spot-on, someone with a particular affinity to Zhuangzi's thought.

There are multiple ways of regarding change, and transformation in the *Zhuangzi* is considerably different from comparative concepts in the *Yijing*, which does not have the same confidence in life, the certainty that one can go along with it. *Yijing* commentaries may speak of "adapting to the changes," but this is different from Zhuangzi's view in the understanding of Dao as providing structure to all transformations through the rhythm of yin and yang. A form of framing Dao, this concept of change makes it measurable and controllable. For Zhuangzi, on the other hand, Dao is empty and all-pervasive, without pattern or structure, just plain change, like a river's ongoing flow.

With all those things around us that we cannot possibly grasp, why not just let go of all grasping? Maybe even to the point of where we no longer add any artificial frameworks. There is no purpose in creating a distinction of right and wrong, win or lose where there is none originally. Zhuangzi distinctly opposes any kind of behavior that might "assist" Heaven. For him, anything we cannot grasp or comprehend needs to be left well alone. Things like that belong to fate, to Heaven. "Life and death are fate—constant as the succession of night and day, a matter of Heaven. There are some things which man can do nothing about. They are part of the nature of things." Human beings should accept their own limitations, the fact that there are innumerable areas in this world that we cannot manage or control. When dealing with these areas, it is wisest to maintain silence and just go along.

The strongest situation to express this kind of alignment to circumstances for Zhuangzi may well be death. Where ordinary people sink into inordinate expressions of grief, what would he do? Would he, like the Confucians, honor all those complex rules of mourning and funerary rites? Or would he, like Mengsun Cai 孟孫才 when his mother died, cry some tears while remaining undisturbed at heart, fulfill the mourning requirements without really suffering? By all means, he would go for the latter: after all, he drums and sings after his wife dies. When Huizi asks him about this reaction, he explains that life and death are nothing but the assemblance and dispersion of *qi*, succeeding each other like the seasons (ch. 18).

This closely matches Mengsun Cai's behavior. "When his mother died, he wailed without shedding tears, his heart was free from distress, and he managed the funeral without sorrow." Despite this lack of obvious grief, people thought him "a top mourner in the state of Lu," Confucius's original home. Even in Confucian funerary rites, the mental sorrow within was considered more important than its outer expression in ritual behavior—as the *Lunyu* says, "Mourning and its changes rest with dignity" (3.4). Still, one must observe specific rituals, such as the three-year mourning period which goes far beyond the internal attitude. How, then, did Mengsun Cai who didn't follow the rules get to be known as a "top mourner"? The same question may occur to ordinary people when confronted with Zhuangzi. And what does he say? Placing words in Confucius's mouth, he praises Mengsun Cai's conduct as "doing all that there was to do" while being "advanced beyond ordinary understanding."

This is reminiscent of the state of oblivion where body and understanding are both eliminated while giving a new twist to "doing away with understanding." It can mean letting go of self but it can also mean going with the flow in great pervasion, moving with the currents of creative change. Here it means the realization that life and death are as natural and as inevitable as the succession of the four seasons, as ordinary as the changes of day and night. Once you see things from this angle, can you still love life and hate death as ordinary people do? Not really. All those complex funerary rites come to look rather petty, maybe even ridiculous, nothing but an expression of extreme ignorance. Then you can let go of them easily.

Like the Confucians, the Mohists, as described in the *Mozi* chapter on "Moderation in Funerals," insisted on proper funerary rites—but they acknowledged that, while being useful and efficacious in antiquity, they had evolved over time to being too complex and were increasingly useless. Zhuangzi goes beyond both these schools in proposing a completely different understanding of life and death, one that is not only simpler but does away with the very effort of understanding. Mengsun Cai still sheds tears although he may not have felt like crying, but for Zhuangzi even that is too much—the tears represent a certain degree of submission to worldly rules. Zhuangzi knows very well that in the course of creative change there is no such thing as life or death, that life and death ultimately form one integrated organism. We come to life as *qi* assembles; we die as it disperses. Whether alive or dead, all states of being are nothing but expressions of the never ending, inexhaustible flow of cosmic change. There is no room for emotions like joy and grief anywhere in this state, let alone for rites and rules.

Yet in this flow of change, is there anything at all that remains unchanging? Speaking of the permanent, what really is the meaning of change we have discovered so far? For us as readers, the meaning of change is clear: the succession of the seasons, life and death, death and life. So what could be unchanging in that? Obviously the factor of creative change itself. All things and affairs are part of the world of change, but change itself is an unchanging factor. "That which kills life does not die; that which gives life to life does not live."

Another factor is the mind. The body is subject to all kinds of changes and the world never stops transforming, but the mind does not change along with them. "His body decays, his mind follows it—can you deny that this is a great sorrow?" (ch. 2). The mind here does not change even while going along with the body's changes. "Though something may startle his body, it won't injure his mind; though something may alarm the house [his spirit lives in], his emotions will suffer no death," Zhuangzi says. Startle and alarm may impact the body while the mind remains free from injury and death and roams beyond change.

However, the fact that the mind is not subject to the same level of change as the body does not mean that it should become inflexible, stuck in any particular state. Rather, as soon as it does hold on to a certain state, it becomes a "fixed mind." Its true unchanging quality arises from being empty and still, remaining without movement or agitation. In a state of emptiness and stillness, the "I" is lost, leaving only an appearance of "me." The difference between "I" and "me" is that the former has form while the latter is formless, the former is solid while the latter is empty. Empty and formless, this "me" can change, becoming a bird and soaring up into the sky, changing into a fish and diving down into the depths, transforming into anything and everything at any moment.

As in chapter 2, Zhuangzi here emphasizes the distinction between dreaming and waking. Mengsun Cai is awake, but Yan Hui and the masses are in a dream. People in a state of dreaming take their "me" to be their "I," vague and unchanging. People who are awake take their "I" as their "me," wandering about the changes in no-mind. Holding on tightly to their dream "reality," ordinary people value this and dismiss that, like themselves and dislike others, are joyful when things go their way and fall into depression when their precious self is hampered. Those fully awake and going along with the changes, on the other hand, see this and that, self and others as part of the same organism. They are comfortable with whatever happens and align themselves with anything, peacefully resting in the process of change. They live a life that is authentic and serene, free from great joys and sorrows. They can smile at all times: "Running around with others is not as good as laughing, and enjoying a good laugh is not as good as going along with things."

Going along with things, moreover, places one in a position where there is nothing much to laugh or cry about, both being a form of attachment, a grasping toward something that is bound to change. Also, anytime there's laughter, crying is waiting just around the corner; anytime you feel smug and well satisfied with yourself, you quickly discover something that makes you feel bad. Can you really laugh while going along with all that happens? Not likely. You will probably continue to live in the ups and downs of joy and anger, sorry and happiness, pulled along by outside things, never quite at peace and resting within. Zhuangzi does not want this kind of life, he wants to "be content to go along and forget about change," content in all situations while releasing the idea of change, going along with things while resting in himself, thus becoming one with Heaven, "entering the mysterious oneness of Heaven," and returning to the great ancestor of all.

Most people have been involved in the human world for a long time, and the longer they are immersed in it the more they lean toward the human side of things, getting farther away from the heavenly. Even to think about leaving the humanly and moving toward Heaven, returning to the origin and recovering the ancestral, cannot be easy. They are so used to follow along with the outside world that they have come to consider it their true home. Heaven being far removed and strange, any lifestyle that emulates it must seem weird. Thus ordinary people think the perfected who truly emulate Heaven are "crazy," strange people who are like the cripples and amputees in ch. 4. But for Zhuangzi, the crazy ones are really "companions of Heaven." Like them, he turns his back on ordinary life and fully matches the patterns of Heaven.

In this chapter, he intentionally fleshes out the perfect blend of the heavenly and the human: what the common world calls a gentleman, described so logically by the Confucians, in the realm of Heaven would be the opposite: a small man who lacks the vast understanding of Heaven, is not awakened to oneness, and only lives within the constricted sphere of the world. In this world, there are benevolence and righteousness, rites and music. "Who makes benevolence his standard of kindness, righteousness his model of reason, ritual his guide to conduct, and music his source of harmony, serene in mercy and benevolence—this is called a gentleman" (ch. 33). He lives in the world of reciprocity where people, like fish out of water, "spew each other with moisture and wet each other down with spit." They never imagine that there is a completely different way of life, where they "could simply forget each other and float about in the rivers and lakes."

Fish are comfortable in water; it is their true home. They do not need to make an effort or be in competition, "spewing each other with moisture and wetting each other down with spit." Comfort at this level means that there is no need to invoke intentional love to create cooperation, i.e., "running around with others is not as good as laughing."

Laughter is an expression of felt joy, but can you laugh forever? When there is nothing to laugh about, you feel stressed and depressed. Love is just like that. Being in a state of "simply forgetting each other and float about in the rivers and lakes" is nothing like living in the constricted realm of benevolent love, which is but a mere branch for people to hold on to while they are drowning in suffering and misery. How can it ever really transform anyone's life from the bottom up?

Love is merely a makeshift stop-gap, providing a brief respite before death yet unable to alter its ugly reality and inevitable reality. On the other hand, when fish swim freely about in the rivers and lakes, finding inner peace and following their fate, there is no need for love, not even the awareness of loving or being loved. They interact naturally without intentionally doing so, live naturally without intentionally creating a particular lifestyle. In their deep pool of rich natural love and nourishing moisture, the fish find their true way of being. And just as fish are in water, so people are in Dao and its arts.

> Fish thrive in water, people thrive in Dao. For those that thrive in water, dig a pond and they will find nourishment enough. For those that thrive in Dao, don't bother about them and their lives will be secure. So it is said, the fish forget each other and float in the rivers and lakes, and people forget each other and flow in the arts of Dao.

This passage can be read variously, but for me the key point is that their "lives will be secure." It means that one lives in the comforting awareness of being at peace within oneself and fully established in one's fate, a feeling best described as being "at home." All is natural, nothing contrived or artificial. Just like fish swimming in rivers and lakes only need water and don't pursue anything else, so people at one with Dao only need Dao and its arts that allow them to return to their true ancestor. They float in true self-realization, resting in nonaction and free from affairs. Here oblivion is complete—no more others, self, life, or death.

This, then, is what Zhuangzi means when he speaks of fish and people forgetting each other. Expanding on this, would fish still be able to float about if there were no rivers and lakes? Could they still remain stress-free under other life circumstances, faced with hardship and death, their own or that of others? According to Mencius, they certainly could not: when someone sees a child about to fall into a well, the submerged compassionate mind arises and comes to the surface. How would Zhuangzi react in that situation? He may be able to avoid this particular case, but he cannot get away from similar scenes. In a world that has lost Dao, where human beings regularly face severe hardships, how can people ever forget each other?

This chapter does not provide a direct answer, but there are hints in the parable of "the praying mantis waving his arms about, trying to stop an approaching carriage" (ch. 3). The text recommends that we "have it in ourselves before trying to give it to others," "understand what we can do nothing about and be content with it as with fate" (ch. 4). So when a child is about to fall into a well and a life is about to be destroyed, how can I not be moved? What can I do? Maybe the toddler is already beyond help and there is nothing I can do; maybe I can reach down and try get him out, only to be pulled into the well myself. Then again, maybe oblivion is my best choice: close my eyes and never let it disturb my inner peace and quiet. I may really have no other choice but to try and forget things around me.

In a world suffused with Dao, this kind of oblivion comes naturally; in Dao-less times, it helps to go beyond suffering. Although there is no Dao in the outside world, I can still maintain it in my mind. People connected to can forget each other like fish in rivers and lakes. The three masters Sanghu 子桑戶, Mengzi Fan 孟子反, and Qinzhang 子琴張 provide an example when they ask: ""Who can join with others without joining with others? Who can do with others without doing with others? Who can climb up to Heaven and wander in the mists, roam the infinite, and be oblivious of life forever and ever?" They have gone beyond others, beyond interaction based on benevolence or love, and are thus able to climb into the skies and float with the clouds, roaming in the infinite. In this state, all distinctions and divisions are eliminated. In oblivion, all is met with the same attitude. At this point, how could there still be any need or use for a ritual system to structure relationships? It would be quite useless.

So Zhuangzi once more expresses his position on how to deal with death and loss. After Master Sanghu dies, the other two do not engage in wailing and mourning as ordinary people would, but drum and sing and play the zither—reflecting their unique approach to death, their particular understanding of the world. Their song goes, "Ah, Sanghu! Ah, Sanghu! You have gone back to your true form, while we remain as men, O!" Death for them is not a separation from life but a return to original form. There is no trace of sadness or regret in their stance, not even a bit of attachment to the other. Death is a form of liberation from this world. Free from ordinary emotions, they feel no need to celebrate or mourn.

From their perspective, why have funerary rites at all? They merely reflect human feelings and have nothing to do with Heaven, nor yet with Heaven-inspired people.

Yet despite being heavenly people, they still have to live among ordinary humanity. How, then, should they deal with the common way of seeing? Wanting ordinary people to truly appreciate Heaven is like trying to make the little quail gain the perspective of the huge Peng—a hard feat indeed. More often than not, they will be not be appreciated or heard but confronted with Zigong's 子貢 reaction: "What sort of men are they anyway?" They are considered strange and called crazy, since they do not practice self-cultivation along the lines of the Confucians, don't make a big to-do over their bodies, easily face death and dying, and instead of crying and mourning like ordinary folk, sing and play music, not showing even a trace of sadness. What kind of people are they? They are perfected, heavenly people, but to ordinary folk they are just plain crazy. Seen from their perspective, the perfected are like the sky: "It looks very blue, but is that its real color, or is it because it is so far away and has no end?" (ch. 1). People of the common world just don't know.

The perfected straddle two worlds—within and beyond ordinary society, one limited by human perimeters, the other far-off, reached by climbing into the skies and floating with the clouds, true endless infinity. In the world limited by human perimeters, they have to deal with ordinary life and relationships—officials, family, relatives, friends, and more—yet even then the perfected are true companions of creative change, wandering about in the oneness of Heaven and Earth. What if any people or things would there be for them? Rather, they "come and go with the pure spirit of Heaven and Earth" (ch. 33), seeing life and death as the mere opening and closing of a flower.

Zhuangzi does not use quite such a pretty image. According to him, the perfected "look upon life as a swelling tumor or a protruding goiter, and upon death as the draining of a sore or the bursting of a boil." There is nothing serious or sacred about the process. Life and death just form part of the universal flow and there is no need to pay any particular attention to them. Really, what is the big deal? Any distinguishing marks dissolve in the great flow of ongoing change. All is completely interconnected, coming and going, beginning and ending—and nobody has a clue of how or why. There appear to be limits and distinctions, but they quickly dissolve in the ubiquitous waves of change. From this perspective, there is no more difference between liver and gall bladder, eyes and ears. In this realm of non-distinction, the perfected soar beyond the world of dust and grime and wander freely in nonaction. Going along with creative change, how could they still submit to the whims of the world and observe some puny funerary rites?

Here the radical difference between Zhuangzi and the Confucians becomes most obvious: the two are as far apart as within and beyond the world. For Confucius, "unless we study the rites, we have no place to stand" (*Lunyu* 16.13), meaning that only rites make people fully human. For Zhuangzi, "rites are a way to follow" (ch. 33), meaning that they must be observed as part of the ordinary world. Confucian thought never once leaves the human world behind and remains centered on human relationships; it strives to set limits to the limitless universe and focuses entirely on the realm "within boundaries." This is the world of rites and distinctions, where relationships between family members, sexes, and officialdom are clearly structured and regulated.

But Zhuangzi wants to go beyond this, into a realm far outside all boundaries, and to this end he questions all and any distinctions, including whether human beings are really so special and why the Confucians single out humanity from the great flow of life. Having reached beyond the limitations himself, Zhuangzi stands firmly in the realm of cosmic change and looks at the world from the perspective of Heaven. For him, Humanity, Heaven, Earth, and all things are all part of one large, integrated organism, where all human-made distinctions are irrelevant. What place is there for petty rites?

More radically speaking, the realm beyond is not really the opposite of that limited by boundaries. The two are only juxtaposed in a manner of speaking. Seen from the perspective of the limited world, yes, there is a distinction between within and without; people here need to hold on to distinctions, after all. But seen from the realm beyond, all just comes and goes, begins and ends. How can there be any distinctions? The realm beyond is much like what Laozi calls the "great realm"—endless and infinite. Formless and without distinctions, it is truly a single organism. Zhuangzi tells the parable of the four masters who ask, "Who can look upon nonbeing as his head, on life as his back, and on death as his rump?" and "Who knows that life and death, existence and annihilation, are all one organism? I will be his friend!"

Here the expression "one organism" (*yiti* 一體) appears for the first time in the text, in a passage that speaks of life and death, existence and annihilation. But it applies to everything in the world. "Heaven and Earth are one attribute; all things are one horse" (ch. 2)—that's another way of saying the same thing. The whole world is one integrated body, connected through veins and arteries. "The hundred joints, the nine openings, the six organs, all come together and exist here [as my body]. But which part should I feel closest to?" (ch. 2). I and all things, all things and I are mutually connected, there is really no distinction between near and far, like and dislike.

The concept of "one organism," however, does not so much reject distinctions per se—as between head, spine, and buttocks—but the attachment to distinctions which turns into one-sided discrimination as, for example, thinking of the head as superior and the buttocks as inferior. Rather than being essentially distinct, these items are in fact constituent parts of the same thing. In order to eliminate the habit of distinction-making, moreover, we must develop a particular understanding. Distinctions are never absolute but different aspects of the same thing, dimensions within the one organism. Nor is this one organism a firm, solid, and stable thing—it flows and changes constantly. In the course of this change, the head can become the buttocks, and vice versa: "The smelly and putrid change into the spiritual and marvelous; the spiritual and marvelous change into the smelly and putrid" (ch. 22).

There are many ways to speak about this one organism, in terms of oneness, *qi*, or Dao, but it centers on the universal fact of creative change. Living beings, including humans, can never escape change. It keeps a firm hold on all, but particularly affects ordinary people and only to a minor degree heavenly beings or the perfected. The perfected have true knowledge of the change process, thus they are like the four masters—with different names yet part of the same structure.[9] Creative change can make a healthy, upright man into a hunchback overnight, turn life into death in an instant—but how to face this when it comes to you or your loved ones?

This requires a particular understanding of how life and circumstances develop. All human beings enjoy being healthy and have an innate desire for life—even Zhuangzi. However, creative change doesn't pay any attention to whether you enjoy something or not. It follows its own rules or has no rules, and there is no way you can stand in its way,

---

[9] Their names are Zi Si 子祀 (Master Sacrifice), Zi Yu 子輿 (Master Carriage), Zi Li 子犁 (Master Plow), and Zi Lai 子來 (Master Come). The first and last refer to death and birth, the middle two indicate the forward movement of life in the here and now. The four are fast friends, providing a symbolic expression of how life and death, existence and annihilation are all part of the same flow.

lest you become like "the praying mantis waving his arms about, trying to stop an approaching carriage." You may well resist the march of change and become a hero. But to what end? You can wail and cry all you want in the face of change, you can pray that change follows your wishes, but it doesn't have human-like natural sympathies, no eyes to see or ears to hear. Any of these reactions are ways of humans assisting Heaven, people structuring nature. It is much better to just be at peace with creative change and come to see all of life as one organism. Then what could there be there to want or reject? Neither have any particular advantage. If change turns my left arm into a rooster, I can "keep watch on the night" and announce the dawn. If it transforms my right arm into a crossbow, I can "shoot down an owl for roasting." If it changes my buttocks into cartwheels, I can "use my spirit for a horse, climb up, and go for a ride." In any case, acceptance is key.

The basic wisdom of Zhuangzi is that "I received life because the time had come; I will lose it because the order of things passes on." He recommends being content with this and dwelling in it with detachment, so that "neither sorrow nor joy can touch you." What is there to resent? In other words, neither the coming nor the going of life has anything to do with "me," and I am in no position to love one or hate the other. It comes and I'm at peace; it goes and I'm still at peace. I am what I am no matter what. With this understanding and attitude, one can be free from the ups and downs of joy and sorrow. As Zhuangzi says, this is what people of old called "detached understanding," an understanding of life based on a state of detachment. On this basis we can develop a position of being at peace with ourselves and resting in fate. If you have detachment but don't feel at peace, you must cut the rope that ties you down—the rope of discrimination and pursuit, especially of things you have no control over. Zhuangzi here again shows his contempt for human efforts, emphasizing once more that "nothing can ever win against Heaven." Humans are powerless in the face of creative change, so why tie ourselves down?

Thus, when Master Lai falls ill, "gasping and wheezing, lying at the point of death, his wife and children gathering and crying," his friend Li comes in and pushes them aside, saying, "Don't disturb the process of change!" This not only vividly demonstrates that death is part of the ongoing process of creative change, but also the proper way to deal with it. Anguish is useless; there is nothing we can do to stop the processes of life and death, so we better get on with it. Li asks the sick man: "Where is change going to take you from here? Will it make you into a rat's liver? Will it make you into a bug's arm?" The patient responds,

> A child, obeying his father and mother, goes wherever he is told, east or west, south or north. And the yin and yang of creative change—how much more are they to a human being than father or mother! Now that they have brought me to the verge of death, if I should refuse to obey them, how perverse I would be.

In the human world, children should obey their parents without question. From a detached perspective, the original ancestor of all beings—Heaven, creative change, yin and yang—has an authority that is just like that of the parents: we should follow their directives without question or complaint. If a lord decides that his minister must die, then die he must. Similarly if Heaven decides that my time has come, can I do anything but comply? Not really. Rather than becoming obstinate, I should just obey, whether what comes is life or death. Change is like a master smith casting a sword. Should it rise up to demand being cast into the famous Moye blade, the smith would certainly think it highly inauspicious. So, if we think of Heaven and Earth as a great furnace and creative change as a master smith, and we rise up to demand being cast as humans—what would they think? That we are highly inauspicious fellows. For Zhuangzi, the proper way to be in the world is to accept and be at peace with whatever we become.

At this point we can truly be one with creative change, develop a nondual awareness of flow, no matter what we become, a rat's liver, a bug's arm, a rooster, or a crossbow—it's always us and yet always not us. We are not firm and solid entities because nothing is firm or solid in creative change. All is change and transformation, and to accomplish anything we have to go along with this change, move in tune with the transformations. To do so, our mind must be completely free from obstacles and blockages, rules and methods. We can get rid of them by following a process.

Here Zhuangzi presents the dialogue between Nanbo Zikui and Nüyu about her disciple Buliang Yi 卜梁倚, who undergoes a systematic progress toward Dao by "putting outside the world, all things, and life itself. "Put outside" (*wai* 外) means eliminate things, and we can do so because these "things" originally do not belong to us. I own neither the world nor all things nor life. Thus I can do away with them, eliminate them completely from my system. As Laozi says, "Learning means to increase day by day; practicing Dao means to diminish day by day" (ch. 48). Putting outside is thus the process of Dao, a daily reduction and diminishing. It takes Buliang Yi three days to get rid of the world, seven days for all things, and nine days for the very concept of life—a day-by-day transformation.

Zhuangzi even fleshes out the contrast to "learning" when he has Nanbo ask, "Can Dao be learned?" and demonstrates his attitude in the answer, "Goodness, how could that be?" Dao can be attained, but not by learning. Learning is a form of increasing things, which means getting further away from Dao. Trying to reach Dao by learning is like directing your wagon's shaft to the south and its tracks pointing north. When it comes to Dao, people are not deficient but rather excessive—in desires, pursuits, and self: thus they have to eliminate these.

The goal of elimination is to attain Dao. After getting rid of the world, all things, and life, Zhuangzi has Buliang Yi attain "brightness of dawn," "seeing one's aloneness," "being free from past and present," and "no life and no death." "Brightness" here means pervasion, so "brightness of dawn" indicates an opening toward Dao, reflecting the expressions "becoming one with great pervasion" (ch. 6) and "joining the pervasion of Dao" (ch. 2). Aloneness is also a characteristic of Dao in Laozi: "Alone it stands and never changes" (ch. 25). So is "no life and no death"—as Zhuangzi says, "it reaches to high antiquity and never ages" and "it has always existed from old times."

The world of Dao is utterly still, free from the ups and downs caused by the movement of *qi* through life and death. It is stillness in the midst of hubbub, containing birth and death, production and destruction. It is thus at the background of all life's fluctuation—killing life and birthing life, destroying creation and producing creation. On the face of it, it seems very busy and laborious, welcoming and sending off, destroying and producing. But in fact it neither welcomes nor sends off, neither kills nor gives birth. Dao is nonaction; it produces things but has no intention. So, however active it may be, nothing ever hinders its peace. Zhuangzi calls this "peace-in-strife: it strives, then always attains completion." This reveals the complex interaction of peace and strife: we must not reject strife in favor of peace but find in it the foundation for a level state. In the same way, in the state of "no life and no death," we cannot reject life and death or seek their destruction but rather must develop a new level of understanding. Thus "putting outside" does not mean getting rid of the world and its features altogether but rather finding a sense of inner peace within its complexity.

Whether speaking of pervasion or peace, of oblivion or putting outside, Zhuangzi wants to penetrate into all kinds of structures and resolve the relationship of self and world, body and mind. There can be no lasting satisfaction in this world: it is full of hardship, unfairness, strife, and pain. We have no power to change that and can only find acceptance. Zhuangzi suffers and works to dissolve this suffering, and to this end he pursues a new understanding, different from the views of the world, that will give him peace of mind. Does he succeed? Master Sang gives an indication, finding himself in dire poverty and singing a haunting song: "Father? Mother? Heaven? Man?" When Yu asks him about it, he says,

> I was pondering what it is that has brought me to this extremity, but I couldn't find the answer. My father and mother surely wouldn't wish this poverty on me. Heaven covers all without partiality; Earth bears up all without partiality - Heaven and Earth surely wouldn't single me out to make me poor. I try to discover who is doing it, but I can't get the answer. Still, here I am - at the very extreme. It must be fate.

This reveals yet another dimension of Zhuangzi's thought. On the background of pursuing inner peace, he is still thrown by waves and eddies. Faced with a difficult situation—in this case, extreme poverty—he has Master Sang cry and wail, questioning his state. There is despair here and, growing from it, anguished protest. But what good is protest? Against the world as it is? Living in abject poverty, I realize it's not caused by my parents, Heaven, or other people. Thus it must be fate. Only by finding acceptance of unalterable fate can the anguished mind finally come to rest, can the soul start to think of its true home and begin the journey there. Then it first glimpses its original ancestor and true master—Heaven and Dao.

Matching them, we can finally float in a realm beyond boundaries—boundaries that, as Confucius mentions in his dialogue with Yan Hui, are in fact Dao. Merging with Dao, we can reach out to Heaven, rise up into the sky and float along with the clouds. This reveals an important aspect of the relationship between ancestor and master: the master is here as a tool that helps us return to the ancestor. The chapter is a continuous song of praise for Dao, but it offers even higher accolades to Heaven—huge and majestic in contrast to small and puny humans. Yet they can turn around and become one with Heaven, as heavenly men or perfected, using Dao as their primary helper and support.

Chapter Seven

Free and Easy Wandering

After an invigorating journey through the *Zhuangzi*, beginning with the chapter on "In the Human World," we are finally ready to take a look at its inspiring first chapter on "Free and Easy Wandering" (Xiaoyaoyou 逍遙遊). Its untrammeled world of ease and self-realization, free from all fetters and boundaries usually makes the deepest impression on its readers. Its position at the beginning of the book, too, is obviously meaningful, providing an indication of its overall content and giving an intentional glimpse of what is to come. Still, I would like to emphasize that, no matter how important personal self-realization is to Zhuangzi, free and easy wandering is the ultimate end point of a long and difficult process that begins in the human world. This process involves the internal fulfillment of virtue, the external radiance of Dao, the complete oblivion of knowledge, the careful prudence of action—all necessary on the path to free and easy wandering. Only after one has walked this path can one begin to wander or flow—not in water but in air: 90,000 miles high in the sky. Flowing in water still meets with restrictions, is still bound by gravity. What, then, would it be like to flow freely in the open sky?

The figure that flows in water in the *Zhuangzi* is "a fish in the northern darkness; his name is Kun 鯤, and I don't know how many thousand miles he measures." We don't know how exactly this creature floats in the northern darkness but he certainly doesn't swim around at ease like the little fish in the River Hao. Still, he is not content with where he is and starts to change. "He changes and becomes a bird whose name is Peng 鵬. The back of the Peng measures I don't know how many thousand miles." A fish changing into a bird sounds pretty crazy, but this is a parable, a myth where all kinds of things can happen. Plus, it is full of symbolic meaning. The fish rests in the depth; the bird soars up into the heights. Since he has huge wings, moreover, he can fly particularly high. "When he rises up and flies off, his wings are like clouds all over the sky. When the sea begins to move, he sets off for the southern darkness, which is the Lake of Heaven."

Flight, and the ascension it represents, is the key topic of this chapter. It allows us to separate from the world for a while and look down upon it, gaining a completely different perspective of life. The chapter deals both with the human perspective and with the nature of the celestial realm. Seeing human beings from the angle of people and from that of Heaven—what a huge divide! "When the Peng moves, the waters are roiled for 3,000 miles. He beats the whirlwind and rises up 90,000 miles." His flight is vast and high, completely different from that of the little quail who remains tied to the earth. He only lands when he reaches the southern darkness, which Zhuangzi describes as the Lake of Heaven.[10] But while in flight, he looks down upon the world, and what does he see?

To understand what the human condition looks like from a celestial perspective, we must begin by looking at Heaven from the human world. Heaven as the sky is high and far-off; to human eyes, it looks bright blue. But when you rise up into the celestial spheres like the Peng, you discover that it is just amazingly beautiful with no particular color. At the same time you find that human beings are very near-sighted and begin to doubt what seems natural and normal to them. "The sky looks very blue. Is that its real color? Or is it because it is so far away and has no end? When the bird looks down, all he sees is blue, too." The sky looks blue, but that is not its original, real color; it is just what it appears to human eyesight which cannot reach that far.

This doubtful appreciation of human perception arises after having reached celestial heights: on the one hand, it reflects what we see and hear in the heavenly halls; on the other hand, it presents a new perspective of looking down from up high. The human world, seen clearly and originally for the first time, looks bright blue, as if concealed in clouds and mist. How is Heaven different from human thinking and intention, then? It really isn't. In the light of Heaven, the whole world blurs: "There is nothing in the world bigger than the tip of an autumn hair, and Mount

---

[10] The myth is recounted a second time in the chapter. "In the bald and barren north, there is a dark sea, the Lake of Heaven. In it is a fish which is several thousand miles across, and no one knows how long. His name is Kun. There is also a bird there, named Peng, with a back like Mount Tai and wings like clouds filling the sky. He beats the whirlwind, leaps into the air, and rises up 90,000 miles, cutting through the clouds and mist, shouldering the blue sky, and then he turns his eyes south and prepares to journey to the southern darkness." This version is slightly different. Here the northern darkness is the Lake of Heaven, and both Kun and Peng live there, with no notion of "change."

Tai is tiny. No one has lived longer than a dead child, and Pengzu died young" (ch. 2).

The first chapter thus focuses on the contrast between the two different perspectives, of Heaven and Humanity. Its purpose is to encourage people to let go of the human angle, rise up to the heights of Heaven, and look down upon this world. But this process is neither light nor easy. Can people let go of themselves? And if so, how?

This brings us back to the parable of Kun and Peng. Being a parable, it contains a deeper meaning, expressed particularly in the two key words "big" and "change." The Kun is big, huge in fact, nobody knows how many miles. The Peng, too, is gigantic, his wings filling the sky. This description makes a deep impression on the reader, not only because the bird's sheer size is completely unreal, but also because it stretches our imagination, creating an unforgettable image in our minds. Plus, it's not the only big item in the text. There are also the big tree that gives shade to thousands of cattle, Huizi's big gourd for floating around the rivers and lakes (ch. 1), and the big fishhook with a huge line made by Prince Ren (ch. 26)—providing different dimensions to a common theme. So, what exactly does "big" mean in the Kun-and-Peng tale?

Most likely, it has many layers. For one, when speaking of provisions, "big" means sufficient.

> If you go off into the nearby forest, you can take along food for three meals and come back with your stomach as full as ever. If you are traveling to a town a hundred miles away, you must grind your grain the night before. If you are off on a thousand-mile journey, you must start getting provisions together three months in advance.

Since the distance traveled is different, what constitutes sufficient food is also different. Inversely, this also means that the amount of provisions determines just how far you can go, just like the depth of water determines the size of boat it will float. "If water is not piled up deep enough, it won't have the strength to bear up a big boat." Being big like the Kun, both provisions and setting need to be substantial.

Provisions here involve not just sustenance; they stand for a preparation that allows one to achieve a great goal or purpose. What are the Kun's provisions for, then? This leads us to the other main term in the story: "change." The purpose of the trip is change or transformation, from a fish into a bird, with the goal of rising up high into the sky. The Kun in his original form has no way to ascend or rise up, thus he needs to change into a different species. He can do so because he is big, which also means that being small makes change impossible.

Small creatures can only hold on to their own little world, live only in their particular setting. Thus, Zhuangzi describes the cicada and the little quail looking up at the huge Peng. They realize that even with effort they can only get to the top of the nearest tree, "but sometimes we don't make it and just fall down on the ground," crashing into the "weeds and brambles." They cannot believe anyone can go up 90,000 miles. "Where does he think he's going?" The little critters stick to their own little world, among the weeds and brambles—an expression rich in imagery and meaning, aptly describing the mental attitude of small beings. They are totally amazed at the celestial flight of the big Peng, "setting off on the sixth month gale." For them, all this big flying is just a huge waste of effort.

In fact, this attitude is not only typical for little birds toward big ones, but for any small being toward larger entities. And this is not unexpected, since how could the morning mushroom ever know the difference between night and day, or the summer cicada ever experience the transition from fall to winter? In other words, each and every living being has its own unique world that is different from that of all others. Thus, for example, in the state of Chu there is the big mahogany tree that takes 500 years for a spring and another 500 for an autumn; there is another long-lived tree that has been around since high antiquity, for whom 8,000 years are a spring and another 8,000 are an autumn. Their duration is far beyond any ordinary kind of tree. Expanding this to human beings, living long means lasting a hundred years, a medium life span is about eighty, and a reduced life is about sixty years—but for the long-lived Pengzu, who reaches 800, any of those life times is a pittance.

This being so, when Zhuangzi speaks of "equalizing all things" or "Dao pervading all things equally" (ch. 2), this is a way of acknowledging the inherent difference between big and small, the inevitable discrepancy among them. Equalizing things does not just mean going beyond the differences between things; more importantly, it means confirming and acknowledging their inherently unique and different natures. It is very clear, as Zhuangzi shows, that those of a short life expectancy cannot reach high longevity, that ordinary people cannot match Pengzu. Similarly, small knowledge cannot attain great knowledge, the little birds cannot match the big Peng. The question arises: Is what the bird and the long-lived master see from their perspective the ultimate truth?

Certainly not. "Life has a limit, but knowledge has none," Zhuangzi says (ch. 3), meaning that there is no way knowledge can ever really pertain to ultimate truth. The position of the big bird and the long-lived master only serves to illuminate the ignorance and limitations of the small and short-lived. It reveals the narrowness of sitting in a well and looking at the sky, the shallowness of trying to control Heaven and Earth with measuring tools. But even if the big Peng eliminates the ignorance and limitations of the little birds, even if we manage to see the world from the perspective of the "big," wouldn't we still be ignorant and limited—only on a larger scale?

For this reason, in the Kun-and-Peng parable, the key question is not really the degree of knowledge but our overall vision, the way we habituate to certain ways of looking at things. Yes, it has something to do with knowledge, but it goes farther than that. The distinction between big and small matches seeing the world from high or low, from 90,000 miles versus ten feet up—naturally they can't be described in the same breath. Such different vantage points really constitute a huge gap. One perspective has every little detail right before the eyes, seeing clearly: mountains as mountains, rivers as rivers, you as you, me as me. The other blurs things: mountains, rivers, you, me—all dissolve in the great universal transformations, like the dust kicked up by a band of wild horses. None of the individual shapes or types is visible anymore; they are merged in radiance as bright as that of ten suns shining together. There is nothing solid or firm any more: the Kun can change into the Peng, Zhuang Zhou can be a butterfly. In this flowing, ever changing world, what is there to hold on to?

This means that there is no point holding on to outside things; instead one can only hold on to oneself. Because small creatures are small, when they hold on to themselves and their world, they think they harbor absolute truth, become rigid, and refuse to change. But when the Kun changes into the Peng, he in some ways goes beyond himself. "Change" here is a metaphor for forgetting and obliterating the self, for going beyond the body. More than just a mythical tale, the story has a deep significance. Change indicates the loss of "I," of any form of unalterable identity, in favor of never ceasing universal transformation. It indicates the state of "I have lost myself" (ch. 2), of forgetting all outside things and letting go of personal identity. But what then? Without me, there is nothing left, and outside things can no longer create fetters. All gone, what is there to hang on to?

This, then, gives rise to a feeling of clarity and lightness, never experienced before. Losing the self means to eliminate all attraction to the human world, to be free from all fascination with wealth and power, success and fame. From here you can be truly like the big Peng bird and rise up, reaching 90,000 miles into the empyrean. This, of course, is not a physical ascent: it happens in the mind. The mind can rise up high, while the body remains earthbound, turbid and heavy. Human beings are embodied and can never escape the body's limitations. Having no wings, they remain physically unable to lift off and leave their heaviness behind. The mind, on the other hand, is empty and open; even without wings, it can fly.

Here we encounter again the strong distinction Zhuangzi makes between body and mind. Many times he speaks of the mind rising up into the heavenly spheres, while the body has to remain in the human world. This leads us to yet another dimension of the Kun-and-Peng parable. The Kun's life in the northern darkness symbolizes the physical dimension of human existence, while the Peng stands for the freedom of the mind. The Kun is big, no one knows how many miles, but this kind of size also means that it is heavy and lumbering, tied down, unable to take flight. This is just like the obligation we have to our parents, the loyalty we owe our rulers—they tie down our minds and remain forever inescapable. Although Zhuangzi does not describe the Kun in these terms, the north in ancient Chinese cosmology stands for yin, darkness, winter, and cold. Familiar with these implications, Zhuangzi's Kun lives in a dark realm, to which he is tied by inescapable fate—quite different from the fish happily swimming in the River Hao.

But while the Kun is tied down by his fate, he also pursues his release. Thus he wants to change, to turn into the Peng. But how can he ever do that? The only part that really can change is his mind. As Zhuangzi describes him, the Peng is still huge but not at all heavy, allowing him to rise up high in clarity and lightness. These qualities are mental, so that in the flight of the Peng we see the mind rising up into the vast empyrean, to touch down in the southern realm—which, unlike the northern darkness, is a place of light and radiance.

This most certainly is the central point of the chapter: body and mind stand in opposition, demanding the release of one and transcendence of the other. For the individual, the person who consists of both body and mind, this means that he has to make use of one while letting go of the other—not an easy feat! The mind has the inherent tendency to follow the body, like water flows naturally down. More often than not, it is subject to the body's whims and has to obey its demands. Don't most people strive to satisfy physical needs? The body is vain: knowledge, virtue, success, fame, and the like are sensory frills that can never be fully satisfied and constantly beleaguer the mind.

Zhuangzi makes this clear when he compares the little creatures with people in official service: "A man who has wisdom enough to fill one office effectively, good conduct enough to impress one community, virtue enough to please one ruler, or talent enough to be called into service in one state, has the same kind of self-pride as these little creatures." This explains what the self-pride of the quail and cicada means in human terms: seeing others in terms of knowledge and ability, striving to satisfy the vanity of the body, and making the mind its slave, leading it to self-satisfaction. It echoes Laozi: "Favor and disgrace create the same inner tension—gaining them is stressful and losing them is also stressful" (ch. 13). Fulfilling the body's vanity, one gains a sense of satisfaction—how can one ever let that go? Certainly not without getting depressed. In this setting, the mind is mired deeply in the ups and downs of vanity, alternately scheming and despairing, soaring to high elation and falling into deep depression, never at peace.

Is this really the state we have to live in? Most certainly not. As long as the mind is the body's slave, people are like the mythical Kuafu, who is forever thirsty and keeps on running after the sun, only to be destroyed by the sun's powerful rays. Living for vanity is just like that: being dazzled by the vainglory of it all while completely losing one's inner authenticity. The perfected, on the other hand, remain unaffected by outward glory because what really makes a person human has nothing to do with the physical body or social status. We have no control over our bodies; by the same token, they do not define who or what we really are. Whether physical or social, the attributes we are born with and what we achieve in terms of reputation, position, honor, and the like, are all "extraneous," to borrow a term from Mencius. What remains truly authentic to the person is the mind alone. How, then, should we deal with that?

The first step is one of elimination. Mind and body are distinctly different: begin by recognizing this fact. Mind is mind; body is body. As Zhuangzi says, "Song Rongzi drew a clear line between the internal and the external"—doesn't that indicate the separation of mind and body? Clearly it does. Thus, Song favors "lessening desires and weakening emotions" to the point where he can "regard it as no shame to suffer insult" (ch. 33). All praise or reprimand that other people offer are extraneous: they don't affect the mind. Quite clearly, Song has completely eliminated all pursuit or even thoughts of "fame." Eliminating fame means opening the mind to a huge new space, but that's as far as it goes. Song may forget all about fame, but he is still tied to his accomplishments. And what about self? He is still attached to that.

Compared to Song Rongzi, Liezi has gone one step further. Historically Liezi is Zhuangzi's predecessor and the disciple of Guan Yin, known best among Daoist thinkers for his achievements in working with *qi*, his ability to ride the wind. "Liezi could ride the wind and go soaring around with cool and breezy skill, but after fifteen days he came back to earth." Riding off on the wind, moving very fast, is a cheerful, enjoyable feeling. More than just an ability, it is a state of being, a way to go beyond the human world. The wind blows away the world's afflictions and futility, taking all pursuit of fame and success with it. One who can ride the wind is no longer bound by duty and obligation, no longer tied down by the world's afflictions and futility. Favor and disgrace have nothing to do with him, success and failure never enter his thoughts.

But, there are still some other thoughts and concerns. He may be free from worries about favor and disgrace, success and failure, even have "escaped the trouble of walking," but he still needs to pay attention to the wind. Without the wind, where would he be? As Shen Dao says, "the coiling snake floats in the mist, the soaring dragon leaps into the clouds; just like the earthworm, they may well lose their ride" (*Shenzi* 慎子, ch. 1; trl. Thompson 1979). Without wind, Liezi is like the coiling snake or the soaring dragon, who may lose their ride: when free floating stops, he lands back on earth, is covered in dust and grime, hungry and exhausted, quite unable to function. Such a person is like the man at the Handan Academy who forgets all his knowledge—a pitiful sight, indeed! And it's easy to fall into that—as long as one still depends on other people, still is connected to this world, even if one is no longer tied down by fame or accomplishments, merely by the wind.

The limitations of riding the wind reveal another level of physical constraint and immersion in the world. Without a body, there would be no need even for the wind. The mind, then, is the entity that does not depend on anything, able to move about freely, like the wind itself. The key question here is how best to discard the body. After eliminating fame, followed by accomplishments, we now deal with the physical and personal self. Once liberated from that, the mind is empty and spiritual, with nothing to hold on to. Like a boat adrift, it can float along, flow about in free and easy wandering. "If he had only mounted on the inherent perfection of Heaven and Earth, ridden the changes of the six *qi*, and thus wandered through the boundless, then what would he have had to depend on? Therefore I say: the perfect man has no self; the spirit man has no accomplishments; the sage has no fame."

Free and easy wandering has no need of the wind: we do not mount the wind or ride it. What we mount instead is inherent perfection, the central core of Heaven and Earth; what we ride is the creative change of cosmic *qi*. This is a not a vague or mysterious thing, but just indicates following the path of nature, going along with the way the world really is. Nor does "wandering" mean the complete transcendence of the world as it is. The world is always there and cannot be avoided; we are born into it and have to live in it until we die. For this reason, any form of wandering has to occur within this world. Still, you have to maintain a certain distance to it; you cannot get involved in it too deeply or let yourself be submerged in it to the point of losing your body and mind. If you get immersed to the point where you can't tell the difference between yourself and the world, how can you ever find true wandering, real flow?

The two essential terms here are "immerse" and "detach." Immersion is described as having the necessary skills and attitude to serve in the world, while detachment appears in Liezi riding the wind. Yet neither fully reaches Zhuangzi's concept of free and easy wandering. It lies somewhere in between, yet completely different from either. "As if immersed," the text says, meaning almost but not quite involved, apparently uninvolved, in the midst of worldly activity while yet also outside it, like a dragonfly sipping water. "As if detached" similarly means to be apparently removed but not really so, at a certain distance to the world yet also in its midst, like a lotus root breaking while its fibers still hold together. We have to be "as if immersed" because there is no getting-away from the world; we have to be "as if detached" because we must go beyond it.

The combination of the two, on the one hand, shows the intricacy and complexity of our relationship to the world: we can neither avoid nor control it. On the other hand, it forms the foundation of true transcendence. Since we cannot avoid the world, we have to find a place in it; since we cannot control it, we have to find a way to go beyond it. Thus, free and easy wandering is a way of freeing up a new space of living in the midst of an inescapable fate. This space, moreover, isn't a firm physical place or set position—as long as we still need anything, rely on anything at all, we are not free and easy. Rather, it is an open state: flow happens anywhere and under any circumstances.

At the same time, you most certainly need some kind of a place, but it does not have to be a concrete location. The mind, the agent that fulfills and manifests human authenticity, lies at the root of all flow or wandering, while the body cannot flow at all, needing to reside in concrete, physical space, always dependent on objects and the interaction with other bodies. It must cooperate with the world, live in codependency with people and things. The mind has no need for that, being a formless, unembodied entity. Clearly put, it is not a thing and, in its formlessness, can change and transform into anything. The mind can construct a light and free world for itself, completely unobstructed. In this world, then, all things dissolve—not physically but spiritually and mentally, into the formlessness of the mind.

Is this, then, what the text means when it says the mind is "without bounds"? It certainly has no limits, structure, or obstructions and can flow freely in the infinite. There is just you, nothing or no one to match or connect to. This is true non-dependence—a state where there is nothing to depend on, nothing to hold on to, nothing to borrow. Most fundamentally it means being without "opposite." No opposite means there is nobody and nothing to match or oppose. It is just as Laozi says of Dao: it "stands alone" in the world—how could it not be free and easy in complete spontaneous realization?

The simple fact is: there are too many things to deal with in this world. As a child you have to deal with the parents; as a citizen, you have to deal with the government; as a traveler, you have to deal with other people, and so on. How can you ever be without opposite? You obviously cannot expect all those various connections to vanish, but to be free from them, won't you have to let go of them as objects? It looks like an impossible task, yet Zhuangzi proposes a way. Even though these various people and things cannot go away as objects in your life, you can let go of yourself. Once you are dissolved in yourself, there will be no more objects or opposites for you. If I don't have a self, how can the world interact with me? From this perspective, the world is still the world, and yet utterly not the world. As the old saying goes: If the mind is not there, the eyes don't see and the ears don't hear. If I as "I" am not there, how can there be a world?

At this point you begin to perceive a new, wide open, vastly spacious world, a world with nothing in it, where you can flow freely and find spontaneous realization. But as long as you still hold to anything in the world, there is no way you can reach this state. And you hold on to something as long as your mind still retains some connection. This is what Zhuangzi means when he says that "the perfect man has no self." The word "perfect" here indicates a person of highest possible quality. But he has no self and no mind—no world. In other words, he has no involvement with the world whatsoever. In comparison, the spirit man and the sage are not quite as accomplished, since they are still connected to outside factors, such as fame and accomplishments. The division be

To release the self it is essential to eliminate fame and accomplishments from one's thinking. In all respects, the freedom from outer considerations is an expression of selflessness. Anyone who finds that they cannot give up fame and accomplishments will never be able to let go of the self. The greatest height of fame and accomplishments is the imperial throne. The king of Chu offers Zhuangzi a position of prime minister, which he rejects summarily. Even though the office brings wealth and honor, to him it is but a trap. But would Zhuangzi reject the position of emperor just as easily? He certainly would, as is made clear in the story of Yao wishing to cede the empire to Xu You who asks why he should take it on. "Will I be doing it for fame? But fame is only the guest of reality: so would I be doing it so that I can play the part of a guest?" He insists that he only wishes to satisfy his personal needs: "I have no use for the rulership of the empire!"

Zhuangzi thus has no compunction in rejecting world rule, just as Xu You does—he's not even tempted! He wants something else. As he makes clear in his interaction with the king's messenger, he wants to "drag his tail in the mud" (ch. 17), live in nature and not in a cage, like the swamp pheasant (ch. 4). Here he uses the tailorbird and the mole to make his point: both only use little to satisfy their needs. The tailorbird has no concept of exploiting the entire forest: she uses only single branches to build her nest. The mole has no desire to own the whole river: he takes no more than a bellyful of water. Like Xu You, Zhuangzi has no urge to become the owner of an empire but only wants to find a place where he can be at peace, burying himself among the masses. It's such a big world—what use would I have for it?

Nor does Zhuangzi think that the empire is too big for him. After all, he holds a far bigger entity in his mind. He just fears that the empire will tie him up, limit the freedom of his mind. Why would anyone want to take over the empire? In reality, one cannot enjoy the happiness of emperors—so why then? For the fame of it, the reputation among men, but this is merely the guest of reality, a secondary factor. Xu You cannot find any reason why he should take on the empire and while he says that Yao is doing a good-enough job, what really is it to him?

From the Confucian perspective, it is easy to criticize Zhuangzi's lack of responsibility for the world, his failure to "serve the empire as he would serve himself." But Zhuangzi's thought is all about how best to live. After all, don't we have the right to choose how to live? Of course we do. Getting involved with the world creates too many limitations; yet even within these limitations you can find a small private space to soar and flow. There is no need to reject our obligations toward the parents or our responsibilities within society. At the same time, we can certainly reject political power and influence. Unlike life which is fated, they are a choice one makes: to accept or relinquish, to pursue or evade.

Zhuangzi has no objections to people enjoying political power or relishing the happiness it may bring. As he indicates in the story about Yao, the emperor in many respects is a celestial entity, like sun, moon, seasons, or rain: benefiting the earth and receiving the veneration of all things. Doesn't Confucius praise Yao as one who follows "Heaven which alone is big"? Zhuangzi may even agree with this kind of evaluation, using Yao as his example. Maybe he feels that the radiance issuing from political power comes back to reflect on him, and that he can die in the radiance he discovers in himself. This being the case, it is still better to remain distant from the very beginning, to escape to a place that has none of it, a dark place where he can rest his body and be at peace with his fate, enjoying the happiness of personal freedom.

Next, the text tells the story of Mount Miaogushe 邈姑射, a world of a totally different dimension, clear and pure, of ice and jade. The word *miao* in the name means "far away," while "mountain" creates a sense of otherness. The spirit folk there live high up and far off, able to look down upon this world. Maybe they have essentially no interest in us, in which case they wouldn't even bother to look down. Their height is different from the loftiness of the emperor—it indicates their coldness and indifference as opposed to the emperor who is surrounded by a crowded and boisterous world, his radiance dancing into its countless nooks and crannies. The world of the spirit folk, in contrast, is lonely and cold, without any dazzling radiance, but full of the brightness and purity of ice and snow.

Zhuangzi here contrasts spirit folk and ordinary people: with flesh like ice and snow, meek and modest like young girls, they make us realize just how immersed and defiled we are. The human world contains people who have lost a foot, strange creatures and odd fellows who do not fit it—how can they ever be like spirit folk? The latter "don't eat the five grains but suck on the wind and the dew": they have no need, like Zhuangzi, to actively reject social involvement and sit quietly by the riverside (ch. 26). Rather than treading on solid ground, they "climb up on the clouds, ride flying dragons, and wander beyond the four seas." The feeling of lightness and clarity expressed here, from the perspective of people living in a turbid and heavy world, is new and amazing.

The spirit folk will never be bothered by ordinary turbidity; ordinary people will have great difficulty feeling spiritual lightness. To attain clarity and lightness requires rejection and abandonment: of the body, of hopes, of conscious knowledge. An embrace of complete forgetfulness, it is a realm created by the mind. Zhuangzi naturally understands that Mount Miaogushe is not a physical place in the real world but exists only in myth—however, it is also a space in Zhuangzi's mind. He most certainly experiences the solitary serenity of the spirit folk—not because he has completely given up on this world, but because he has separated himself from it and does not interfere with it. He made the active choice of living like the spirit folk: a life that ordinary people have no way of comprehending. As the narrator, Jian Wu 肩吾, says about the parable in the text: "I was listening to Jie Yu talk—big and nothing to back it up, going on and on without turning around. I was completely dumbfounded at his words—spacious like the Milky Way, wild and wide off the mark, never coming near human affairs!"

This really is far beyond ordinary living. But if there is such a world, why shouldn't there also be people who don't eat ordinary food? Is such a life possible? Or is it so far beyond that one can never get there? Of course, one can get there. It is not only possible, but actually constitutes true authenticity, complete perfection.

Here we come to Zhuangzi's most authentic way of life, one that is completely free from physical constraints and goes beyond the body. The body has no way of leaving this world behind; it can only suffer from being immersed in it, be subject to defilement and pollution. But the mind can become light and numinous, clear like ice, untouched by the world. Zhuangzi knows that ordinary people have no way to comprehend this kind of life. Their minds are deeply immersed in the physical reality represented by the five grains; they are so full of it that there is no space left. Anything else their ears do not hear, their eyes do not see—they are as if deaf and blind.

Thus, when they do hear of the spirit folk, they are "completely dumbfounded" and feel that these beings are so extraordinary that they "never even come near human affairs." What is their reaction, then? As Laozi already says, "When high thinkers hear about Dao, they earnestly practice it. When medium scholars hear about it, they accept and then lose it. When those of the lowest class hear of it, they laugh out loud. If they didn't laugh, it would not be Dao" (ch. 41). Little people cannot deal with it, thus they laugh—not only at anyone resembling the spirit folk but even at the very idea of going beyond the world.

The story is obviously a parable, full of strange and improbably ideas, each part carrying its own unique meaning, just like the various characters in the other chapters represent certain aspects of Zhuangzi's thought. The text ascribes the tale to Jie Yu, the madman of Chu, a highly exceptional character who admonishes Confucius in a song, "Leave off, leave off! People who pursue politics today will perish" (*Lunyu* 18.5). The ordinary world being dark and polluted, how can you pursue anything in it?

Zhuangzi would second Jie Yu's admonition. Tao Yuanming, too, says in his famous poem *Guiqulai ci* 歸去來辭 (Come Away Home): "The world and I are mutually opposed. If again I made to leave, what would I be seeking?" He has nothing left to pursue in the world and is only left with personal craziness. People who pursue useful things in the world can never be crazy like this: they live by rules and regulations, find joy in the crowd, and hold on to established virtues and social values. But Jie Yu can be crazy; thus he is called a madman. This kind of craziness is quite different from the faked madness of Qizi—which really is a survival skill, expressed for a specific social purpose. This craziness is a way of life, a particular attitude of mind. Craziness as survival skill is temporary, the expression of the mechanical mind; real craziness is permanent, the manifestation of true authenticity and inner perfection.

Is Zhuangzi crazy like that? A person who is empty and free from the world may appear a coward to others; certainly no hero, he's not an outcast either. Bravery and cowardice are measured by the standard of courage. Zhuangzi values neither, so how can we speak of his courage? Bravery and cowardice are simply not terms that apply to him. Craziness, on the other hand, might fit the bill, since "crazy" means not caring about lots of things such as fame, accomplishments, profit, and position. It means to be indifferent to right and wrong, praise and slander, not even thinking much about oneself. With this kind of attitude, withdrawal does not mean weakness, advance does not indicate valor. Also, since he is crazy, he spouts lots of crazy words. His style of writing is crazy, what he says is also crazy. To get to the root of it, he has a crazy mind, and thus is a crazy guy. Being a crazy guy, he speaks crazy words.

In this craziness, then, Zhuangzi exhibits a clear contrast to ordinary people. In his pursuit of being without a match or opposite, he sets himself up in juxtaposition to the world. Unlike him, the spirit folk have no connection at all with this world. "With their unique virtue, they embrace all things and merge them into one." Current society may urgently need reforms, but "why should they wear themselves out over the affairs of the world?" They remain aloof, beyond all harm. "Although flood waters pile up to the sky, they do not drown. Though a great drought melts metal and stone and scorches the earth and hills, they do not burn."

People like these, with no ties to or agitation about the world, have stable, unmoved minds. Fully self-aware, they contain their feelings and remain untouched by heat and cold, beauty and ugliness. In our rich and variegated world, with its innumerable trees and flowers, full of emotions such as joy and anger, delight and sadness, they have returned to oneness in a state of nonbeing. All things to them are dissolved in an inner radiance that is more intense than the sun and the moon. Seeing all in this radiant brightness, things for them are but floating dust.

On a certain level this is a form of craziness, which "destroys" all things yet still focuses centrally on self-protection. The way Zhuangzi describes the spirit folk connects them to the mind, and thus in our eyes "have to do with humanity, never harming all things." This simple expression seems to reveal the secret of Zhuangzi's mind: starting out rather weak-kneed, his transcendence may be a mere escape, a running-away from harm inflicted by the human world. But in a situation where nothing is there any longer, when you have nothing to pursue in the world at all, how can the world still be your enemy? It can't, most assuredly not. Zhuangzi thinks it possible for the individual to completely forget the world so that, though still physically there, it is as if not there. Yes, it's there, right before your eyes, yet as far removed as the outer reaches of Heaven. This makes you invisible, a shadow person: you can see the world, but the world cannot see you.

To understand this kind of craziness as merely a mode of survival is to underestimate Zhuangzi. As noted earlier, craziness is an expression of the authentic, the perfected mind—also called the mind of the infant—where spirit resides fully in the person. It centers on a different kind of pursuit: the pursuit of spirit, which raises the self to a higher level, to the creation of a purer person, a purer world. A person like this is quite strange in certain respects, as is reflected in the myths of old which tell of spirit people who are half human and half animal, in whom the human and the nonhuman are merged together.

Quite possibly human existence is like that: right in the middle between beast and spirit, body and mind. This split makes it possible to choose what kind life to live: that of the beast or that of spirit, purely physical or purely spiritual, or somewhere in between. Human beings certainly experience animal pleasures, but they also relish spiritual delights—depending entirely on their choice. Zhuangzi's choice is clear, as outlined in his description of the spirit folk. Although still human, they have opted to represent spirit fully in their lives. These mythical people are the clearest and most convenient expression of his vision, and their mountain represents the pure residence of spirit.

To pursue spirit means to live the life of the mind while letting go of the animal aspects of human nature and abandoning the body. If the body was able "to climb up on clouds and ride flying dragons," if we could ride the wind like Liezi, there would be no division between the realms. But they are certainly different. Zhuangzi recognizes that body and mind are not the same, that each can only do certain things. Climbing up on clouds and riding flying dragons are feats only the mind can accomplish, impossible for the body. While the body remains caught in the fires of the human world, the mind can rise into the sky and float with the mists. This reveals another level of meaning of "sit and race around," the body sitting while the mind is off somewhere else. This kind of "racing around" frees the mind from being immersed in the physical realm, connected to material things, lets it separate itself completely, transcend all, and come to rest in peace and freedom.

Each individual has this mind, just as each person has a body. The bodies of people are all vastly different, but their minds are essentially the same. Zhuangzi never actually addresses the issue of the original mind, he doesn't need to. But there certainly is an original mind underlying all, and while it may or may not be the same for everyone, one thing is certain: the ways people use their minds are vastly divergent. How people use their minds determines what kind of person they become and what kind of life they lead. You want to activate your mechanical mind? Just be like the raccoon dog: "It crouches down and hides, watching for something to come along. It leaps and races east and west, not hesitating to go high or low-until it falls into the trap and dies in the net." It lives by its mechanical mind, labors its body—and where does it end?

The world is huge, living things are amazing, people's minds are unfathomable, desires are hard to contain, and there is no way to comprehend the innumerable ways the mechanical mind is used. Ceremonial hats may be popular in Song, but when you take them to Yue to sell, you soon discover that people there shave their heads and tattoo their bodies and have no use for hats. At this point you come to the limits of the mechanical mind. Under Yao, the empire is at peace and the people do good and remain content, but if he went to the spirit folk on Mount Miaogushe, he might feel differently. He might reach a state where, as Zhuangzi puts it, "he was dazed and had forgotten the world." He might find that the empire and his position of emperor were not really a place to rest his body and be at peace with his fate, that fame and accomplishments are highly ephemeral. Isn't whatever I achieve today only a short-term resting place, quickly lost tomorrow? Thus I am always anxious, like a dog that has lost its master, never feeling restful and at peace.

My true place of rest is elsewhere—not anywhere outside but in the mind. Different kinds of mind produce different worlds, different lives, and different experiences. Zhuangzi describes this in terms of the piping of Heaven that blows on things differently, creating many different kinds of sound (ch. 2). Each individual ultimately creates his or her particular meaning of world and life. Meaning is not a preformed entity that can be placed in the world or into anyone's life, nor does it spontaneously manifest before us. Rather, it is gradually created by our mind. Essentially the same, it manifests in various shapes and representing different things in different individual minds.

An example is the anti-chapping salve—some use it to keep their hands safe while dying cloth, others apply it to conquer land and earn a fiefdom. Another is the huge gourd—for Huizi it is useless and should be destroyed, for Zhuangzi it is a fun tub, good for floating around the rivers and lakes. Yet another case is the big tree, too gnarled for measuring and cutting—passing carpenters don't even spare it a glance, Zhuangzi in his mind sees it as a gateway to Not-Even-Anything Village (*wuheyou zhi xiang* 無何有之鄉) and the Field of Broad-and-Boundless (*guangmo zhi ye* 廣漠之野), where one can relax and do nothing, lie down for a free and easy sleep. What kind of freedom and ease we can have with it! We don't have to worry about anything. Like the tree, we remain whole, free from harm and pain because we are useless.

Whether a big tree or a huge gourd, what Zhuangzi really discusses here is the great man, the person with an expansive mind. This expansive mind arises after we have forgotten ourselves and let go of the world. What he calls Not-Even-Anything Village and the Field of Broad-and-Boundless is not a far-off place on the planet, no real or concrete space in the world, but your own inner wilderness, your own personal big tree. As long as your mind is crowded with worldly concerns, full of creatures and things, you cannot reach it and will never be free and easy.

Not-Even-Anything Village is not just any relaxed state of mind, though. It is the state you reach after you have completely forgotten self and world, characterized by no fame, no accomplishments, and no self. In this state, the mind is free from things, free from others, free from self. All is dissolved, and the mind is just one huge, empty chamber. But you must never think of this as absolute nonbeing, because in this huge, empty chamber a bright white light arises—the pure light of life and meaning. Then you may discover how from this originally dissolved world, all things (and yourself) gradually come forth, blurred to begin with, then gradually more distinct, until they are reborn and look quite like they did earlier but on a completely new level. The ten thousand things have passed through the purification of the mind, their original defilements have been washed away, and all that is left is purity and clarity.

This is reminiscent of Chan master Qingyuan Weixin 青原惟信 who said, "Thirty years ago, before doing *chan*, I saw mountains as mountains and rivers as rivers. Later, as I became aware of my own knowledge, I entered a different state and no longer saw mountains as mountains and rivers as rivers. Today, I have reached the point of completion, and I now see mountains as just mountains and rivers as just rivers" (*Wudeng huiyuan* 五燈會元 17). Passing through a stage of completely different perception, he returns to his point of origin but in a much larger space. "Just as" is not the same things as mere "as"—there is an empty space here that goes far beyond the acknowledgment of concrete reality. Mere reality constitutes a blockage of the mind; reality with emptiness signifies a blockage-free mind. Mountains and rivers are mountains and rivers, no matter what, but their impact and meaning for the individual have changed completely. This matches Zhuangzi's position on "use." The world out there is the same, but its impact on the spirit-based mind is not at all like that on the ordinary mind.

The difference is symbolized in the contrast between Zhuangzi and Huizi. The latter receives the seeds for a huge gourd from the king of Wei, plants them, and is now faced with a gigantic tuber. He hopes to put it to use: "I tried using it for a water container, but it was so heavy I couldn't lift it. I split it in half to make dippers, but they were so large and unwieldy that I couldn't dip them into anything." Deciding that the thing was completely useless, he destroys it. Zhuangzi, in contrast, tells him the story about the anti-chapping salve used by cloth dyers in Song.

A traveler hears about it and sees its potential. The dyers sell the recipe to him, and he takes it to the king of Wu who, in the process of fighting Yue, gets his navy to apply it. Winning a decisive victory, he rewards the traveler with a fiefdom. "The salve had the power to prevent chapped hands in either case: but one man used it to get a fief, while the other one never got beyond silk bleaching—because they used it differently." By the same token, Huizi's gourd could be a great tub for "floating around the rivers and lakes," providing pleasure and leisure to its owner.

The episode presents a story within a story, like a dream in a dream. This is classic Zhuangzi. The way he uses his mind is completely unique: not only unlike Huizi's, it differs from that of all people. More specifically, it serves to show just how special and amazing he is. In a certain sense, Zhuangzi himself is the humongous gourd—he has no match anywhere in the ordinary world. In fact, with his lifestyle that eschews all wealth and position, he might well be seen as essentially useless and cast aside. He never matches others' expectations, since he relishes what ordinary people simply cannot comprehend, living in a different world that remains beyond their reach. Small knowledge cannot comprehend big knowledge; small use never reaches big use; the short-lived cannot understand the long-lived—this is the core message of this chapter.

The world is without limit; the mind is immeasurably vast. But as long as you fill yourself up with what is "useful" in front of your eyes, you crowd your mind and will never be able to see beyond a small portion of the world—or even a mere portion of a portion. You will be like the original owners of the anti-chapping salve, the family that for generations used it to keep their hands healthy while dyeing silk. Limited by their desire to hang on to the limited income from their business, they never dreamt that the salve might have a different, more potent use.

What is Zhuangzi saying here? Simply put, what really counts is not the particular object or entity we face, but our attitude, the way we use our mind. The very same tool or technique is put to different uses by different people to noticeably different effects. Zhuangzi himself, of course, has no interest in receiving a fiefdom; he just wants to be his own master. He may well think that each and every individual has their own equivalent of the anti-chapping salve, just waiting to be used in its own unique way. Anything apparently useless can be of exceptional use. Like the big gourd—you cannot make it into a dipper but it can serve as a big tub for floating, offering ease and freedom. What could be better?

A great vessel works fine on water, but what if you are on dry land? For this case, Zhuangzi—in a final episode—offers the parable of the big tree that, according to Huizi, is "too gnarled and too bumpy to apply a measuring line to, its branches too bent and twisty to match up to a compass or square." Carpenters have no use for it, but Zhuangzi sees its potential. "Why don't you plant it in Not-Even-Anything Village or the Field of Broad-and-Boundless, relax and do nothing by its side, or lie down for a free and easy sleep under it?"

Here again Huizi stays within the world of utility, classifying all he encounters according to useful or useless and enjoying only the useful. In his view, the big tree that cannot be straightened is totally useless; it rightfully is not spared a single glance by passing carpenters. Zhuangzi's thinking is much like the big tree—a point he certainly wouldn't deny. The big tree is useless for cutting up into lumber, reflecting a thinking that only looks for the useful. The big tree is useful, however, for relishing its shade, frolicking or napping under its foliage. Its canopy protects people from the sun and the rain—what is useless about that?

The useless always has its own unique use. The more useless it is, moreover, the more it helps to liberate the mind from the body and from human affairs, allowing it to reach Not-Even-Anything Village, a state of being completely vast and empty, where you can be free and nondependent. Then you have no need to run around like the raccoon dog, foraging hungrily with your mechanical mind, planning until you die, trapped and hurt. You are much more like the big yak, so tall he reaches the clouds in the sky, but useless for catching mice. It's not that he couldn't catch them, you know, but that he has no mind to do so. And it is precisely because he has no mind for the petty, little things that he can be as big as he is. Thus Zhuangzi, refusing to be entangled by worldly things, can flow through life at ease.

Being in Not-Even-Anything Village means to be empty and open, light and airy; it is a bright and luminous state, free from all obstruction. But even here we can still feel the burdens and troubles of the world. "Axes will never shorten its life, nothing can ever harm it. If there's no use for it, how can it come to grief or pain?" Thus even in Not-Even-Anything Village, Zhuangzi constantly thinks about the ideal life free from all suffering. It may appear ridiculous—Not-Even-Anything Village being like the mythical dragon king's palace at the bottom of the sea, a magic kingdom woven from dreams. We wake up to discover that this is actually a vast and magnificent world. But unless we learn to flow through it in ease and freedom, this same world becomes cursed and burdensome, causing us to despair of the pursuit of free and easy wandering.

Chapter Eight

Going Along as Emperor or King

"Going Along as Emperor or King" (Yingdiwang 應帝王) is the seventh and last chapter of the Inner Chapters. Judging from its title, it seems that after all his rejection of the world Zhuangzi still retains some interest in rulership. And in fact many commentators have connected this chapter with the issue of being "sage within, king without" (ch. 33), taking it to contain an exposition of how to be the latter. There is certainly some justification for this viewpoint. Since we live in a world that has governments, in a universe where death and taxes are inescapable, we must face the reality of politics and deal with issues of governance. This is different, however, from discussions of specific ways or theories of governing, which are highly limited and never connect to questions of actual living. For Zhuangzi, how to rule is secondary to his discussion of life in general. Rightfully so, since who in human society would ever be able to live without relating to some ruler or the other?

Zhuangzi tends to use rulers as symbols of tyrannical government and, like all of us, hopes that they can be influenced in their thinking to open up a living space for themselves and for the people, so that no one falls into the hardship of being considered "not like us." He speaks of "emperor" and "king," evoking a feeling of antiquity and also implying a certain criticism of rulers in his time. In Warring States theory, rulers were sovereigns, emperors, kings, or warlords (hegemons), but in Warring States practice especially the latter dominated political life. Rulers in Zhuangzi's time were particularly warlords, strong men who forcefully imposed their will on others, not like true emperors or kings at all.

In Zhuangzi, the notion of emperor or king carries a special significance. This cannot be separated from his overall vision of life, unlike Laozi whose thought—as described already in the literary section of the *Hanshu*—can easily be classified as dealing with the "art of rulership" or the "art of emperors and kings." Zhuangzi, in contrast, has no interest in these specific arts. In governing, there is only one emperor or king, but in life, everyone can be his or her own emperor or king. In this sense, the expression "art of emperors and kings" takes on a different dimension, including behavior and techniques of managing our relationships to the world and all things. Each individual needs to learn the right way and art of living—this is what the chapter provides.

Its title has been interpreted variously, most importantly by Guo Xiang: "Going along with the spontaneous transformations in a state of no-mind, one should be an emperor or king." The first part sounds good, but "should" doesn't quite do it. The word *ying* in the chapter title means both "should" and "go along;" it also occurs in the phrase "go along and don't hold on" in the sense of "following along" with things. This can only be accomplished in a state of emptiness, where one does not "contain" anything or hold on to things. The *Guanzi* says, "Emptiness means no holding on" (ch. 36). Without holding on, one can go along with things, never imposing one's ideas or will on others, but approaching them without adding or diminishing, just letting them be as they are. This is the way of calm accordance—the focal point of this chapter. Its key idea is that by simply going along with all, we can each be our own emperor or king. For Zhuangzi, this means that to be an emperor or king, or any kind of ruler in the world, does not involve putting one's imprint on others like a warlord. Rather, it is the exact opposite—going along without even a thought of changing the world, thereby realizing the highest art of living.

Since this "going along" requires an emptiness and calmness of the mind, it begins with knowledge, or rather with not knowing. The chapter accordingly sets out with Nie Que 齧缺 questioning Wang Ni 王倪. "Four times he asked a question, and four times Wang Ni said he didn't know." Nie Que then takes the issue to Master Puyi 浦衣 who refers to two rulers of antiquity, Shun and Yao. Shun "still held on to benevolence and worked to win men over," never leaving the realm of "making others wrong." On the other hand,

> Yao lay down peaceful and easy, and woke up wide-eyed and blank. Sometimes he thought he was a horse; sometimes he thought he was a cow. His understanding was truly trustworthy; his virtue was perfectly true. He never entered [the realm of] 'making others wrong'.

Looking at this closely, we soon realize that the story never actually provides the exact content of the question asked nor does it give any answer, a phenomenon that helps us understand Zhuangzi's use of mind.

What is he trying to tell us here? Maybe he thinks the content of the question is irrelevant: what counts is the attitude we exhibit when faced with a question. What kind of behavior do you exhibit? Are you happy to become someone's teacher? Or would you rather not?

Under ordinary circumstances, "ask" indicates a request for instruction, and the recipient of the question easily falls into the role of teacher. In ancient Chinese thought this is best known from the Confucians who just love to go and lecture people. The *Lunyu* is full of people asking all sorts of questions, but you won't find a single instance where the answer is, "I don't know." In Zhuangzi, on the other hand, the answer is "I don't know" four times in a row. This may indicate a lack of knowledge or the inability to answer, but to me it more pertinently constitutes a refusal to answer, an unwillingness to engage.

It is, in other words, a refusal to take on the position of teacher. Wang Ni is unwilling to serve as anyone's teacher. Maybe he feels that he lacks the proper qualifications, matching the earlier statement that nobody is really qualified to judge anything (ch. 2). Obviously, this assumed lack of qualifications is not due to insufficient knowledge. Rather, reflects a profound skepticism toward the very idea of knowing. Can we truly know anything—things, people, ourselves? In reality, if we truly believe that there is no common ground among living beings, that people can never truly know one another, we cannot but deeply appreciate our individuality and fully accept each other's uniqueness. That makes it very hard to take on the role of teacher.

This refusal to be anyone's teacher is a radical avoidance of imposing our will or thinking on others—the central topic of this chapter. Emperors or kings represent control over the people as their subjects. How exactly does this control manifest? Does it mean forcing one's will on the people, or letting them all be themselves? Zhuangzi bases his thought here closely on Laozi's idea of nonaction, in contrast to the Confucian vision of transformative education, Mohist universal love, Legalist rule by law, and Mencius's benevolent government. Except for Laozi, who lets people be natural, all these involve some degree of forceful imposition, most obvious among the Legalists who favor law, strict rules and regulations imposed by the ruler, as the main norm all people have to obey, whether they like it or not.

The Confucian way is a bit gentler, establishing rules that are based on human nature. As Mencius puts it, "Benevolence, righteousness, propriety, and wisdom are not infused into us from without. We are fundamentally endowed with them" (6A6). Confucians accordingly claim that their rules are not imposed on people, but encourage them to become more self-aware and self-controlling. A softer and gentler mode, Confucian government casts the ruler in the role of teacher and master educator. Unlike the Legalists who govern by force, Confucians rule by virtue, but both equally bend people to their will.

Zhuangzi's central question here is: Why bend people at all? "Bending" means subjecting people to the will of others. This implies that one thinks one has all the right ideas while everyone else is dead wrong in their thinking and acting. Of course, the style of suppression varies; it can be hard or soft, like that of the Legalists and Confucians. But they all share the common premise of "making others wrong." Zhuangzi says that, even though Shun "won men over," he never left the realm of "making others wrong": he never gave up thinking himself right and others wrong. He thus remained focused on how best to get them to accept—happily and voluntarily—his particular thinking. Shun's mind never got to be really empty, but always harbored some sort of benevolence with which he tied people up. And what about Yao? He slept easily, woke up blankly, and went along with the changes in no-mind, flowing through the world with an empty mind.

The Confucians—Confucius, Mencius, Xunzi—all make a strong distinction between humans and animals. Their rationale is that, unless people are educated in the Confucian mode, they easily revert to being mere beasts. Thus Mencius criticizes Mozi and Yang Zhu: "Yang's principle is 'every one for himself,' which leaves no room for the ruler. Mozi's principle is 'love all equally,' which leaves no room for the father. To acknowledge neither ruler nor father is to be in the state of a beast" (3B14). Yao, in contrast, thought that he was a horse or a cow—not in physical reality but as a way of eliminating all ideas of thinking himself particularly wise or beautiful. He "knows his true essence and has inherent trust in Dao" (ch. 6)—an expression echoing Laozi's description of Dao. The worlds "knowledge," "essence," and "trust" indicate that he has realized Dao and from there embodies genuine virtue, which he spreads throughout his environment. Thus all perception of right and wrong dissolves, and he is nowhere near "thinking others wrong."

Entering or leaving the realm of thinking others wrong is a central point for Zhuangzi. Later discussions of his thought often point to his refusal to evaluate things in terms of right and wrong while remaining part of the ordinary world (e.g., ch. 33). The subject of the text here seems to be Zhuangzi himself, but it could just as well be anyone. The path of not evaluating things according to right and wrong starts small, then extends to all life and through all one's years, until one reaches a higher level and opens to free and easy wandering. But what if one is a lord or ruler? Is not evaluating an efficient basis for government? Maybe. Not evaluating according to right and wrong means not giving directions to the world, not making oneself the master of the universe. But I'm afraid that's precisely what rulers tend to do.

In another parable, Zhuangzi describes a figure called Rizhongshi 日中始, whose name literally means "Come from Sun Central," indicating that he is the center of the universe, radiating through all. His advice on governing is: "When the lord establishes principles, who among the people will not follow?" That is to say, the ruler issues rules and standards based on his own will and requires the people to observe and obey them. This forceful procedure of getting people to follow one's rules means to set oneself up as the center of the universe—like the sun. No one else is allowed to have a will of his own: they call it being "educated." First, they try to modify the mind, and if that does not work, they modify the body. Under this impact, even if the mind resists, there is at least the appearance of conformity.

The madman of Chu calls this "bogus virtue" and compares it to efforts of walking on water, drilling through a river, or making a mosquito shoulder a mountain. Bogus virtue implies contempt for virtue, contempt for the very existence of authentic people. In governing the empire, this forceful mode really means setting oneself up in opposition to all people, it is hard if not actually impossible. A sage rules differently. "He makes sure of himself first, and then he acts. He makes absolutely certain that things can do what they are supposed to do," and leaves it at that. All creatures detest captivity: birds fly up high to escape arrows; mice burrow deep to get away from diggers. Respecting this, the sage ruler never thinks of changing people and only occupies his own place. He realizes that nobody takes guidance easily, that people, when confronted with governmental imposition, may go underground, flee to safety, or rise in rebellion—somehow they always find a way to keep themselves safe, they never just sit still and wait for the ax to fall.

In Zhuangzi's view, the ruler is just the ruler—neither a representative of the world nor the teacher of the masses. Rich and variegated as this world is, you don't have a hope of controlling or managing it. Thus Tian Gen 天根 (lit., Root of Heaven), wandering on the sunny side of Yin Mountain, meets Wuming ren 無名人, the Nameless Man, and asks him about governing the world, only to be rudely rebuffed. "What kind of a dreary question is that? I'm just about to set off to flow with creative change. And if I get bored with that, then I'll ride a light and lissome bird beyond the six directions or go off wandering in Not-Even-Anything Village and the Field of Broad-and-Boundless." When Tian Gen repeats his question, the Nameless Man advises him to let go of all and wander in freedom and ease.

Just look at the names of these characters: Come-from-Sun-Central and the Nameless Man! While the former takes delight in the power of managing others, the latter hangs out in Not-Even-Anything Village. He thinks that ruling the world is a most inauspicious undertaking—how much worse if one directly interferes in its functioning? And even the strongest interference comes nowhere close to the simple recipe for success: "Let your mind wander in simplicity, blend your spirit with vastness, go along with things the way they are, and make no room for personal views—then the world will be governed."

In this state, all ego is completely rejected and eliminated, not just in terms of personal profit but as all ego-centered thinking. For the ruler, this means that it is most important not impose one's will on others. This reflects Laozi's statement that "the sage has no fixed mind of his own, he makes the people's minds his" (ch. 49). Laozi and Zhuangzi hold somewhat different positions here—the former sees the overflowing of Dao as pervading the empire and proposes a certain art of rulership, while the latter thinks this impossible. Zhuangzi wants to join relative change and flow along with all, leaving the world behind. He wants to fly like a bird to the end of the world, roam about in complete freedom like the spirit folk of Mount Miaogushe (ch. 1). At this point, what can political power possibly be to him? Yet this does not mean that he leaves the world, which cannot be escaped. It means that he opens a way to find peace within it while maintaining a healthy distance to it.

For ordinary people, someone either has political power or not, and governing is a Heaven-given duty. But what if it's you in the role of emperor or king? Will you react like the hermits Boyi and Shuqi and choose to run off into the wilderness? Or will you sit on the throne and enjoy its pleasures sit in freedom and ease? Or, as Guo Xiang puts it, will you physically be in the halls of government yet mentally withdraw into the wilderness? Zhuangzi asks the same question. To expand Guo Xiang's position into Mencius's contrast of "allow" versus "violate"—which will it be? Different people will obviously make different choices, and really crafty ones will leave all options open. Zhuangzi, as this chapter makes clear, although unwilling and under duress, would acknowledge the ruler's existence and even think like one. As he has Lao Dan say about the enlightened king: "His achievements embrace the world but seem to be not his doing. His transforming influence touches all things but people do not depend on him. There is no promotion or praise—he lets everything find its own enjoyment."

"Achievements embracing the world" and "transforming influence touching all things" as well as the central Confucian concept of "widely expanding to the people in order to save the masses" (*Lunyu* 6.30)—how do attitudes like these relate to the sage king? From the words themselves, there is no difference. But the Confucian sage king is full of glamour, like the North Star he receives the adulation of all the constellations. At the same time, he remains free from all anguish and sorrow. In Zhuangzi's writing, the enlightened king "takes his stand on what cannot be fathomed and wanders in not possessing anything at all." And since he has nothing and is without ego, he can go along with all.

Thus, for the "enlightened" king, there is nothing he cannot do. He does it all, since all creatures do their own thing—and this is how he realizes himself. "Enlightened" here indicates a form of shadowed darkness—a hidden quality because the ruler does not promote any discernment of right and wrong, good and bad among the people. Nor does he pursue any status of high or low, noble or humble for himself. He is as if unknowing, completely different from the enlightened king as commonly envisioned. "He is a man swift as an echo, strong as a beam, with a wonderfully clear understanding of the principles of things, studying Dao without ever letting up—someone like this could compare with an enlightened king, couldn't he?"

The enlightened king is swift-witted and efficient. He distinguishes fact from fiction and never tires of learning. This sounds much like the Confucian ideal, with its emphasis on the three virtues of benevolence, wisdom, and valor. Most important among them, for our discussion here, is wisdom or knowledge. From Confucius to Xunzi, all ancient thinkers demand that people should practice self-effacement and keep in the shadows, be they lowly peasants or the emperor on high. Only in self-effacement can one truly shine forth—Xunzi calls this the radiance of "great clarity." In this state, the distinctions among things are highlighted. But what does that do? For Zhuangzi, the enlightened or sage king achieves things that greatly affect the world yet they don't seem to issue from him. How is this different from the beautiful fur of the tiger or the nimbleness of the monkey? These creatures are being captured for their particular radiant features, so how would the radiance of the enlightened king be any different?

The enlightened king may not in fact be captured and exploited by others, but he will most likely become the prisoner of his particular radiant feature and from there lead others into deep darkness. He thinks that he understands all, but does he really? What the world considers enlightened only pertains to distinctions among things, speaking of affairs and creatures from a particular perspective. It means being like Huizi and going after things without ever turning back, weak in virtue and strong in possessions. What they call enlightenment is just about enough to create a shield. For Zhuangzi, affairs and possessions only exist because of creative change and can only be comprehended through it. In this understanding, any distinction made on the basis of ordinary wisdom soon dissolves and dissipates. All things are essentially one, completely themselves while merged in chaos. This kind of pervasion, rather than discrimination, is the mark of true enlightenment. As Zhuangzi says, "the best thing to use is radiant clarity."

Lao Dan (and through him Zhuangzi) understands perfectly well that the enlightened king as seen by the world still has some unenlightened dimensions, some dark spots. He still actively undertakes lots of things, but the people think they are doing it all themselves and the king just sits there. His rule is hidden and invisible, "deeply concealed as if empty," as the *Shiji* biography puts it (ch. 63). Thus he can "take his stand on what cannot be fathomed"—realizing a potential that is based on his ability to flow freely in nonbeing.

To demonstrate just what this means in more detail, and also to explicate the dark dimensions of ordinary enlightenment, Zhuangzi tells the parable of the Gourd Master who, urged by his disciple Liezi, lets himself be analyzed by Jixian, a spirit shaman who "could tell whether men would live or die, survive of perish, be fortunate or unfortunate, live a long time or die young." Coming repeatedly to the master, he sees a different personality or mind image each time, making predictions that reach from immediate death to great good fortune. Eventually he runs away, spooked by the never-ending change and inconceivable depth of the master's expression.

The technique of the shaman is face analysis or physiognomy, a form of fortune-telling or divination like the oracle bones or the *Yijing*. He never goes beyond the world of form, never sees beyond the outer image. For Zhuangzi, who pursues the ultimate beginning of things and rests in Not-Even-Anything Village, this is obviously small potatoes, not really worth getting one's teeth into. When the shaman analyzes someone's features, he keeps his focus on what can be seen. How can he possibly deal with the invisible, with the never ending change that propels the world? The Gourd Master demonstrates this change, showing him the workings of true virtue, the ways of goodness, the patterns of balanced energy, and the state before emergence. He is never stable but always changing—causing the shaman to take fright and run off.

Ordinary people, amazed at enlightenment, cannot even comprehend the shaman's skill at prediction. Unlike them, Zhuangzi presents him as representative for a world whose thinking is limited by concrete matter, tends to hold on to one side of things, and remains forever locked in by apparently solid entities. For example, the pattern the Gourd Master shows the shaman called "workings of true virtue" has to do with the ongoing rhythms of life and thus also implies death. The phase called "ways of goodness" shows the brightness of nature's path and thus represents life. Focusing on only one of them is a form of ignorance. By centering on stability, one blocks change; by centering on obstructions, blocks pervasion. Focusing only on what can be solidly determined is futile when "whatever you think you know is essentially not fixed" (ch. 2). From this position, how can you possibly appreciate the ever changing and impermanent dimensions of the world?

"Where the swirling waves gather there is an abyss; where the still waters gather there is an abyss; where the running waters gather there is an abyss. The abyss has nine names and I have shown him three." The Gourd Master points to nine mental and energy patterns, possibly increasing in complexity. Three forms are most likely those mentioned earlier: the workings of true virtue (standing water), the ways of goodness (flowing ripples), and the pattern of balanced energy (swirling eddies). Showing even these basic changes, the Gourd Master makes it clear to the shaman that nothing is really stable. And what about the great, overarching change of all? If one were to show how the entire universe incessantly transforms? Could the likes of shaman ever grasp that? To Zhuangzi, they don't stand a chance.

Thus, outside-based knowledge is nothing to cherish. Seeing the world from the perspective of mere knowledge is like looking at the sky from the bottom of a narrow well. This kind of knowledge just shows ignorance. On the other hand, this ignorance can also open the pathway to true knowledge. True knowledge is not the kind of knowledge of things that people acquire without effort. On the contrary, in all respects it develops after one has forgotten all knowledge of things. Thus this chapter begins with the story of the question that remains unanswered four times. This is a clear expression of true knowledge. One who has this is an authentic person or perfected. Ordinary people are transformed through knowledge, transformed through others, since they are mere things among things. Only the perfected can go beyond things, release all ties to them, directly connect to their origin, and from there treat things as things. This kind of person is fit to be an emperor or king in the world. He can rule and control the world without ever being in opposition to it. In this sense, the emperor or king of the world is also its slave.

Extrapolating further from the Gourd Master parable, we can see it as a journey from things through people to Dao. First there is the pattern of Earth, then the great pool of Heaven in balanced energy, and finally there is "not yet emerged from the source." As in the transformation from the Kun fish to the Peng bird, the movement here is from low to high, entering the nine levels of Heaven. The pattern of Earth stands for the world of form and physical shapes: one can clearly see them. The great pool of Heaven represents the world of symbolic images and underlying structures: one can discern them from afar. Balanced energy is the state of emptiness and nonbeing: one can imagine it internally. Not yet emerged from the source is "the not yet beginning of the not yet beginning of things" (ch. 2), the pure Not-Even-Anything Village, the origin of all things. One cannot grasp it through physical shapes or symbolic images, or know it through mind and senses—any knowledge of things is powerless before it. This is the ultimate point of the ascent, the end of worldly knowledge and the beginning of true knowledge.

The knowledge of things and of Dao cannot be mentioned in the same breath. The former is divisive and thinks itself right; the latter is unitive and remains free from right and wrong. When the two meet, they have no way of communicating or interpenetrating—just like the Gourd Master and the shaman don't have a common platform. Zhuangzi's position becomes clear from this. In the parable, the Gourd Master does both—ridicule and diminish the shaman while yet giving guidance and instruction to his disciple Liezi. Just like this, Zhuangzi ridicules and diminishes the world while giving guidance and instruction to his readers.

Similarly, the shaman's running off has two meanings. First, more superficially, it shows Zhuangzi's attitude toward shamanic skills as essentially irrelevant. When discussing Zhuangzi, we must never forget that he lived in a time when shamanism was rampant and all sorts of divination and fortune-telling ruled the day. More vague and fanciful than the practical skills of daily necessity, they were yet concrete in that they all worked with outward shapes and appearances. Zhuangzi presents many kinds of skills in his work, but they are not all equal. As Cook Ding puts it, "What I have is Dao, it goes beyond skill." Dao is not skill—this is what Zhuangzi is really after. Skill goes only as far as the world of things; Dao dissolves all things and affairs, apparent when Cook Ding dissects the ox: "I no longer see the whole ox."

This brings us to the second meaning of the shaman's flight: a retreat from the appearances of things, from dealing with things and affairs merely on the worldly level. All things and appearances change incessantly; your mind and senses cannot possibly keep up with them. The abyss has nine forms, but even after seeing only three, the shaman's world is in tatters. What to do? Leading us beyond concrete things, Zhuangzi shows the path to higher levels, to the source of all, to true knowledge of the inherent nature of this world. In this understanding, all things are dissolved and embraced, their mental constructions erased, their fetters untied.

Going beyond things and affairs—being an emperor or king in the world—does not mean becoming disrespectful toward them. On the contrary, as the chapter title indicates, it means going along with them. Thus, after the affair of the shaman,

> Liezi concluded that he had never really begun to learn anything. He went home and for three years did not go out. He replaced his wife at the stove, fed the pigs as though he were feeding people, and showed no preferences in the things he did. He got rid of the carving and polishing and returned to plainness, letting his body stand alone like a clod. In the midst of entanglement he remained sealed, and in this oneness he ended his life.

In Liezi's life, therefore, the traditional division between husband and wife dissolved, the borders between human and animal, kin and stranger gave way. After all the particularities were gone, he could return to his original state. Unhearing, unseeing, he perceived all phenomena like a piece of stone. "His body like a withered tree, his mind like dead ashes" (ch. 2), he "cast off form, did away with understanding, and became one with great pervasion" (ch. 6). In this state of mind, going along with all is completely natural.

An unknowing mind is empty and free from harboring anything. Anything you still hang on to in your mind will turn into limitations for you. For example, if you have the idea of fame, you will spend your time running after that. If you value affairs, your mind will be occupied with accomplishments. Your life is soon controlled by them. So, if you really want to be an emperor or king in this world, you win over things rather than being defeated by them. For this, you need to be empty on a most fundamental level. Thus Zhuangzi recommends to give up running after fame, harboring plans, undertaking projects, and amassing knowledge. "Be empty, that is all, like the perfect man who uses his mind like a mirror—going after nothing, welcoming nothing, responding but not storing."

All these—fame, plans, projects, knowledge—are fetters that tie you down from within and without. You use plans to pursue fame and knowledge to go after projects—but can you really plan to become famous, really know how best to pursue your projects? The shaman is a planning, knowledgeable person, but what did he do when faced with the constant change in things? For Zhuangzi, fame and projects should both be forgotten, plans and knowledge both be eliminated. Facing the world while never harboring even a trace of the mundane mind: this is emptiness. Like the perfected, using the mind without really using it: this is greatest use. Then the mind is like a mirror that contains all things but does not hold on to them. The mind becomes choiceless—anything can appear in its mirror. As you rest in emptiness and remain free from harboring, things will come to you to go along with you. Then you can truly experience the happiness of fish diving to the bottom of the sea, of birds soaring to the heights of the sky. Free from all obstructions, you can be free and fully yourself, flowing along with the great cosmic changes of creation.

This is "flowing in nonbeing." Nonbeing here does not mean that the world is not. The world is the world, but seeing it as solid and real makes it into an obstruction for the mind. Without such an obstruction, the mind is free as if the world was not there at all. With such an obstruction, even if there's nothing around physically, the world will still be present—the best you can ever do is waddle, never flow. In a world that is not there for you, however, you can enter the state of free and easy wandering. A world not there is a state where both self and things are dissolved: there is no more self, there are no more things. This dissolution is not physical but mental; it happens in our personal experience of light and darkness as one state, when we don't add anything to our just being. This is the experience Zhuangzi is after. It is not complicated—it just requires letting go of the mind. Once the mind is let go, things have no place to roost and cannot leave traces or cause obstructions. At this point, the mind is like a mirror that reflects all things, neither adding nor diminishing.

A mind let-go is by no means dead. On the contrary, it is part of a new way of living—no longer drowning in the ocean of things, no longer being treated as a mere thing by others, but the master of all. Being fully ourselves, we can listen to our personal directions instead of receiving those of others. In fact, there are no specific directions within us other than to return to our initial state of purity and chaos. Without outward impressions, we remain free from expectations and desires. Then the world of things dissolves fully in our mind, and we reach a level of pervasion in change. This is the point of freedom from toil and labor. On this background, and to conclude all seven Inner Chapters, Zhuangzi tells the myth of the emperor of the center, Hundun 混沌 or Chaos, who had no sense openings. Still, he was hospitable and hosted the emperors of the South and North, Shu 倏 (Brief) and Hu 忽 (Sudden). Wishing to repay his kindness, they decide to drill the seven sense openings into him. "Every day they drilled another hole, and on the seventh day Hundun died."

This tale has been interpreted in many different ways through the ages. In terms of mythology, it has been linked with ancient folk heroes, such as a figure called Hundun in the *Zuozhuan* (Wen 18) and a character of a similar name described as "red like cinnabar flames" in the *Shanhai jing* 山海經 (Classic of Mountains and Seas; trl. Mathieu 1983; ch. 2). Be that as it may, our interest lies elsewhere: why is this and no other story at the very end of the chapter on emperors and kings?

Hundun has no sense openings and thus does not perceive or know anything. Zhuangzi sees these openings as gates of knowledge. Just as Laozi demands that we "close the windows, shut the doors" (ch. 52), he says "don't listen with your ears" (ch. 4), "let your eyes and ears communicate with what is inside and put mind and knowledge on the outside" (ch. 4), and "let the six parts of the body be only a dwelling, make mere ornaments of your eyes and ears" (ch. 5). "Dwelling" and "ornaments" are as if not there: without sense openings there is true nonbeing. No senses, no knowledge means no-mind. This means there is no good and evil, self and others—the whole world is merged into one organism. Free from all distinctions, as his name indicates, Hundun is chaos, an entity that flows with all changes in no-mind.

For the emperor or king, this means resting in nonaction and letting all things follow their nature. In nonaction, all things can be at peace in their own unique way. As Laozi says,

I rest in nonaction, and the people transform naturally;
I relish stillness, and the people become correct naturally.
I remain free from affairs, and the people become rich naturally;
I am free from desires, and the people attain simplicity naturally. (ch. 57)

Hundun is just like that, he rests in no-mind and therefore cannot do intentional good. He is just like Heaven and Earth who are "not benevolent and treat the ten thousand things like straw dogs" (*Laozi* 5). Zhuangzi would agree to this, then add that for things with discriminating senses and a conscious mind, Hundun creates a challenge. The two emperors of the North and South are like that, receiving Hundun's generous hospitality, then reciprocate his kindness by drilling openings into him.

The word "drill" in the story startles the reader. It evokes both, a strong and pushy effort as well as the pain Hundun must feel. Hundun is a weird entity, without sense openings—what would he do in the human world? He inspires compassion and helpfulness in people, just like when they encounter a madman. The other emperors see him that way and develop the good intention to make him more like others, more normal. This is much like what Confucius means when he says, "He who wishes to establish his own character, establishes the character of others; he who wishes to have attainment, promotes attainment in others" (*Lunyu* 6.30). This attitude is full of enthusiasm and well-meaning—but can we move away from it, let go of ourselves? Like Hundun, after they drill the seven openings into him, we can only die.

Hundun dies under the best of intentions. He is like the seabird captured by the Duke of Lu who is caged and feasted to death (ch. 18), like people suffering suppression under all the good intentions of the Confucians. In all these cases, "drilling" represents a violent infringement on the personal space and development of the individual. The process inevitably means leading people by imposing outside standards. But the moment anyone changes to become like us or is remade in our image, he or she perishes as a unique individual, leaving behind only a bleak and monochrome world. Once in such a world, you may well become an emperor or king, but will you be truly sovereign? Maybe, in this variegated and ever-changing world you can find the happiness of an emperor or king—but the only way you will ever get there is by fully going along with all beings in who they truly are.

Chapter Nine

The Inner Chapters

Reading this book, a number of questions may have come up—some that the author cannot answer or has no need to answer, but others that relate to the text itself. For example, why did I limit the discussion to the Inner Chapters, excluding all other parts of the *Zhuangzi*? Why did I present them in this particular order and not start with chapter 1? I think it is appropriate to answer them at this point.

Let me begin by clarifying that my goal in this book was to think through the philosophy of Zhuangzi, not of *the Zhuangzi*. I decided to place my main emphasis on the man rather than the book. In ancient China, the relation between a philosopher associated with a certain text and the work itself tends to be highly complex. Scholars generally assume, as Fung Yulan says, that "books from the Warring States associated with the name of a certain thinker are best regarded as coming from his school of thought rather than being written by the person himself. For example, texts like the *Mozi* and the *Zhuangzi* should be considered as works of disciples following Mozi and Zhuangzi rather than something authored individually" (1988, 1:34-35).

This means that *Zhuangzi* does not equal Zhuangzi. On the other hand, the only way to know the thought of Zhuangzi himself is through the text. We therefore must distinguish the two—following guidelines established over the millennia, such as the distinction between the Inner, Outer, and Miscellaneous chapters. We may never know the complete history of how the text and these particular sections came about, but they are helpful to provide some insight into the distinction between Zhuangzi the thinker and the *Zhuangzi* the text.

The Inner Chapters are special, not only because they are placed in the beginning of the text, but also for other reasons. For instance, they each have titles consisting of three words that indicate the overall intention of the chapter, while other chapters carry titles of only two words taken directly from their beginning with no attempt at thematic summary. In addition, each of the Inner Chapters is structured systematically to create a self-contained whole. Most importantly, they all revolve around a single topic: how best to live in the world. This closely matches the thought and life of Zhuangzi himself, as documented both in the *Shiji* and the *Zhuangzi*.

Many commentators and scholars over history have believed that the Inner Chapters were written by Zhuangzi himself, whereas other parts of the text go back to later followers. They have presented arguments in favor of this position, which I follow as well, but for reasons of my own. More specifically, I think that the Hundun fable at the very end of the Inner Chapters has some implied meaning apart from the fact that it reinforces what has appeared earlier. The number of sense openings in the story matches that of the Inner Chapters. Is this mere coincidence or a deliberate arrangement? If the latter, can it be used as evidence to support the idea that Zhuangzi wrote this part himself?

The earliest discussion of Zhuangzi's work appears in chapter 33 of the standard edition, which presents a critique of various schools of thought. Wang Fuzhi considered this the postface of the original edition, matching a preface that now appears as chapter 27. I think of the discussion of Zhuangzi in chapter 33 as an epilogue particular to the Inner Chapters rather than the entire *Zhuangzi*. It begins by asking certain questions that, to me, are at the center of Zhuangzi's thought.

> Blank, vague, formless, transforming, changing, never constant—are we dead or alive? Matched with Heaven and Earth? Moving in spirit radiance? Or confused, uncertain of where are we going? Distracted, with no idea where are we headed? Among all the things around us, there is none worthy to serve as destination.

Next, it confirms that Zhuangzi listened to various views on these issues and pondered them, developing a vision of his own which he expounded in a strange language. "He used goblet words to pour out endless changes, grave words to give a ring of truth, and lodged words to impart greater breadth." In addition, he was unique, connected to the spirit of Heaven and Earth, but never developed a sense of superiority or argued over right and wrong.

The presentation thus begins with a general overview, followed by a description of Zhuangzi's literary style and his attitude to the world. Especially the last part seems directed at the Inner Chapters, presenting points that match the order in which they appear in the text. "He communed with the spirit of Heaven and Earth, never developing arrogance toward the world." This may well allude to chapter 1 and its ideal of mounting the truth of Heaven and Earth and wandering through the boundless in complete freedom and independence. Next it says that "he never argued over right and wrong, but lived within the world and its vulgarity." This connects to chapter 2, which speaks of equalizing right and wrong and discusses the relationship between self and outside things.

It also relates somewhat to chapters 3 and 4 since they focus on the world. "Though his words fully matched reality, they remain inexhaustible." This is reminiscent of the idea of "fully matching virtue" in chapter 5. Chapter 6, next, is represented in the following passage.

> Above he roamed with creative change; below he was friends with those beyond life and death, without beginning and end. Closely connected to the root of all, he was vastly open and unimpeded, deeply profound and free. Never far from the ancestor of all, he may be said to have harmonized and aligned himself with him, following him in all things.

Not only does the passage contain the words "great" and "ancestor," but expressions such as "roam with creative change" and "friends with those beyond life and death" are directly taken from the chapter.

Chapter 7, finally, is reflected in the following. "In responding to change and expounding on things, his principles will never cease to be valid, his approach will never be cast off. Obscure and dark, he cannot be fully understood." The word "respond" here is the same as "go along" in the chapter title, while "obscure and dark" is reminiscent of Hundun. Really, is such close correspondence between this outline and the sequence of the Inner Chapters simply coincidence? Certainly not. The sequence supports the conviction that they go back to Zhuangzi himself.

Also, in the Han dynasty, when this summary that is now in chapter 33 was written, the Inner Chapters most certainly were already in place and had received their particular order and titles—which of course did not stop later writers from expanding the book. This, too, is common: the *Lunyu*, for example, probably only had ten chapters originally. Five were added somewhat later, and another five after that (see Wang 2001). The same holds also true for the *Mengzi*, which originally had only seven chapters, but in the literary section of the *Hanshu* is listed as consisting of eleven.

The *Zhuangzi* must have grown early. Sima Qian, in his Zhuangzi biography, mentions the titles "The Old Fisherman,""Robber Zhi," and "Rifling Trunks," now part of the Outer and Miscellaneous chapters (chs. 31, 29, 10). He also claims that the book consisted of "over 100,000 words" (*Shiji* 63), which would match the *Zhuangzi* in fifty-two chapters as mentioned in the *Hanshu*. Maybe Sima Qian believed that it all went back to a single author named Zhuang Zhou, but Guo Xiang certainly did not, nor did other early commentators, such as Xiang Xiu 向秀 and Cui Zhuan 催譔. They all edited the text to get closer to Zhuangzi's thought—Guo Xiang in particular eliminating nineteen entire chapters so that the standard edition since then has had thirty-three. Guo Xiang describes his editing in a postface to his commentary, found in an edition that survived in the Kōzanji Temple near Kyoto, Japan. It matches what the Tang scholar Lu Deming 陸德明 cites from his work in his *Jingdian shiwen* 經典釋文 (Explanatory Notes to the Classics) (Cui 1996, 299-337). The text runs:

> This humble scholar sees his virtue as lying in the ability to deal with what is easy to understand, but he does not think very highly of his talent to study strange doctrines.
>
> Now, Zhuangzi possessed extensive skill and exceptional abilities, so that his work is really full of daring terms and lofty expressions. Sometimes the immediate meaning of a word is as good in understanding the text as its metaphorical sense is. Thus, an unlearned person like me is unable to clarify his vast ideas.
>
> Instead I randomly revised his parables and metaphors. Especially chapters like "Eyi," "Yixiu," "Weiyan," "Youyi," and "Zixu" are extremely artful and complicated. Texts of this kind make up about thirty percent of the book. Some passages have to be stretched to appear somewhat reasonable; others are so distorted that one can only call them absurd.
>
> There are parts very similar to the *Shanhai jing*; others resemble the scripts of dream-interpreters. Some come from the *Huainanzi*; others again belong in the category of speculation about names and reality.
>
> The text sounds very lofty, with profundity and shallowness side by side. On the other hand, there are vulgar and far-fetched expressions, without any essence or depth whatsoever. In vain one undertakes the effort to understand those, supposing some concealed meaning underlying them.

> All this causes enormous hindrance in commenting and makes one often lose track of the argument. Taking this into consideration, how could one ever succeed in finding Zhuangzi's real intentions?
>
> Thus I content myself with summarizing all and refrain from intensely inquiring into its logic, reducing the text to thirty-three chapters. (Knaul 1982, 54-55)

This documents that Guo Xiang did not believe the entire book *Zhuangzi* to be the work of a single author, thus lending justification for his massive cuts. Later commentators followed a similar route and continued to express doubts about the text. For example, men like Su Shi 蘇軾 (1037-1101) and Wang Fuzhi never stopped questioning the division of the Outer and Miscellaneous chapters, yet also came to some affirmative conclusions, such as the contention that Zhuangzi wrote only the Inner Chapters, while others are by later hands (Cui 1996, 64-65).

It is hard to find people agreeing on these issues in the course of history, and even in *Zhuangzi* interpretation today there are two major tendencies: a focus on the text that integrates all parts and a focus on the thinker that sees a major divide between the Inner and other chapters—plus, as is inevitably the case in situations like this, any combination of the two. Typically people either completely eliminate the Outer and Miscellaneous Chapters from "Zhuangzi" proper or they recognize a more or less close connection. In my view, each understanding has something valuable to contribute to the issue of text versus thinker. Of course, each differs according to the ultimate trajectory of the particular research and interpretation—whether you want to understand the text, the thinker, the school of thought, or whatever else.

The central focus of my work has always been the thinker, but I don't think of him as a single, unchanging entity. Like everybody else, he underwent changes in the course of his life, which manifested in his life-style and his understanding of the world. There are many examples of such changes, showing how people change over time, and this applies to Zhuangzi as much as to any number of philosophers. In our own time, in the 20th century, only few thinkers have maintained the same position throughout their lives, although most have not gone as far as the *Zhuangzi* expression, "change fifty times in fifty years." Examining the sources, we can discern the patterns and causes of these changes.

Still, there is something underlying that does not change, a feature beneath the surface that remains permanent, a pattern that illuminates the transformations. At what period in your life did you write this? Were you just reaching maturity, were you well established, or was it during a time of decline? As Mencius says, "When the will is active, it moves *qi*; when *qi* is active, it moves the will" (2A2). Will and *qi* are not the same, neither are their expressions in life and thought. Don't we often see young, hot-blooded revolutionaries turning into sedate conservatives in their later years? These are people who first radically state that "killing the tyrant Zhou is not regicide" (*Mengzi* 1B15), yet eventually change their tune to the much more sedate "unless the world changes, Dao doesn't change either" (*Hanshu* 56). These two, moreover are not mutually exclusive. In their youth, certain thinkers are revolutionaries—that's a fact. In their later years, some turn conservative—that's a fact, too. Each position matches a certain period in their lives, yet they all return to an underlying steadiness.

If we assume, then, that the Inner Chapters are Zhuangzi's writing, what period of his life would they match? The *Mengzi*, as documented in his *Shiji* biography, goes back to Mencius's later years, when he had numerous disciples. Unfortunately we don't have similar information on Zhuangzi, but there are some hints to follow. For example, he refers to various masters, such as the zither player Zhao Wen, the musician Master Kuang, and the orator Huizi, who were all "close to perfection, masters whose names were transmitted through the ages" (ch. 2).

Huizi was Zhuangzi's compatriot and close friend, probably about his age. Due to enormous stress on body and mind, he died early, as we know from the passage where Zhuangzi passes his grave (ch. 24). The above reference doesn't mention Huizi's death, but it speaks of his name being "transmitted through the ages," in which respect he is similar to the other masters. Both Zhao Wen and Master Kuang are figures from antiquity, but Huizi is ranked right next to them, the passage referring to the transmission of skill and admiration over several generations. This means that, if we accept this passage as authentic, chapter 2 of the *Zhuangzi* cannot have been written by a babe in arms but must go back to an older person, someone like Master Ziqi, who "sat leaning on his armrest, staring up at the sky and sighing."

Without considering the style and content of the Outer and Miscellaneous Chapters, their mere placement indicates that they are later than the Inner Chapters (see Liu 1987; 1994). This makes it hard to argue that they issued from Zhuangzi's own hand. Also, if the Inner Chapters are the product of Zhuangzi in his later years, how could he have written all the others? In years beyond his decline? Not likely. They are full of an entirely different spirit in their criticism and arguments, showing mature philosophical principles and a great concern for governing—overall moving to a tune and rhythm, as well as performance mode, completely different from the Inner Chapters.

The Inner Chapters are like the piping of Heaven, each hollow producing its own unique sound and returning to open emptiness in the end. The later chapters are more like a professional symphony, different people climbing the conductor's dais and creating entirely new structures.

Both in style and content the Inner Chapters are a work of art—from the contrast between the northern darkness and southern sky (ch. 1) to the meeting of the rulers of the South and North (ch. 7). From north to south, from south to north, in the end all return to Hundun, who unlike people does not have the seven sense openings. People want to use human means—whether production or reception, as authors or readers—to open Hundun to their world. To this end, they take their tools and drill holes into him—seven, just like the Inner Chapters. But never forget: these seven are not intrinsically part of Hundun, they are just a means toward opening him up. Since he lacks them originally, they are not part of his authenticity.

In the same way, if the reader takes the Inner Chapters as written, he will hold on to them too tightly and stick too much to their surface. The seven chapters are not separate entities—they form one integrated whole, the unique and unified expression of Zhuangzi heart. They are like Cook Ding's ox: a complete, integrated animal yet neither complete nor integrated. Once you realize this, division and integration, completion and destruction are all one—division is also integration, completion is also destruction. Ultimately things have neither, but are all part of overarching cosmic oneness. As the *Liezi* has it, "Cosmic change occurred and oneness arose. Oneness changed into seven parts; the seven parts evolved into nine. The nine changed in turn and reverted back to oneness" (ch. 1; Graham 1960, 19).

The number seven, moreover, is no accident. Why not have six chapters? Or eight? But seven, like the *Mengzi*? The ancients were very aware of the power of numbers and the order they represent. The year is divided into twelve months—why not eleven? Each month has thirty days, why not twenty? Each has its particular rationale—one that does not come from human beings but goes back to nature, to Heaven. The number seven may well have to do with the seven sense openings. Using our seven sense openings, we can discern what kind of person another is.

Using the seven Inner Chapters, we can figure out what kind of philosophy Zhuangzi presents.

Historically, there are various models of understanding the inherent structure of the Inner Chapters. The first among them appears in the subcommentary by the Tang Daoist Cheng Xuanying. He says,

> The Inner Chapters illuminate principle and origin, the Outer Chapters speak of essential reality and manifestations, and the Miscellaneous Chapters focus on principle and reality. Although the Inner Chapters illuminate principle and origin, they do not overlook reality and manifestations. Although the Outer Chapters speak of reality and manifestations, they are still full of wondrous principle. However, to establish distinct teachings and set up a chapter division, they were divided into various treatises.
>
> Thus, the discussion of "Free and Easy Wandering" stands at the beginning because it presents masters who have attained Dao: radiant in wisdom and efficacious in virtue, they go along with all creation, flowing with things in ease and freedom. They use this ease and freedom to command things. Sages in complete independence of all, they reflect all situations like a bright mirror, in full command of both applied and substantial wisdom. This allows them to equalize all mental projections, which is why "Equalizing Things" comes next in the book.
>
> Connecting to the later chapters, "Horses' Hoofs" (ch. 9) and "Heaven and Earth" (ch. 12), the text after this shows how to unify and merge all things, keeping the mind concentrated and serene and thus preserving life: therefore, "Nourishing Life" appears here. Once good and evil are both forgotten, mental projections and wisdom both wondrous, you can go along with all in ongoing transformation, and move freely about the human world—as discussed in "In the Human World."
>
> With well-rounded virtue within, you can manage life well; with a close connection to living beings without, you can follow them in their ups and downs. In perfect accord both within and without, you can skillfully complete all sorts of things: this is the theme of "The Great Ancestor and master." The perfected and sages of old knew Heaven as much as they knew Humanity; they joined their merit with creative change, rested in serenity and moved in accordance, thus able to work equally well with all there is. Here "Going Along as Emperor or King" has its place.

This makes it very clear that the order of the Inner Chapters is by no means accidental, but represents a systematic structure. Flowing in freedom and ease allows one to equalize all things, which in turn makes it possible to nourish life, live in the world, and so on. This kind of interpretation is obviously not new, and although we can never be sure if there was a similar line of reasoning prior to Cheng, we know that in his time the chapter order was thought intentional. The earliest example of a similar structure is in the *Yijing*, which sets up the sixty-four hexagrams in this and no other order. Why do they begin in Part I with Qian 乾 (Heaven) and Kun 坤 (Earth), followed by Chun 屯 (Difficulty at the Beginning) and Meng 蒙 (Youthful Folly)? Why does Part II start with Xian 咸 (Influence) and Heng 恆 (Duration)? Why does the whole sequence end with Jiji 既濟 (After Completion) and Weiji 未濟 (Before Completion)?

Each reader can try and figure it out for herself, and while you may not fully buy into their version, you can still be inspired and get to thinking. Other classics scholars, too, select particular models of classification and arrangement. Thus there are the "Four Beginnings" in the *Shijing*, the "Prime" system in the *Chunqiu*, and others more. They all impact the interpretation and later vision of these works. For the *Zhuangzi*, Cheng Xuanying has proven such an influential exegist.

Despite this clear order and obvious internal structure of the Inner Chapters, we cannot expect there to be a single, unified interpretation. Interpretation always means multiple viewpoints. Here is the take of the Ming Buddhist exegete Hanshan Deqing:

> As regards Zhuangzi's book, his words have an all-comprehending principle, its subject has an inherent authority, and his language is truly masterful—there is nothing vague or random about it. It divides into an inner and outer section which, according to experts, reflects the divide between sage and king. That is to say, as great Dao fills one's mind, one is a sage within; as one goes steadily along with the world, one is an emperor or king without. This is a teaching of substance and great utility—it is not just empty words!
>
> The seven Inner Chapters have a set order. "Free and Easy Wandering" illuminates the fullness of the sage, as particularly characterized by being big and changing. It is the foundation of the whole book, setting up its central theme.
>
> Next, "Equalizing Things" discusses how people in the old days and today, hoping to understand the origin of Dao, each thought of their own view as right. Thus the interdependent values of right

and wrong came about. First it outlines the views of the Confucians and the Mohists, who have not awakened to Dao but follow their particular leader and think that his teaching must be right. Deeply attached to this belief, they resist all change; losing track of the true master, they stick to their particular views in delusion. However many truly enlightened people there may be in the past and today—none of them can straighten them out! As the world mired in deplorable delusion with no chance at resolution, each individual is totally attached to his or her personal viewpoint.

"Nourishing Life" explains how people in the world have rejected the true master and come to believe that this body of flesh and blood is their authentic self. They each only know their own particular plans and ideas, then pursue fame and accomplishments, profit and wealth to nourish their bodies, moving ever farther away from the true master and never coming even close to awakening. None in the world, whether in the past or today, really know how to nourish themselves. If they ever made nourishing life their first priority, they could easily shed their addiction to material cravings and their lives would no longer be empty. Let them master nourishing life, so they can recover their heavenly perfection, find wholeness in Dao, and attain full sagehood.

"In the Human World" deals with the question of how to survive in society, emphasizing that we have no intentional control over the world and cannot easily move through it. Trying to deal with it intentionally, we tend to hanker after praise and waste our inborn talents, constantly hurting our vitality and injuring our inner nature. Neither Yan Hui nor Zigao accepted their fate, instead pushing forcefully forward without true self-knowledge. They should rather, like the sages, forget themselves and empty their minds to flow through the world and continuously go along with all: this way they can avoid coming to grief. The trick of living like this is to see the nooks and crannies. Flowing through the world without affliction—this is the great utility of the sage!

"Full in Virtue" illuminates how the sage forgets his body and discards wisdom to be whole in both substance and function. Relating to the world in no-mind, he floats along with Dao, thus he exhibits all the signs of being full in virtue.

"The Great Ancestor and Master" presents a culmination of the six chapters so far. It shows how, with Dao complete and virtue whole, one can merge with universal change. Forgetting self, merit,

> and fame, one can become a perfect man, a spirit man, or a sage—truly making the great ancestor of all one's personal master. This gives the chapter its title. The key figure here is the "great sage of complete wholeness," described specifically as having reached the ultimate of the study of internal holiness. Having fully mastered the universal substance, he can go along with the world in all he does: a sage emperor or enlightened king! Described in "Going Along as Emperor or King," this concludes the Inner Chapters. (Hanshan 1956, ch. 6)

The phrase in the beginning of this passage—"His words have an all-comprehending principle, its subject has an authoritative law"—goes back to the *Laozi* (ch. 70) and does not actually cite Zhuangzi. Hanshan also uses quite a few Buddhist terms, including "deluded," "awakened," "attached," and "cravings." He follows the established order of the chapters, indicating that he considers it firm and unalterable. He thus understands "Free and Easy Wandering" as the root of the whole piece and sees it as setting the central tone, while appreciating "Going Along as Emperor or King" as its ultimate resolution in the best way of continuously going along with the world.

Another commentator discussing the seven Inner Chapters is Qu Fu 屈复 of the Qing. In his *Nanhua yao* 南華遙 (Far Out in Southern Efflorescence), he says.

> These seven Inner Chapters are by Zhuangzi's own hand. "Free and Easy Wandering" sets his intention. "Equalizing Things" illustrations his understanding of knowledge. "Nourishing Life" focuses on the power of action. "In the Human World" presents ways of living in society. "Full in Virtue" is about the practice of self-cultivation. "The Great Ancestor and Master" illuminates the ultimate merit of internal sagehood. "Going Along as Emperor or King" focuses on the potential service of rulership.
>
> All seven form one integrated piece, with nothing to add or subtract, reverse or straighten. The greatness of Kun and Peng represents a life free from hardship and suffering; the loss of self and opposite forms the foundation of moving along with the changes. My life has a limit, but the flame of life burns without end; encountering punishments is not as good as avoiding them. Being formless yet with mind complete creates Heaven within; events ordained by Heaven manifest as fate. Questioned four times, the answer is, "I

don't know"—this truly is like Hundun before the drilling. This is what I mean when I say that the seven chapters are one integrated piece, with head and tail well matched and a single strand of meaning throughout.

"Free and Easy Wandering" is about realizing greatness in freedom from hardship and suffering. "Equalizing Things" is about changing along with all. "Nourishing Life" is about firewood being exhausted while the flame burns on. "In the Human World" is about being useless and avoiding punishment. "Full in Virtue" is about realizing one's mind in formlessness. "The Great Ancestor and Master" is about attaining Heaven and knowing fate. "Going Along as Emperor or King" is about governing in nonaction.

Each chapter can thus be summarized in a single sentence, like the dragon guarding his pearl: rivers may roil and oceans churn, but his palace is quiet and stable. The only thing not at peace is the self; thus the perfect man has no self.

"Free and Easy Wandering" encourages us to focus on meaning, let go of the self and transform with all things, thereby to reach the ultimate state of no-self. "Equalizing Things" centers on core principles, so we can understand that life has no limit and in substance has a true master. "Nourishing Life" and "In the Human World" describe the vicissitudes of life, then admonish us to practice mind-fasting and uselessness while following the guidance of the central channel. "Full in Virtue" allows us to pervade the world outside through inner cultivation, floating our minds in harmony and fully fasting the mind. "The Great Ancestor and Master" teaches us to appreciate fate and reach out to Heaven, realizing its fullness in our unique aloneness. "Going Along as Emperor or King" presents ways to rule in nonaction while finding deep peace through sitting in oblivion.

Seen from this angle, the whole text reads like a single paragraph. The perfect man has not self; his inner nature and body are both empty. Losing oneself and transforming with all things is the ultimate in emptiness and public spirit. Following the center line is flowing in emptiness. Mind-fasting is emptiness on the inside; uselessness is emptiness on the outside. Virtue full and pervading all solidity, we are protected internally and do not let outside factors become overbearing. They never disturb our harmony or enter our spirit storehouse: this is exceptional emptiness. Sitting in oblivion

> and nurturing inner peace is how we firmly establish emptiness throughout.
>
> Looking at the text on this basis, we can reduce it even further, so that it becomes a single sentence. How so? Well, it always focuses on pervasion. Among all the different writings in the world, it is the most spacious and strange, constantly changing: none of the others can hold a candle to it. There is only *Southern Florescence*. Therefore, if we read it diligently and carefully play with it, we can see how it really a single chapter, a single paragraph, a single sentence—with pervasion throughout. We see how it can be condensed into a single paragraph, even into a single sentence. With its extreme pervasion, it is the most amazing piece of literature in the world. There can't be anything it does not pervade—trustworthy to the last (Yan 1972, ch. 21).

As this indicates, the author pursues the idea of "pervasion" in the *Zhuangzi*. Pervasion is the opposite of division and classification. To attain it, we must throw all kinds of divisions open to pervasion. The first such division is into chapters, such as the seven Inner Chapters. For Qu Fu, they are really just one single chapter. But not only that, they form essentially a single paragraph, a single sentence: "Float the mind in emptiness." The reader may not get a full grip on all of Zhuangzi's thought from this sentence, but it may well set him up to appreciate his basic notion of pervasion, and in this sense it presents a powerful condensation of his entire writing. What he means by pervasion, moreover, is flowing in and through oneness. As Zhuangzi says, "One single energy pervades the entire universe." Similarly, we can say, "One single sentence pervades all of Zhuangzi."

This understanding means that all seven Inner Chapters are nothing but explanations of this single sentence from different perspectives. Of course, Qu Fu recognizes the traditional division into seven chapters and describes the particular focus of each. Still even here, in their very difference, he presents them as unobstructed and focused on a single principle, a single question.

A critical take on his approach was expressed by Li Yuanchun 李元春 who says, "No previous commentator has ever seen the whole book as a single thread." This does not mean that earlier commentators never thought of seeing the book's coherence, but they never expressed it so radically. He also says, "Not commenting on the Outer Chapters—that's true pervasion!" These words seem ordinary, but they pack quite a punch, almost making one's mind feel moved by compassion or another variation of "being labored." To those who see the entire *Zhuangzi* as an authentic document, this may seem extreme or even nonsensical.

Still, Li Yuanchun here follows Qu Fu in accepting only the Inner Chapters as written by Zhuangzi himself and thus acknowledges their internal coherence. Zhuangzi's Dao can pervade all things: "Whether you point to a little stalk or a great pillar, a leper or the beautiful Xi Shi, things ribald and shady, grotesque and strange: Dao pervades them all in oneness" (ch. 2). But how about our minds as readers? If Dao really pervades all things, does that include those hard to understand? Naturally as we face this particular reading material, if we really develop an attitude of openness, we can pervade it and it opens into one whole, or we can divide it and it splits into parts—this is true pervasion. On the other hand, firm divisions may be described as "pervasion," but they are really not.

This is leading us somewhat astray, so let us return to understanding the relationship among the seven Inner Chapters. Can we somehow get away from their original order that begins with "Free and Easy Wandering" and pursue a fresh way of looking at them? Free and easy wandering is vague and airy, like clouds drifting in the sky, on which we can ride into fantasy land—but this is the end point of the journey, not a place to take a firm grip or find a good foothold. When Qu Fu says, "neither straight nor upended is possible," is that really so? From a position of pervasion, right and left, up and down should be equally fluid.

It should be like the Hall of Light or *Luoshu* 洛書 (Writ of the Luo): the numbers two and eight present the shoulders; four and six are the feet; three and seven are left and right; and five is the center—whichever way you add them, the sum is always fifteen. There is neither a clear starting point nor a definite end. Given this fluidity, why shouldn't we go ahead and find a new way of arranging the chapters to understand Zhuangzi? For example, why not start with "In the Human World" (ch. 4)? Wouldn't that make a lot more sense? Be a lot more practical? This, in turn, reminds us of Cangyun Shanfang zhuren who says:

> Question: Since each of the seven Inner Chapters has a particular topic, is there any discernible order to them?
>
> Answer: The Inner Chapters have a well-defined order. Chapter 1 presents an extension of Laozi 1. It reverses the duality of creation to describe the perfect man, the spirit man, and the sage as models

of attainment. Reflecting the overarching theme of the seven chapters, this occurs in the beginning.

Chapter 7 runs from an account of external cultivation by a person called Yu to a discussion of internal cultivation, and on to the full realization of Dao. This responds to chapter 1, "the perfect man has no self, the spirit man has no accomplishments, the sage has no fame." It thus brings all seven chapters to a conclusion and is accordingly placed last.

Chapters 2 through 5 separately discuss knowledge, behavior, Dao, and virtue. Chapter 4 is in the very center of it all, providing the pivot for the entire discussion. Head and tail connected in a single line of energy, a steady pulse runs through the four limbs, while a steady movement from the heart transforms the entire body. Seen separately, each chapter stands on its own; seen together, they become one. Along a revolving and twisting path, the gifted craftsman charts his course. Unless manifesting ultimate Dao in ultimate writing, how could it be possible? (Yan 1972, ch. 15)

At first glance, the author seems to join Cheng Xuanying in his emphasis on the inherent and unchangeable order of the Inner Chapters. Yet he also suggests a new approach, pinpointing chapter 4 (In the Human World) as the central pivot. This not only refers to its placement in the chapter sequence, but more importantly invokes its particular role as the dynamic center that transforms the entire body and sends blood through all the limbs, connecting top to bottom in a single flow of energy. The image is reminiscent of the pivot of Dao, creating a position of core stillness that allows a limitless response to all that goes on in the world (ch. 2)—like a gifted craftsman charting his course along a revolving and twisting path through endless. Is chapter 4 then the real nub?

I am convinced that it is. Everyone knows that Zhuangzi's goal is free and easy wandering and that he advocates equalizing all things, but why should he do so? No worthwhile philosophy is based on vain speculation, certainly not one with life as its central focus. Such a philosophy must flow from a feeling of life's immediacy, and this can only come from the human world, and not from some imaginary realm like paradise, hell, or pure thought. This immediacy determines your view of the world, the attitude you take, and how you handle your relationships. At this point, the human world becomes the key for understanding Zhuangzi's thought.

How does chapter 4 in its pivotal function effect transformation throughout? Zhuangzi uses the expression "twofold motion" in this context, i.e., walking in two directions. In one direction, moving outward into the world, are chapters 5 through 7 on being full in virtue, connecting to ancestor and master, and going along as emperor or king. In the other, moving inward into the mind and body, there are chapters 3 through 1, on preserving life, equalizing all things, and wandering in ease and freedom. The Master of the Cangyun Studio summarizes four of these chapters (2, 3, 5, 6) with the words "knowledge," "behavior," "Dao," and virtue"—each word representing one chapter, and each word perfectly matching the others.

In other words, chapters 3 through 1 focus on knowledge, while chapters 5 through 7 develop the theme of virtue. We must gradually eliminate discriminating knowledge, thus the chapters increasingly emphasize emptiness to the point of remote detachment: Cook Ding in his butchery sees the living as dead and the solid as empty. We must gradually get stronger in virtue, thus the chapters increasingly emphasize substantiality to the point of perfect dealings with the world: Yan Hui sits in oblivion, beyond things and self.

Yet, dealing with the world and being detached are not radical opposites but come together in a way of life that involves participation without immersion, harmony without complete separation. Not separating from the world does not entail becoming deeply immersed in it; not fully participating in it does not entail being completely separate. This is "flow" or "wandering": neither entering nor leaving, neither not entering nor not leaving. It is the core message of chapters 1 and 7, what binds all the seven chapters together.

If chapter 4 is the pivot of all transformative motion, then chapter 3 presents a world full of danger and futility, a world that requires you to proceed cautiously as you find ways to hide from it or cope with it, but also one where you can tread lightly and with confidence, such as Cook Ding cutting up the ox. Chapter 2, with its butterfly dream, similarly presents a resigned attitude toward people contending over right and wrong, a mode of coexistence with the times that involves the elimination of all distinctions from the mind, not just indulgence in some far-off fantasy. Chapter 1, finally, with its huge bird mounting the whirlwind and rising up into the sky, presents a vision of flight, a release from bonds and limitations. It encourages us to release our emotional attachments to the world and not just enjoy the sensation of looking down on it.

By the same token, chapter 5, with its description of severe physical disabilities, reveals a sense of sorrow and suffering under tyrannical rule, including a complete lack of solace from the external world that goes beyond coming to terms with life by developing inner virtue to the fullest. Chapter 6 contains the plaintive cry of bereavement—"Father? Mother? Heaven? Earth?" Powerless, we have no choice but to follow the will of Heaven, which does not give us a carefree and unrestrained life like that of the fish forgetting each other in the rivers and lakes. Chapter 7, then, in its various stories, provides hints of how people hide from reality. Like fish diving for the depths, they enter deep concealment to avoid punishment, instead of simply abiding in the unfathomable and roaming in nonbeing.

The human world is full of obstructions; like the planet that houses it, it possesses a force of gravity that prevents people from soaring. It appears in children's obligation to their parents, citizens' duty to their sovereigns, and most fundamentally in a fate that people can neither escape nor resist. From the very start, you are controlled externally and entirely helpless before the greater forces. Often you find that things have already been arranged for you ahead of time, neither by your parents or your government nor by the deliberate design of any person or thing, but by fate. You have no control over your birth, your death, or the course of your life, even though you may sometimes feel that things happen because of particular choices and decisions you make.

How can people live this way? They are like slaves, statues, or buffoons, but not like real masters. Of course we can always dream. The *Liezi* mentions a slave who dreams every night that he is his country's ruler. But then what? He wakes up and is still a slave. If we rely on a dream, we need one that never ends but continues day and night, through sleep and waking, until we are no longer aware that we are in fact dreaming. The best dream to have, then, is one of the spirit, guiding it go beyond the ordinary world. In this dream, we see ourselves beginning our ascent out of worldly mire, slowly at first, gradually gathering momentum, accumulating strength, wisdom, and virtue. First we see the clouds close up, then we can touch them. From there we reach a realm beyond physical existence, vast and boundless, where there is no seeing or hearing, no quibbling or quarreling, no suffering or injury, no need to step cautiously and talk in whispers. Here, there is only you. You are the master, and if you wish, you may declare yourself emperor or king.

But have you really become a ruler, or are you still a mere slave? Maybe both, maybe neither. Physically, you are still in the human world, still controlled by fate. In this sense, you are still a slave. But your mind soars up high, even to 90,000 miles like the legendary Peng bird, and you look down from afar upon worldly life. Zhuangzi has both feet firmly planted in the human world. With chapter 4,"In the Human World," as his central pivot, he shows the inevitable struggle of living in it. The advice given by the Master of the Cangyun Studio, to "let the mind roam through emptiness," would be too light and insubstantial for him, presenting only one facet of Zhuangzi, albeit an important one.

Zhuangzi reaches yet farther, to the desire to "live out one's Heaven-given years" right here in the concrete world of form. In almost every chapter, he calls to us from the deepest reaches of life. If we dedicate ourselves completely to equalizing things and wandering in ease and freedom, we see Zhuangzi as more carefree and unrestrained than he actually is. To me, more than this carefree and unrestrained approach to life is the shadow behind: Zhuangzi's seriousness and sense of futility. It is because of them that he pursues being carefree and unrestrained, just as the pursuit of liberation comes from a sense of being tied up. This, then, is the main reason why I place "In the Human World" at the center and use it as my prime point of departure for understanding Zhuangzi.

Appendix One

Key Concepts

Terminological necessity determines that every philosophical system contains a set of essential concepts, categories, and themes. Zhuangzi's thought is no exception. In his case, though, drawing these concepts out and opening them for analysis is a bit like destroying Hundun by drilling sensory holes. For this reason, the book so far has focused on common threads and general patterns. This had the clear advantage of allowing the major themes of Zhuangzi's thought to come to the fore, but it also meant that we had to treat essential notions in a rather superficial manner, unable to present a deeper analysis of concepts and categories. This appendix serves to remedy this shortcoming.

Dao 道

Dao is obviously of essential importance in all of Daoism. The word originally means "way." As the *Shuowen jiezi zhu* says, "Dao is the way one walks on. All passages are called Dao." Already in the Spring and Autumn period (770-479 BCE) it was common to speak of the Dao of Heaven and that of Humanity. As Zhang Dainian points out, the Dao of Heaven involved the regular course of the sun, moon, and stars, while that of Humanity concerned rules to follow in life on earth (1996, 475; 2002, 14). This reflects the earliest dimension of the concept. In actual, concrete application, the Dao of Heaven involved a much wider range of meaning. No matter what, at this point the term "Dao" essentially meant something like "way" or "course."

The meaning of the word first changed with the *Laozi*. He took it to refer to the original source or "mother" of Heaven, Earth, and all things, describing it as being "in chaos yet complete, preceding Heaven and Earth; silent and solitary, it stands alone and never changes" (ch. 25). He also placed it at the root of creation, "producing the One" from which arose the two, the three, and eventually all things, "relying on yin and embracing yang" to create overall harmony (ch. 42).

As the underlying source of the universe, Dao further contains the concepts of existence and latency, described as the "named," i.e., the mother of all things, and the "nameless," i.e., "the origin of Heaven and Earth" (ch. 1). They stand in a relation of mutual productivity, "bringing each other forth" (ch. 2) and reversing into each other as "the fundamental movement of Dao" (ch. 40). In this manner, Dao provides a model for human activity: "Humanity patterns itself on Earth; Earth patterns itself on Heaven, Heaven patterns itself on Dao, and Dao patterns itself on the self-so" (ch. 25).

In the wake of Laozi, the Daoist take on Dao underwent various developments, most importantly in connection to emptiness and nonbeing. Laozi does not speak directly of these concepts, for him Dao is still essentially a way of being, a rule of life or tangible force that can in no way be described as empty or nonexistent. In the Huang-Lao school, however, this changes: here the rule of life is associated with the visible way of Heaven, while Dao is understood more abstractly as empty. Thus the Mawangdui manuscript *Jingfa* says, "Dao has no form; it is dark and obscure. The ten thousand things are born from it." The *Daoyuan* similarly has,

> In the beginning of all-encompassing nonbeing, all was great emptiness. Emptiness was oneness, and all that existed was this unifying oneness. It was blurred and indistinct, without the differentiation of light and darkness. Spirit was subtly contained in it; essence was submerged and not shining forth. Thus there was nothing and the ten thousand things did not yet exist. There was no form, all was enveloped in cosmic namelessness. . . . This state is part of all humans, but none knows its name. Human beings all use it regularly, but none can see its form. If one were to call it something, "emptiness" would be its frame, "nonbeing" would be its element, and "harmony" its application. (4.1.5)

According to this, Dao is empty, formless, and nameless, completely superseding its understanding in Laozi.

Zhuangzi inherits both these visions of Dao and continues its transformation into a cosmic phenomenon of emptiness. At the same time, he has a completely different focus from other early Daoist thinkers and develops the concept in various respects, creating his own unique take. Only a few passages in the Inner Chapters speak directly of Dao. For example, "Dao has essential reality and manifestations but is free of action and form." It cannot be managed or transmitted, but remains dark and obscure (ch. 6). This quite obviously reflects Laozi who says, "Profound it is, dark and obscure; it contains an essence. This essence is utterly perfect; it contains ultimate truth" (ch. 21). "Essence" is the same as "reality" in the old language, thus Zhuangzi's statement closely matches this passage.

The same holds true for his statement that Dao is "free of action," which matches Laozi's concept of nonaction. His notion that it has "no form," moreover, can be linked to Laozi's characterization of Dao as "a great symbol without form" (ch. 41). When Zhuangzi says that "it is its own source, its own root," this is reminiscent of Laozi saying, "Standing alone, it never changes" (ch. 25). "It gave spirituality to spirits and high gods; it gave birth to Heaven and Earth," moreover, matches Laozi's words: "Its appearance precedes the gods" (ch. 4) and, "It preceded Heaven and Earth" (ch 25). In other words, Zhuangzi inherits many of Laozi's formulations about Dao in relation to Heaven and Earth, spirit and human life, but he goes beyond Laozi's key concern for order in the world and focuses dominantly on life as such.

In this most fundamental way, Zhuangzi is completely different from Laozi. Where the latter still sees Dao as an entity, Zhuangzi clearly goes beyond, claiming the purest understanding "of men in ancient times" who were at one with Dao was the belief "that things never existed." At this level of unknowing, a long time before conscious classifications and "right and wrong," Dao was still whole and uninjured (ch. 2). This original stage of "things never existed," moreover, is not the same as Laozi's description of Dao as "a being in chaos yet complete." Rather, it represents a clear development.

At the same time, Dao goes beyond other concepts and can no longer be described in terms of "beginning," "being," or "nonbeing."For Zhuangzi, there is always "a not yet beginning to be a not yet beginning to be a beginning," a being or a nonbeing. All these suddenly arise and continue to change, so that we can never be sure which is really which (ch. 2). In contrast, for Laozi Dao is the ultimate beginning; he uses both "being" and "nonbeing" to describe it. Zhuangzi has obvious reservations about this. If there is a "beginning," mustn't there be a time when this was not yet? Similarly, if there is "nonbeing," mustn't there be a state when this did not exist? Pursuing the question in this manner makes it increasingly difficult to pinpoint Dao. In fact, for Zhuangzi Dao is utterly ineffable. As he says, "Great Dao has no name" (ch. 2).

Dao is ineffable because it is nothing but emptiness and nonbeing. For Laozi, it still has some solid reality, a specific content and a certain determined nature. Huang-Lao thinkers already go beyond that, but

Zhuangzi really pushes the emptiness aspect, so he can say that "Dao gathers in emptiness alone" when speaking about mind-fasting (ch. 4). All things all have form and name, but Dao is without them—pure emptiness, utterly ineffable.

Emptiness opens another aspect of Dao, that of pervasion, openness, or free flow. Zhuangzi calls Dao "great pervasion" (ch. 6) and says, "Whether a little stalk or a great pillar, a leper or the beautiful Xi Shi, things ribald and shady, grotesque and strange: Dao pervades them all in oneness" (ch. 2). This way of presenting Dao shows obvious Huang-Lao influence. While "pervasion" does not occur in the *Laozi*, the *Daoyuan* speaks of "pervading and merging in emptiness."

When Zhuangzi connects pervasion with Dao, he does so in three dimensions. First, it is the state where "Dao was free from boundaries," a state of mind without distinctions limitations, and divisions, utterly open and fluid. Second, it indicates the fact that there are no obstructions between Dao and all things, that "there is no place where Dao is not" and that "things go along with all others without break" (ch. 22). And third, it means that all things form one single, complex, integrated organism: "Heaven and Earth are one attribute; all things are one horse" (ch. 2). The one parable that best expresses this notion of pervasion is Zhuangzi's butterfly dream. All distinctions between man and butterfly are gone; there is complete openness, fluidity, and pervasion. It is called the "transformation of things" (ch. 2).

Underlying this change in terminology is the fact that Zhuangzi's fundamental philosophical questions are not the same as those of other Daoist thinkers. While others always think of Dao as the "way of rulership," in Zhuangzi it is all about human behavior and how best to live in the world. The emptiness and nonbeing of Dao then form the foundation of a certain state of mind, which in turn enables people to "equalize all things" and engage in "free and easy wandering." Zhuangzi's discussion of Dao is less about order than about life. Whether by mind-fasting or through sitting in oblivion, he is after the ultimate unity of mind and Dao which alone leads to pervasion and harmony and the best understanding of life and world.

Virtue 德

Virtue is a concept that is always connected to the mind, a fact that becomes clear by merely looking at the character. The original graph follows the "heart" radical, and when Laozi uses the expression "contain virtue" (ch. 55), he means that it can be harbored within. The person who contains an abundance of virtue is the infant: "Unaware of sexual congress, his member is erect—the height of vital essence. All day long he cries without getting a sore throat—the height of inner harmony" (ch. 55).

Essence and harmony represent a state where virtue is abundant; it matches a state of no-mind, where the conscious mind is calm and at peace. No-mind, moreover, also means nonaction, so that high virtue indicates a situation where one does nothing and yet there is nothing that is not done (ch. 48), while low virtue means effort by intentional action. Laozi also speaks of "mysterious virtue" (ch. 10), "all-embracing virtue" (ch. 21), and the like, saying that its "full expression comes only from Dao" (ch. 21), is thus closely related to it. On another level, and as defined by the *Shuowen jiezi zhu*, the character for "virtue" implies "ascent," which means a way of becoming one with Dao. Based on the close connection of Dao and virtue, then, Laozi defines one through the other: "Dao is esteemed and virtue honored—without anyone giving an order, this is so spontaneously" (ch. 51).

In the Inner Chapters, virtue is also an important concept, particularly in chapter 5, "Full in Virtue." It appears here as a particular way of how people use their mind, closely related to thought and emotion in contrast to the physical body. It is a mental attitude that connects people with Dao, so that Zhuangzi's understanding of virtue can be summarized as "flowing the mind in Dao." He presents stories about amputees and cripples to illustrate the relation of body, mind, and virtue, showing the overarching predominance of the latter. "If virtue is preeminent, the body will be forgotten"(ch. 5): it is the most important, centrally potent factor of human life. "Full in virtue" is thus a state where the mind within never wavers and reaches beyond form.

> Among level things, water at rest is the most perfect, and therefore it can serve as a standard. It guards what is inside and shows no movement outside. Virtue is the establishment of perfect harmony. Though virtue takes no form, things cannot break away from it. (ch. 5)

The metaphor of water represents the unmoved mind as it rests in complete stillness. Since it remain without movement, it cannot expand toward the outside, but is fully at peace within. This echoes the statement, "virtue is destroyed by fame" (ch. 2), placing outside considerations of name and fame in opposition to virtue. By the same token, sounds and sights can agitate people's minds, causing virtue to suffer and be destroyed.

Another term Zhuangzi uses in this context is "natural endowment" or "talent" (*cai*), speaking of the inborn qualities of the sage (ch. 6). He contrasts this with his way of being in the world and thus describes the inherent, natural, predestined abilities we have, our inborn characteristics and abilities (*xing*). These are significantly different from the vagaries of ordinary life, expressed as "life and death, preservation and loss, success and failure, poverty and riches, favor and disgrace, reputation and slander, hunger and thirst, cold and heat" and described as "the ongoing patterns of the world, the workings of fate" (ch. 5).That is to say, all sorts of outer events and developments are the workings of fate, yet even in this complex and variegated world, the mind can maintain inner peace and happiness, a harmony that remains immune to outer impacts. This is being whole in one's natural endowment or in a state of being full in virtue. Throughout, Zhuangzi sees a close connection between virtue and fate: "To understand what you can do nothing about and to be content with it as with fate—this is the perfection of virtue" (ch. 4).

Zhuangzi's sense of virtue is thus quite different from that of the Confucians who define it in terms of specific concrete virtues, such as benevolence and righteousness, propriety and wisdom. Zhuangzi denies this level of virtue. In this he is close to Laozi who sees particular moral attitudes as the opposite of highest virtue and says, "Highest virtue is not virtues, only without them can one possess true virtue" (ch. 38), poking at the Confucians. Zhuangzi occupies a similar position, maintaining the need to forget all concrete, specific virtues (ch. 6) and taking care to avoid living in "crippled virtue" (ch. 4), which is the opposite of being "full in virtue." He thus implies that whatever the Confucians propose is just a distorted, crippled form of the real thing. Only by giving up the latter can one attain Zhuangzi's level of fullness in virtue.

Heaven 天

Heaven is an important and complex term in ancient Chinese thought. Fung Yulan describes it in terms of five major levels: "1. The Heaven-given inner nature of beings, in contrast to their earthly form; 2. Heaven as the divine ruler of the universe, described as celestial sovereign, and his manifestation on earth in the figure of the emperor; 3. Heaven-given fate, the factors of life we can do nothing about, what Mencius calls "what proceeds naturally;" 4. Heaven as nature, indicating the natural flow of things, what Xunzi calls "heavenly process"; and 5. The heavenly principles of existence, the factors that govern life from within, what the "Zhongyong" refers to when it says, "Fate is the mandate of Heaven" (Fung 1988, 43).

Ancient thinkers used "Heaven" in all these different dimensions, but with varying emphasis. Thus, in the *Lunyu*, Heaven is mostly the divine ruler of the universe, while for Laozi it refers mainly to the natural flow of things, representing the spontaneity of life and often used in the combination "Heaven and Earth." Heaven and Earth, the text says, are "eternal and everlasting"(ch. 7). Although "not benevolent" (ch. 5), they "unite to drip sweet dew" (ch. 32).

In the Inner Chapters, the term "Heaven" is of particular complexity, containing a number of different meanings plus one underlying strand. Simply put, Heaven for Zhuangzi is not primarily a divine ruler or cosmic principle, but the inner nature of beings as they are, in close connection to the spontaneous flow of life. Often he juxtaposes Heaven with Earth, indicating that the inner nature of beings is closely connected to the former. "The sky looks very blue—is that its real color?" he asks (ch. 1), questioning the true nature of living beings. Heaven and Humanity are often in opposition, so that knowledge of Heaven does not necessarily mean one also has knowledge of Humanity (ch. 6) and the human can quite easily "destroy the heavenly" (ch. 17). The human, moreover, tends to be "tiny and small" while the heavenly is "massive and vast" (ch. 5), and what is called a gentleman in the human world is a mere small man in the eyes of Heaven (ch. 6).

Instance like these show that Heaven here does not so much represent the natural processes in juxtaposition with Earth, but the basic so-being, the inherent nature of people and things. Zhuangzi also speaks of the "piping of Heaven" (ch. 2), which is not a particular kind of music but the natural sound things make. "It blows on all things in a different way, so that each can be itself—all take what they want for themselves, but who does the sounding?"Any form of human artificiality, then, means the distortion and even destruction of this heavenly naturalness. Much better to "just let things be the way they are and not try to help life along" (ch. 5), thereby not allowing "the human part to destroy the heavenly."

Heaven also represents the ongoing changes and universal transformations that human beings cannot manipulate or control, a factor Zhuangzi on occasion calls "creative change." "Think of Heaven and

Earth as a great furnace, and creative change as a skilled smith" (ch. 6)—this means that creation is nothing but the universal transformations of Heaven and Earth. These transformations are beyond human control and thus part of Heaven, which here refers to the process of life as such. All things and humans ultimately issue from this heavenly dimension: "He who knows what Heaven does and also knows what Humanity does has reached the peak" (ch. 6). Human beings have this within themselves: "Dao gave him a face; Heaven gave him a form" (ch. 5). In this sense Heaven is their ancestor (ch. 33), their ultimate father. "Nothing can ever win against Heaven" (ch. 6): we can go along with and match Heaven but we can never change or alter it. For this reason, Zhuangzi demands that we diminish the human part and return to the heavenly, thereby becoming a perfected, a person who models himself on Heaven, reaching what Xunzi calls the state of "being shadowed by Heaven and unknown to Humanity."

Fate 命

Fate is a crucial issue in all ancient thinkers. Confucius and his school firmly believe in it: "Life and death are fated; wealth and honor rest with Heaven" (*Lunyu* 12.5). Fate and Heaven stand in a subtle, mutual relationship and at times are obviously connected as in the combined phrase "Heaven's fate," better known as the "mandate of Heaven"—a factor both acknowledged and feared by the Confucians. This stands in strong contrast to the Mohists who oppose the idea and firmly deny fate ("Against Fate;" Johnston 2000, 318-49). Mencius speaks of it variously and also links it with Heaven. "That which is done without human doing is from Heaven; that which happens without human cause is fate" (5A6).

In Zhuangzi's thought, fate plays a significant role and the term occurs numerous times. To him, there are "two great mainstays in the world, fate and duty. That a son should love his parents is fate—you cannot erase this from his heart. That a subject should serve his ruler is duty—there is no place he can go and be without a ruler, no place he can escape to between Heaven and Earth" (ch. 4). Fate here represents a factor one can neither comprehend nor escape; people must accept it in their mind. Plus, it is obviously not limited to obedience toward the parents but reaches throughout all areas of life, governing all its changes and vicissitudes (ch. 5). Fate covers areas such as life and death, wealth and honor—things the Confucians like to talk about—but also other things like praise and blame, wisdom and stupidity, and so on. It is always linked to Heaven, indicating a highly meaningful connection. In fact, anytime we try to flesh out the concrete meaning of the workings and boundaries of Heaven, fate crops up—what Fung Yulan describes "as the heavenly principles of existence."

The concept of fate is essential in Zhuangzi's thought, representing the idea that there are things in the world "people can do nothing about," a sphere that sets firm boundaries on human activity. Fate gives people the feeling of futility and powerlessness, leading them to desist from outside pursuits and reflect on their limitations. Zhuangzi's position is that we have to accept and relax into fate, since it can be neither avoided nor changed.

Bodily Form 形

Ever since Laozi, Daoists have understood the world in terms of form as opposed to formlessness. In philosophical terms, these two can be equated with ontology and metaphysics, literally the realms "below" and "above" form (as described first in the *Xici* commentary to the *Yijing*, 1.12), i.e., of concrete entities and Dao. Dao is formless, above all forms, and metaphysical; it is, to speak with Laozi, "a great image without form" (ch. 41). Beings have form, rest below the forms, and are ontological; as Laozi says, "Dao gives them birth, virtue raises them, beings give them form, concrete reality completes them" (ch. 51).

These two realms are not equal. Formlessness is the ancestor, the origin, the mother; form is the child, the result, that which is brought forth. The tradition develops the distinction further, so that Huang-Lao thinkers, in texts like the Mawangdui manuscript *Jingfa*, describe Dao as empty, formless, and nameless, while characterizing beings as constituting the world of form and names (1.1.2). Ancient records, such as the *Lüshi chunqiu* (ch. 99; 17/7) and the *Guanzi* (ch. 36), show that other early Daoist thinkers, notably Liezi and Guanzi, held similar views, making it clear that the fundamental division into form and formlessness was a major common thread in the tradition. No doubt, it is also essential in Zhuangzi.

A classic way of looking at humanity and the world in ancient China is by analogy: seeing the world as a huge human being, and the human being as a miniature cosmos, i.e., in terms of microcosm and macrocosm (e.g., *Lüshi chunqiu*, ch. 62; 13/1). Based on this, the division of form and formlessness also applies to the human being, resulting in the division of body and mind.

Already Laozi makes this distinction: "Empty their minds, fill their bellied; weaken their will, strengthen their bones" (ch. 3). Mind and belly, will and bones are different, even opposing areas. Similarly the *Guanzi* says, "Heaven issues their essence, Earth brings forth their form, both together create the human being" (ch. 49; trl. Roth 1999). This, too, emphasizes the distinction and links it to Heaven and Earth. It also notes, "The mind resides in the organism like a ruler. The nine openings each have their particular task just like officials in state administration" (ch. 36). This divides the person into mind and sensory openings, again revealing a body-mind split.

In the *Zhuangzi*, the division appears variously: "Blindness and deafness are not confined to the body alone—knowledge has them too" (ch. 1), he says and asks, "Can you really make the body like a withered tree and the mind like dead ashes?" (ch. 2). In addition, the mind may be free during sleep while the body works hard in waking hours (ch. 2), but often enough it follows the body: "His body decays, his mind follows it—can you deny that this is a great sorrow?" (ch. 2). When the mind or spirit is gone, moreover, identity dissolves, even if the physical form is still present: "In loving their mother, the piglets loved not her body but the thing that moved her body" (ch. 5). Mind supersedes the physical: "If virtue is preeminent, the body will be forgotten" (ch. 5); "though something may startle his body, it won't injure his mind." (ch. 6)

These citations make it clear that Zhuangzi places a heavier emphasis on the mind (spirit, virtue) than the body. This means that, although form and formlessness are linked in one organism within the human being, they yet have their clear boundaries. In the world, formless Dao is like the ancestral master, which for human life means that it is more fundamental, just as the mind is in relation to the body.

Mind 心

The human mind as a central feature of philosophy is a hallmark of pre-Qin thought, most obviously so in Mencius and Zhuangzi. Both see the mind as the most fundamental aspect of the human being, but disagree on exactly how to understand it.

For Mencius, the mind has specific content, notably the Four Beginnings, the roots of benevolence and righteousness, propriety and wisdom. He thus speaks of "reaching to the depth of the mind" in order to understand one's personal character and the nature of Heaven (7A1): it is the ultimate root of morality and social order.

For Zhuangzi, in contrast, the mind is empty, free from anything at all: it is the foundation of transcendence, of going beyond the world of form, and of becoming one with Dao. He contrasts it with the physical body, which has form where the mind has none. Formless, it represents the inner authenticity of the individual and serves as the true lord and master of the body. The mind "has identity but no form"(ch. 2); it is the true lord, the authentic master of life, which means it should rule and guide the body, and not vice versa. For Zhuangzi, ordinary people tend to let their minds be run by their physical needs: "When their bodies change, so do their minds" marks a truly deplorable state. He calls this being of "fixed mind," set in ways of "right and wrong," likes and dislikes, pulled about by outside things, and never at peace. This kind of mind needs to be eliminated and replaced by the "constant mind."

How do we do that? "The way to go about it is to use knowledge to get at the mind, then use the mind to reach the constant mind" (ch. 5). Really, "use" here should be read "cease"—first knowledge, then the fixed mind need to be stopped for the constant mind to emerge. The reason is that knowledge focuses on things outside and any mind determined by it will forever change along with whatever goes on there. The constant mind, on the other hand, is unchanging and unmoved, independent of outside things.

To realize this, moreover, Zhuangzi provides specific methods, notably mind-fasting and sitting in oblivion. Mind-fasting works by unifying the will and letting go of the senses. Instead of listening with the ears, we learn to listen with the mind, then move on to listen with pure *qi* in open emptiness, where alone Dao assembles (ch. 4). Similarly, sitting in oblivion means the obliteration of personal perception, doing away with all concepts of self and other, body and mind, life and death, and opening to the great pervasion of Dao. This only occurs after benevolence and righteousness, propriety and wisdom have been obliterated completely; it signals a state where the mind is everywhere, completely empty, open, and still, without any movement whatsoever.

Zhuangzi often also uses the expression "body like a withered tree, mind like dead ashes" (ch. 2) to indicate this state, meaning that the mind is utterly still yet very much alive, like "an empty chamber that gives rise to brightness" (ch. 4). Completely free from all outside things and the world of form, it can reach Not-Even-Anything Village and become one with Dao.

The originally empty and nonsolid nature of the mind allows it—even requires it—to discard all limitations of embodied beings. But this discarding presupposes that one acknowledges the limited nature of the body and its close connection to fate. In this acknowledgment, the mind partially goes beyond the body's grasp and frees itself from the hold of its limitations. The body alone cannot limit the mind; it cannot tie it down. Seen from another angle, once the mind is no longer subject to the body's hold, it can go beyond it to the point where it "treats things as things but is no longer treated as a mere thing" (ch. 11).

With an empty, pervasive mind we can go beyond the limitations of the body—both ourselves as embodied beings and the entire world of form, "coming and going with the essence and spirit of Heaven and Earth" (ch. 33). The body then becomes a mere "residence" of the mind or spirit, so that one "governs Heaven and Earth, stores up the ten thousand things, lets the six parts of his body be only a dwelling, makes ornaments of his ears and eyes" (ch. 5).

Equalizing 齊

Equalizing is not just a Zhuangzi concept, but also plays a role in the thought of Peng Meng, Tian Pian, and Shen Dao. The underlying rationale is that all beings have their particularly uniqueness: "Heaven is capable of sheltering but not of bearing up; Earth is capable of bearing up but not of sheltering. Great Dao is capable of embracing all things but not of discriminating among them" (ch. 33). Because of this, there is no point making distinctions and engaging in comparisons; it is much better to equalize all.

In Zhuangzi specifically, equalizing does not mean that one sees all beings as the same, but is a way of interacting with them on a nondiscriminatory basis. As Mencius says, "Where beings are not equal is their identity" (3A4). It is quite obvious that people and things are all unique—they each have their particular shape, name, attitude, and behavior. But Zhuangzi wants to do away with our perception of this distinction and see and treat them all as equally valid and acceptable. Inheriting the emphasis on their unique natures from Peng Meng, Tian Pian, and Shen Dao, he contends that there is no point in having any sort of dispute on their relative value or position.

For example, he notes that to human beings certain people are beautiful but fish or birds get scared by them (ch. 2). In other words, there is no universal standard of beauty among different species—or even within the same species—nor is there any firm knowledge of "what all beings have in common." Each individual creature sees the world from the particular position it occupies at any given moment. Each has its own unique angle and sees itself as "this" and anything or anyone else as "that." From there, they engage in disputes about universal right and wrong. What a waste of time! Zhuangzi knows that such disputes can never deliver a true perspective of the world. Instead, we have to go back to the source that underlies all to find proper understanding and evenly balanced perception. This allows us to discover that the entire universe is pervaded by the same unifying flow, is ultimately one and not divided.

Value judgments are accordingly turned on their head, and what is usually seen as tiny can appear huge (like the tip of an autumn hair); what is usually seen as gigantic is now tiny (like Mount Tai). All is part of everything else, with no measurements, no judgments: "Heaven and Earth were born at the same time I was, and the ten thousand things are one with me" (ch. 1). All things are still the same: the real difference between them remains undissolved. Our view point is what changes. Limited by living among creatures, we are physically one of them and thus cannot make them equal. In order to equalize all, we must first do away with our perception of ourselves as defined by the world. We must allow the mind to roam in the beginning of all and begin to flow with Dao. Therefore, all equalizing starts with "I have lost myself," as described in the beginning of chapter 2. It means that I have eliminated the discriminating mind that grasps and holds on to things; from there I can go beyond and reach to formlessness.

There is a big difference between looking at beings from the perspective of a concrete, living entity and from that of Dao. In the former, we see distinctions, such as noble and humble; in the latter, we are free from differentiation and can equalize all. Firmly rooted in Dao, we can see all beings as who and what they are originally, realizing that there is no fundamental difference between them, that they are all equally pervaded by Dao, all equally form one organism within the flux of universal change. This, then leads to the appreciation of the "transformation of things," the central point of the butterfly dream (ch. 2).

It is important to understand that equalizing is not primarily a matter of knowledge but one of behavior, a way of treating others. Zhuangzi proposes that we go along with the world and keep our minds unmoved—there is no meaning in making distinctions among beings. Only in this way can is equalization possible. It does not really change what things are but completely alters our way of looking at them.

Free and Easy 逍遙

The expression "free and easy" first appears in the *Shijing*, where it stands for a relaxed and light-hearted way of being. In the Inner Chapters, it occurs only twice, including the heading of chapter 1, which shows just how essential it is in Zhuangzi's thought. "Free and easy" means relaxing "in Not-Even-Anything Village and the Field of Broad-and-Boundless," drifting around in nonaction, resting under a tree, floating about the rivers and lakes (ch. 1). It is a way of being in the world, an attitude toward life that connects to nonaction, relaxation, and flow with a feeling of freedom from hardship and suffering. It happens best in Not-Even-Anything Village, a realm beyond the world of form, far removed from earthly limitations. Here one can wander or flow, free from obstructions, released from worldly ties.

Being free and easy means to let go of all dependence. Zhuangzi tells of "Liezi who could ride the wind and go soaring around with cool and breezy skill . . . but still had to depend on something to get around" (ch. 1). Just like he still needs the wind to find his ease, so anyone who still has to rely on anything for peace and happiness is not fully open and cannot be truly free and easy. Better to ride the "truth of Heaven and Earth" and go along with "the changes of the six cosmic energies," reaching a state of non-dependence. These cosmic powers are not the same as the wind used by Liezi. Wind has its own rhythm: it may blow hard or stop completely. But cosmic forces are like Dao, infinite, formless, and permanent. Using them to get around means not to depend on anything; it is a true attainment of non-dependence. We can be free from all dependence and wander in the infinite because our self no longer holds on to anything and we have become free from it. No-self is thus the precondition for true non-dependence, the basis for being free and easy: "The perfect man has no self."

"Free and easy" has been read variously by later commentators. Guo Xiang says,

> Although big and small are different, when they relax into spontaneous self-realization, follow their own unique nature, fulfill their unique abilities, and each stay within their allotments, they all are equally free and easy—how can there be the distinction of better or worse among them? (ch. 1).

Cheng Xuanying outlines different views current in his time:

> What we call "free and easy" has been interpreted differently over the years. Today there are mainly three readings.
>
> First, Gu Huan 顧歡: Free means "dissolve;" easy means "far-off." Dissolving all means to loosen all ties to the world; being far-off means to see nonbeing as the underlying principle of all. On this basis one can flow or wander, thus the text speaks of "free and easy."
>
> Second, Zhi Daolin 支道林: Treating beings as beings but not being treated as a mere being means freedom and non-dependence. Being stimulated but not react with urgency or haste means ease and having nothing to do. On this basis, one can wander through the world, thus the text speaks of "free and easy wandering."
>
> Third, Mu Ye 穆夜: Free and easy is an expression for letting go of all and finding spontaneous self-realization. Virtue is complete and full within, and one goes along with all at all times. One forgets all concerns and moves with beings—what would not be open? Moving like this through the world, that is "free and easy wandering." (Guo 1982, 1:6-7)

This shows that being free and easy is a very important concept in the history of the *Zhuangzi* that evoked much interest among its commentators. Despite the wide divergence in readings, though, it always points to a way of being in spontaneous self-realization.

No Feelings 無情

Feelings usually mean things like joy and anger, happiness and sorrow, love and hate. All people have these, which is why Xunzi speaks of them as "Heaven-given." The Confucians take them very seriously, seeing them as emerging from inner nature, on the one hand, and as the foundation of social order, on the other. This is expressed in statements like "Feelings arise from inner nature" and "Dao begins with feelings," as found in the Guodian 郭店 manuscript *Xing zi ming chu* 性自命出 (Inner Nature Arises from Fate; see Perkins 2010; Tang 2003). As a result, Confucians tend to control or regulate feelings, notably with the help of rites and music.

Zhuangzi, in contrast, speaks of having no feelings, asserting that it is possible to have "the form of a human being but not his feelings." This means that "we don't allow likes and dislikes to enter and burden who we are, but always go along with our inherent naturalness. We never even try to improve on life and never allow likes or dislikes to get in and do us harm. We just let things be the way they are and don't try to help life along" (ch. 5).

As this makes clear, what Zhuangzi means by having "no feelings" does not mean being completely without love, hate, and so on, but rather not allowing these emotions to do us harm. In this sense, he speaks about using our proper understanding of the structure of the universe to transform our feelings so they no longer have an impact. No feelings here is thus a particular way of using the mind: "Don't use the mind to diminish Dao; don't use the humanly to assist Heaven" (ch. 6).

Using the proper understanding of the universe to transform feelings means that we no longer hold on to them. Holding on to feelings, in Zhuangzi, is "hiding from Heaven and turning one's back on the essential." This expression occurs in the story on Lao Dan's funeral, where Qin Shi gives three cries and leaves, expressing obvious contempt for the Confucian system of rites and music, then revises his appreciation of the great thinker since people there were mourning him like a close relative. "He made them weep for him, though he didn't ask them to weep," behaving in a way that made him turn his back on the essential (ch. 3). The word "essential" is the same as that for "feelings," but used in a different sense—more like in the expression "no feelings." Holding on to feelings goes against the essential reality of the world; it means moving against Heaven. Thus Zhuangzi speaks of the "crime of hiding from Heaven." Having "no feelings" is a way to be liberated from this state.

Uselessness 無用

Uselessness is a key concept in Zhuangzi. While ordinary people tend to pursue being useful, Zhuangzi prefers to guide them to the useless. He says,

> The mountain trees do themselves harm; the grease in the torch burns itself up. The bark of the cinnamon tree can be eaten, so it gets cut down; the sap of the lacquer tree can be used, so it gets hacked apart. All men know the use of the useful, but nobody knows the use of the useless!" (ch. 4)

He prefers the useless because there is use in it: the usefulness of the useless lies in the ability to avoid harm. All kinds of things and beings in nature have aspects that can be of use to others, as a result of which they get hurt, killed, or cut down. People, too, when they are useful in society, often run into danger to life and limb. In contrast, the tree without any obvious use can grow big and live long; people who are of no use to others can live free from harm—the most obvious examples being cripples and amputees (ch. 4). By the same token, the huge gourd Huizi receives from the King of Wei is useless for making into ordinary utensils, but can serve as a great tub "to go floating around the rivers and lakes;" the anti-chapping salve use by silk dyers to keep their hands safe can serve as a means to win naval battles and may earn its owner a fiefdom; the big tree that is too gnarled and twisted to be made into lumber can give shade for rest and relaxation (ch. 1). All these examples show that "use" is relative, depending on perspective; it is directly related to the divergent way in which people use their minds. Being useless is thus just another way of looking at what is commonly perceived as useful.

For Zhuangzi, uselessness is a particular attitude toward life, including a way of hiding one's true abilities in order to keep oneself safe and avoid misfortune. He says, "Act by not using [anything] and instead rest in the ordinary. The ordinary is a form of use; use leads to pervasion, which means realization" (ch. 2). "Not using" means having the ability to use things but eschew doing so; people who may be useful should give themselves an added sheen of plainness: "rest in the ordinary." "Rest" here refers to a choice one makes, a way of pursuing the useless, of manifesting use in the useless and thereby preserve life.

Uselessness as an attitude toward life is Zhuangzi's reaction to the inherent tension between self and world—it involves both opposition and cooperation. He presents a number of crippled and mutilated figures to show how uselessness can play out in life. Intentional uselessness, moreover, is a form of self-mutilation, a way of hiding one's true talents and abilities in order to keep oneself safe. At the same time, it also means leaving the ordinary world while enhancing one's inner freedom and ease.

In the wider context of Daoist thought, use and uselessness stand in a mutually productive relationship. Laozi presents the examples of the hub and spokes that make a wheel, the walls that make a room, the clay that makes a vessel—in all cases it is the empty, open space that creates utility (ch. 11). What is not there is just as important as what is there—the useful and the useless depend on each other. This thinking of Laozi's quite obviously is at the root of Zhuangzi's concept of the usefulness of the useless.

Forgetting 忘

The word "forget" occurs quite often in the Inner Chapters to the point where it can be regarded as a key concept in the text. "Forgetting" has two aspects.

First, it concerns the elimination of all intentional efforts at cultivation. For example, "if virtue is preeminent, the body will be forgotten" (ch. 5), which means that one should forget physical reality but not inherent virtue. "But when people do not forget what can be forgotten, but forget what cannot be forgotten—that may be called true forgetting" (ch. 5). True forgetting here is not the same as ordinary forgetting, rather it is eliminating what one should not forget and remembering what one should not retain. The most prominent passage in the text speaks of "sitting in oblivion," beginning with forgetting benevolence and righteousness, followed by giving up on rites and music. This makes it clear that the text is concerned with forgetting any personal cultivation efforts.

Forgetting here also means to put things outside: the world, all things, and life as such (ch. 6), eliminating them completely from the mind. The main reason for doing so is to liberate oneself from the their impact and control. Similarly, Mencius speaks of "pursuing things outside of ourselves" (7A3). By forgetting them all, the mind can be still and at peace, and from there we can strive to attain oneness with Dao. Zhuangzi says, "Instead of praising Yao and condemning Jie, it would be better to forget both of them and transform yourself in Dao" (ch. 6); "Forget the years; forget distinctions: leap into the boundless and make it your home!" (ch. 2). "They borrow the forms of different creatures and house them in the same body. They forget liver and gall, cast aside ears and eyes" (ch. 6).

The second major aspect of forgetting appears in the specific practice of "sitting in oblivion," where one sits down and forgets everything—body and limbs, perception and intellect—to merge with great pervasion (ch. 6). In this state all efforts at self-cultivation have been given up and no-self has been reached. In no-self, we are one with the world and attain great pervasion, open to all and fully in a place of non-dependence. Thus, by forgetting we reach the realm of free and easy wandering and can "forget each other in the rivers and lakes" (ch. 6) in a state of complete spontaneous self-realization.

Appendix Two

The Recluse Phenomenon[1]

When we speak of recluses today, we think of men withdrawing from a vibrant cultural and intellectual environment that actively integrates the three teachings. But this is only one way of being a recluse, quite different from those in earlier days, when life was characterized more by specific teachings such as those prominent in my own student days. Why is that? It is because in those days, the three teachings were not strongly regarded, and our culture was a rather desolate field—not even sporting any basket ball courts! Since then, culture and society have undergone vast changes, and so has the life style of the recluse.

It is well known that ancient China was had strong social stratifications. Among them was a group of men known as knights (*shi*). There were many types of knights, recluses being one, wanderers being another. Wanderers were men who traveled, moving about between different local states to offer their services. Prominent examples include Confucius, Mozi, and more. Then there were warriors, characterized by courage and martial prowess, described by Mencius as "not flinching from any strokes nor looking away from any thrusts" (*Mengzi* 2A2). This sounds frightful, a state we cannot reach unless we close our eyes firmly, something these warriors must never do. Beyond that, knights also included odd fellows, strategists, moral paragons, and others, each with their own unique lifestyle, which in turn depended on a particular worldview or "philosophy." To discuss the lifestyle and philosophy of seclusion, then, we must first ask: "What is a recluse?" Then: "How do recluses live?" and "Why do they live like this?" Such are the perimeters of our discussion today.

Let us begin with the first question. The word for recluse in Chinese is *yinshi* 隐士, combining the two words "hide" and "knight." A recluse is thus a hidden knight, and inevitably a man. Women could not be recluses, and there is not a single female recluse in Chinese history—mainly because women were already secluded in traditional society and had no opportunity to go out and leave it.

[1] Paper presented at Peking University in 2002.

Another group of people that needs to be exempted are men who are not "knights" in the proper sense of the term. Knights, that is to say, include two kinds of men: warriors and eminent men. Warriors are the more original type: the word *shi* originally indicates a weapon, and martial prowess formed a strong part of traditional culture as seen, for example, in Japanese *bushidō*. Eminent men come second, but are no less important; they can be learned intellectuals or moral paragons. In addition to women, then, men who are neither warriors nor eminent have no recluse potential. Even with potential, moreover, not all of them elect to live a life of seclusion but, as noted earlier, make all kinds of different choices on how to live—wandering, preaching, etc.

Recluses are thus a special kind of men, those that pursue a lifestyle of hiding. Why do they hide? Most commonly, going into hiding indicates the desire for concealment, secrecy, or escape. To round out our basic definition, then, recluses generally are warriors or moral paragons who wish to conceal themselves; more specifically, they are escaping from something. But this alone does not provide a firm standard, since in some cases people go into hiding for a period because they owe money or clear out temporarily because they got into a fight with their neighbor. None of these are properly speaking recluses. They hide but in order to achieve a worldly goal, which leads us to the observation that proper recluses go into concealment for a lofty, superior purpose.

Underlying this trend is a universal human tendency toward concealment. All children—no matter from what country, historical period, or culture—play Hide and Seek, and I'm sure we all have done so. What is the attraction? I'm not sure, but it obviously reflects some deep, inborn urge or, in more philosophical, metaphysical terms, a latent desire. Not everyone can fulfill this desire in their adult life, but it still forms the backdrop of the recluse phenomenon.

The earliest known recluses in China go back to the Shang and Zhou dynasties. As described in the biographical section of the *Shiji* (ch. 61), the most prominent among them were Boyi and Shuqi. Who were they and what made them go into seclusion? Sons of the Duke of Guzhu 孤竹, Boyi was the oldest and Shuqi the third. They were of similar minds and temperaments and quite different from the middle brother. Their father, seeing their characters, decided to make Shuqi his heir, which went against the social standard of inheritance by primogeniture. After the father's death, Shuqi refused the throne, ceding it to Boyi, who in turn refused to accept it. While they kept offering it to each other, the state remained in administrative limbo. Finally the middle brother put his foot down and took over the government. "When the snipe and the mussel grip each other, the fishermen gets the profit," as the *Shiji* puts it. In the event, Boyi and Shuqi elected to leave the duchy altogether.

The story makes it clear that the brothers faced a moral dilemma and were ensconced in two conflicts. For one, there was the conflict between their father's will and the established rules of inheritance, which in turn led to the conflict between them—each offering the other the throne—and caused them to seek resolution by leaving. Both were exceedingly moral people, and their ethical convictions propelled them to depart. When they first left, they hoped to find a happier place, but the land at the time was ruled by King Wen of the Western Zhou. While they were on the road, King Wen died and his son, King Wu, succeeded him. Without even completing the burial formalities for his father, he raised an army and went to attack the Shang tyrant Zhou.

This behavior made Boyi and Shuqi despair. They had left home in the hope of finding a moral stronghold, but reality turned out different. It presented yet another moral dilemma, manifest in the destruction of social order as symbolized by the proper relation between ruler and vassal. As far as they were concerned, King Wu was a vassal of the Shang and by raising arms against the tyrant Zhou, he was breaking his vow of loyalty, causing the downfall of the political order. At the same time, since he moved into battle before completing the burial rites for his father, he behaved without proper filial piety. Lacking both loyalty and filial piety, in the thinking of Boyi and Shuqi, he could not possibly provide a morally sane place to live. The despair they experienced at this point was even more poignant than when they decided to leave their original home. It led them to make a yet different choice: to leave the world altogether. As Confucius describes the different kinds of escape, "Some worthy men leave the world altogether, others retreat from particular areas; some escape because of disrespectful looks, others leave due to contradictory language" (*Lunyu* 14.37).

The initial urge of Boyi and Shuqi was just one of getting away from a bad situation. It was like me having an enemy and leaving Beijing for Shanghai, or like the medieval poet Xi Kang 嵇康 (223-262) moving to north China to avoid his foes. Boyi and Shuqi similarly left their home duchy to seek refuge in the Western Zhou kingdom. But then they discovered that this place was not acceptable either and they fell into moral and ethical despair, losing all faith in the political order. From this extreme disappointment, they then made a yet different choice: to leave the world.

But where to go? If we don't like the three teachings and want to get totally away from people, we naturally go into remote wilderness such as, for example, the mountain ranges north of Beijing. We climb one or the other peak or enter a forest so deep that we don't encounter any more people. Naturally, to do so we don't have to become mountain climbers. Rather, we look for a place that is far away yet still somewhat accessible. In all cases, this kind of refuge would most likely consist of "mountains and forests." When leaving the world, this is our first choice—a place without people, social structure, and political conflict.

Historically this idea is also reflected in the *Yijing*, whose Hexagram 33 is called Dun 遯 (Retreat) (Wilhelm 1950, 129). It consists of the two trigrams Qian 乾 (Heaven) over Gen 艮 (Mountain)—showing just how perceptive its compilers were in seeing mountains as connecting to Heaven while offering people a place of refuge. The *Yijing* was compiled in the Western Zhou period, when many people became hermits, Boyi and Shuqi being the best known among them. At this time of massive change, living in the mountains was significantly different from life in the villages, reflecting the option of either working with or being separate from the laboring masses.

Still, these early recluses were not trying to get away from people but from the political and (im)moral order of the day. For Boyi and Shuqi, this means that they wanted to get away from ordinary society, political power, and moral iniquity. They thought of themselves as being seriously different from society, a difference best characterized by the contrast between purity and pollution, flowing and brackish water. Thus the *Mengzi* describes them as "the purest of sages" (5B10). Purity is the opposite of pollution, and those ancient recluses not only thought of the world as mired in filth but feared that they would be tainted by and submerged in it. Thus they decided to get away. Highly aware of the distinction, they found that the world with its pollution was not at all a suitable place for them to live and set out to find a location of higher purity.

Seeing their situation from this angle, it is easy to imagine the bone-deep sense of isolation and abandonment they must have felt. In contrast to most people who still lived in the ordinary world and labored under the illusion of a functioning moral and political order, they must have felt massively disjointed. From their abandonment, they then set out to find a like-minded community, and when there was none, they retreated to the mountains.

Sima Qian records a song they composed (*Shiji* 61). It begins, "Climbing West Mountain, pulling out ferns," indicating that Mount Shouyang 首陽山 where they retired did not grow grain, so they had to live on grasses and ferns. The next line is, "Trying to fight violence with violence, and not realizing this is wrong," referring to King Wu's attack on the tyrant Zhou. The latter is obviously a violent ruler; however, using violence to vanquish him only generates more violence and is fundamentally and morally wrong. King Wu does not think of it that way. He commits two faults: using force and attacking his liege lord. "Shennong, Shun, and Yu all gone—where can we find a true home?" This refers to sage rulers of past dynasties who are no longer there, leaving the brothers with no place to go.

The song reflects as much a profound despair of the world as an intense longing for a home—not a physical home but a safe place of the mind, a soft place to fall, a community of shared values and concepts. Boyi and Shuqi were unable to find that and elected to retreat to the mountains and live on grasses and ferns. In the end, they died from starvation and became famous. Of course, had they been unable to hold out to the very end and left their aerie for material sustenance, they would never have reached such a high profile in later generations.

Even though, there were quite a few people over the course of history who did not find their behavior praiseworthy, criticizing it from various angles. For example, some said that they acted purely for vainglory, disregarding their own life and setting a bad example for others. Be that as it may, the story provides some fundamental insights into the recluse phenomenon. For one, recluses are people who go into seclusion as a form of escape from this world. For another, they do so not just because of pettiness or annoyance, but for some deep fundamental reason that has to do with their particular ethical value system and the political order of the time. This holds true for recluses of all kinds and historical periods, from the times of Zhuangzi and Confucius through the Han dynasty and into the Wei-Jin, which saw famous figures such as Xi Kang and Ruan Ji 阮籍 (210-263), even Guo Xiang and Tao Yuanming, who elected to leave the world and return to their estates rather than serve a corrupt government.

Another point Boyi and Shuqi's fate makes clear is that ultimate starvation is not part of the recluse ideal. Human beings are instinctually set up to cling to life and most people, including most recluses, have no desire to die. They thus need to find an alternative lifestyle that allows them to survive. How to do that? The mountains offer only minimal support in terms of sustenance, and so recluses have gradually come to give up on them and find other ways of seclusion. Just like Boyi and Shuqi, though, this created a another dilemma for them: still somewhat connected to human society, they would refuse to serve, failing in their duty toward family and state—just as Shuqi refused to honor his father's will and thus failed to meet these two obligations of traditional society.

The *Lunyu* records Confucius's encounter with a recluse and his rather negative response toward him. Now, we know that Confucius traveled far and wide among the various states, hoping to interest any local ruler in his political concepts, but was never employed and kept wandering, agitated like a dog that has lost his master. In many ways he is in no position to criticize the recluse, but his disciple Zilu, a man of great courage, speaks up, telling his family: "Not to serve in office is failing righteousness. The family relations between old and young must not be neglected. How could one ever abandon the duties between ruler and minister? Wishing to maintain personal purity, you let more important relationships disintegrate" (18.7).

That is to say, rather than standing up for a better moral order, by his refusal to serve the recluse causes social harmony to disintegrate. He places his personal convictions and feelings, his rejection of the world's pollution, before the key relationships that provide the foundation of all society and, in doing so, actually causes harm. The "more important relationships" he lets disintegrate are, especially in traditional China, the relationship between individuals and family members, but most importantly, the connection between ruler and subject. We can see here how this would be a serious question for anyone choosing to follow the path of Boyi and Shuqi. As we noted earlier, they face two dilemmas: their particular ethical position plus their mode of subsistence—and have to find a resolution for both.

In comes a third person, a different kind of recluse, and that is Zhuangzi. Deeply aware of the fundamental recluse dilemma, he proposes a resolution by establishing core values that anyone must honor—be they wanderers, conventional ethicists, or recluses. These values center on personal relationships and social duties. "There are two great containing forces in the world: fate and duty" (ch. 4).

What, then, is fate? "The love of a child for the parents is fate; it can never be extirpated from the heart." That is to say, a child's love is a natural bond that can never be dissolved or avoided. What is duty? "The obedience of a citizen to his country is duty; wherever you go there is always a ruler." This means, no matter how far you remove yourself, there is always some political and social structure: "Anywhere under Heaven, all is land governed by a ruler; even at the farthest shores of the Earth, you will always be subject to a ruler." So, even if you escape to the height of Mount Shouyang, you are still under the jurisdiction of the Western Zhou, still subject to the king's rule: "You cannot get away from it anywhere between Heaven and Earth" (ch. 4).

Zhuangzi is very clear on this point. You may want to escape, you may even take measures to get away—but no matter how far you run, as long as you live on this earth, you cannot possibly escape the two fundamental relationships. By insisting on the need to honor these, Zhuangzi provides would-be recluses with a new, different and alternative lifestyle—a way of life that no longer necessitates flight into the mountains. Instead, you can fulfill your purpose here and now, go into "inner emigration" and live as a recluse within society. This also resolves the issue of subsistence. Living in society, you can do some basic work to provide for yourself, avoiding illness and starvation. Still, most recluses left the world not for some self-realization or love of nature, but for very real threats posed by people, society, and government—in other words, manmade situations that put life and limb in jeopardy.

For example, the *Zhanguoce* mentions the younger brother of the ruler of Qi, whom many think of as a proto-Daoist (Qi, 1; trl. Crump 1970). His name, as supplied in the *Xunzi* (6.3; trl. Knoblock 1988), was Chen Zhong 陳仲, *chen* meaning "field" and replacing Tian 田 (field), the family name of the Qi rulers. Chen Zhong was a recluse along the lines of Boyi and Shuqi who wanted to live in the mountains, but in the end both his personal situation and Warring States politics interfered. At the time, many people wanted to get away; having heard of him, they all tried to follow him into seclusion. We can just about imagine the situation: large numbers of people with no love for political power and no joy in the world, giving up on government, stepping on each other's heels as they crowd the trails into the wilderness.

As the Legalist Han Feizi says, criticizing the Confucians: if all started living according to the Confucian moral code and it became state doctrine, all would have to give up on this world of corruption and nobody would be left to govern. The same holds true for the ideal of filial piety: if everyone decided to be a filial son, "the parents are there, no need to go far," just stay with the family (47.6). But if the child dies or leaves due to high moral sentiments, what are they to do? And if all did so, who would still support the family? Han Fei, in his exposition to a Confucius-loving ruler, makes it very clear that these ideals are useless—and even harmful—to self and society. These early recluses, although praised by Confucians, were in fact detrimental to social order and political power. Why? Because they set up a model of keeping distance to government and pointed the way toward escape from society.

Later on, the same holds true for Buddhism. Its advocacy of the monastic life meant that its followers would not reproduce, work, or fight battles—doing harm to political and social functioning. Rulers thus found them useless. As a woman asks Chen Zhong's brother, the Qi ruler: Why not kill him? What good does he do? This means, recluses in highly unstable times who leave in large numbers face a direct threat to life and limb.

But there is yet another issue. Although wanting to get away and go into hiding, by establishing a formal way of confronting the world and increasing in numbers, these recluses become highly visible and even prominent, establishing a position that becomes socially relevant in a new way. They also begin to live in semi-worldly ways, judging each other according to levels of seclusion, establishing power structures within their groups while pursuing fame and accomplishments, profit and wealth. All highly special and uniquely gifted people, they start out by wanting to live in seclusion but then rise to prominence, at times even become government officials. Lonely stars of purity in an ocean of corruption, they hinder the majority and are soon subject to persecution. Their prominence thus creates a new level of social instability and personal insecurity, making their existential dilemma even more obvious. Zhuangzi, very much aware of this situation, accordingly insists on the fulfillment of fate and duty and proposes a new model: be a recluse in the world.

Zhuangzi himself was a sort of recluse, rejecting the King Wei's offer of employment. Like the early recluses, he saw a clear delimitation between purity and pollution, continuous from antiquity into his own times, yet opened up a different resolution by suggesting varied ways of living in seclusion. He thus developed a new model: live physically in the world yet remain detached from society. To do so, radically divide body from mind.

All people have body and mind: different and each with their particular requirements, they metaphysically belong to the spheres of Heaven and Earth, opening different venues for living in seclusion. The life of Boyi and Shuqi was body based: they physically removed themselves from society and eliminated all human contact, sort of like playing Hide and Seek with the world. Zhuangzi, recognizing the problems with that, proposed a mind-based form of seclusion. In other words, the body stays openly visible within society and interacts with people on a daily basis, but the mind is special: different from others and detached from the world.

This, however, brings up yet another question. As you live in the world while maintaining a position of detachment, how exactly do you relate to ordinary morality, political power, social values, and the like? Yes, you may be able to maintain a unique attitude in your mind, but how does that translate into concrete, physical behavior? Even in mind-based seclusion you make demands on your body, possibly of reticence and withdrawal but certainly of purity versus pollution, lest you be tainted by the corruption of the world. Beyond this, there is also the issue of your physical needs within society that necessitate a certain degree of interaction and cooperation with others.

This has two dimensions: the physical upkeep of the body and the demand for socially acceptable behavior—you have to find some sort of balance between the two. How does Zhuangzi deal with this? He proposes a state of oblivion toward the body combined with a letting-go of personal needs. He says, "In the body it is best to go along." That is, we should match the dominant circumstances and do whatever society may require, but not all the way. "Go along but don't get involved." Going along is not the same thing as getting involved, which indicates the full immersion of the body in the world, which would be the opposite of seclusion. Going along thus means finding a middle path between escape and involvement, a balance between detachment and connection.

Zhuangzi then advances many reasons why this balance offers the perfect lifestyle while arguing that physical forms are particularly unsuited to create ultimate guidelines. For example, he discusses their differences in terms of size, noting that Mount Tai is huge and an autumn hair is tiny, then says, "There is nothing bigger than an autumn hair, and Mount Tai is small" (ch. 2)—creating the basis for a life in complete oblivion of emotions and value judgments. Still, this life requires the maintenance of the body since, as long as one is in this world, certain things must be honored. At the very least, one must prevent the body from coming to grief. This, of course, resolves to a certain degree the question Zhuangzi received from the early recluses, allowing him to offer some form of a resolution.

Zhuangzi's personal pursuit of seclusion, then, is a form of inner emigration and occurs predominantly in the mind. He hopes to achieve a way of life where the mind is free and autonomous in a state of non-dependence. Without hiding from the world, it remains separate from society. Zhuangzi discusses the mind frequently, insisting that it can reach non-dependence while the body cannot, being more of a passive, receiving factor. The mind can be cultivated and refined, raised to a higher state, far removed from ordinary people and worldly thinking. With his vision of mind-based seclusion, Zhuangzi therefore creates a new model of eremitism, expressed best with the phrase "floating on dry land."

The expression is familiar today from the time of the Japanese invasion, when people spoke of the "sacred homeland floating away." Zhuangzi means something different, "dry land" indicating life among ordinary people, the concrete existence of the body, while "floating" refers to a particular mental state. Since body and mind are different, the two don't have to be in the same place. While the body stays within the world, the mind can take off into a different sphere, rising up into Heaven. That is to say, when Zhuangzi speaks of "floating," he means a form of ascension, symbolized by the big Peng bird spreading his wings and rising up 90,000 miles.

Not only central in Zhuangzi, this also had a major impact on the later tradition. In the middle ages, numerous recluses took their clues from Zhuangzi's thought and lifestyle, using them as the foundation for their own particular way while also moving on one more step metaphysically. In this additional step, they did away even with Zhuangzi's delimitation between seclusion and the ordinary world, dissolving his radical division between simple living and political power. This delimitation is common to all recluses and always expressed as the contrast between purity and pollution—however, different recluses draw the dividing line differently.

Thus, Boyi and Shuqi saw the core division between themselves and all ordinary society, and accordingly removed themselves physically from it. Zhuangzi saw it between simple living and political power, allowing him to live in the world while staying away from government. The first removes recluses from people; the second separates them from power. Zhuangzi insisted on an absolute separation from political power, creating a good, solid foundation for simple living. Taking his model to its logical conclusion, however, and following his particular choice of inner emigration or mind-based seclusion, we have to make sure the mind remains detached and solitary, so that when we allow the body to relax, anything it does stays secondary to the mind. If we now take this yet another step further, why in the world would we be content to just live among the common people and not engage in social activities?

Later recluses faced this question squarely and saw no reason why they shouldn't. Doing away with Zhuangzi's delimitation, they began to serve in the imperial administration. A good example is the well-known figure Dongfang Shuo 東方朔 who lived under Emperor Wu of the Han and has a biography in the *Shiji* (ch. 126). He was very talented, excelled at writing, and authored many books, which he took to present to the emperor. At the time books consisted of bundles of bamboo slips or stacks of rolled-up silk, and it took several porters to transport all Dongfang's works to the palace. The emperor read through them over a few days, liked what he saw, and offered him official appointment.

He accepted it, but lived a unique lifestyle, reflecting his essential nature as a recluse. For instance, the emperor would invite him to banquets and feast him with wine and meat. After eating his fill, Dongfang Shuo would fold the left-overs into his gown, causing it to get oily all over, which was not seemly at all. Despite recriminations from other officials, he continued stubbornly to march to his own drummer—to the emperor's delight. Another example is his family morals. He would take a new wife almost every year, sending the previous one back to her family. After a while, he ran out of money for this, but the emperor stepped into the breach and provided him with the necessary funds.

Dongfang Shuo, drinking heavily and breaking into song at odd moments, was to all intents and purposes crazy—not unlike Jie Yu mentioned in both the *Lunyu* (18.5) and the *Zhuangzi* (ch. 4). Later recluses similarly tended to exhibit eccentric characteristics and behave in crazy ways, establishing a connection between seclusion and being weird. Where earlier recluses eschewed all society, however, they just gave up on its niceties, separating themselves intentionally from official court behavior.

Dongfang Shuo of the Han marks a major shift in traditional Chinese recluse culture, away from the seclusion of the mountains and toward living in society and even at the imperial court, in the center of political power. Like Zhuangzi, he "floated on dry land while joining ordinary society, avoided the world while entering the palace gates." Being able to maintain an attitude of seclusion at court, why would he even think of moving into the mountains and live in a thatched hut? Going beyond Zhuangzi, he represents a third type of recluse with yet a different rationale. Unlike Zhuangzi, who was a philosopher with a focus on ideas and a quiet scholarly lifestyle, Dongfang Shuo was expansive and radical, maintaining his personal uniqueness in the midst of officialdom and opening the sphere of potential seclusion to include all dimensions of the world.

Each age and culture has its own particular values and ideals; each individual has what he or she desires most. By the same token, recluses over history have developed several visions of who they would like to be. In the early stages, this involved living secluded in the mountains, that is, in a rather small and narrow space. Later this space expanded, to include first ordinary society and then the imperial court. This means, recluses were able to experience all kinds of worldly joys while yet maintaining their mind in aloneness and living in spiritual seclusion.

The same overall development also occurred in Chinese Buddhism. In the early middle ages, monks would retire into the mountains for personal cultivation, but by the time the Chan school came along in the 6th century, there was no need for this anymore and it was thought possible to practice within ordinary society. "Carrying water and chopping wood are all activities of Dao." No matter where one is or what one does, one can be in seclusion, even in the center of political power. Both the greater development of history and the unfolding of the individual share this progress, so that Dongfang Shuo, followed by many later intellectuals, embraced this third model of seclusion, choosing and enjoying a unique lifestyle on the border between withdrawal and involvement.

This is especially evident in the Wei-Jin period, when quite a few aristocrats made similar choices, notably Ruan Ji and Xi Kang and other members of the Seven Worthies of the Bamboo Grove. Ruan Ji, for example, was very fond of drinking, but would turn maudlin and depressed under the influence. Still, he kept on drinking, because it provided relief to this spirit and let him escape from this world for a while. He also served in government and held a minor post, changing places as the dynasties unfolded. How is he a recluse? Well, he exhibited a unique and rather eccentric lifestyle and his writings reveal his inner world, plus he was just as crazy as Dongfang Shuo and other people of his type.

Ruan Ji lived just as he liked, not letting anything interfere. For example, when his mother died, he was engaged in a game of chess and, upon hearing the news, insisted on completing the game. Throughout the mourning period, he still continued to drink and have fun—a behavior many people thought highly inappropriate. This is one way in which his craziness showed up, the physical directly reflecting his inner mental state. Like Dongfang Shuo and unlike most people of his time, he expressed his mind clearly in the interaction with others.

Another important figure of the period was Guo Xiang who also showed similar inclinations toward seclusion. Best known for his *Zhuangzi* commentary, he successfully combines the text's presentation of a reclusive lifestyle with official service, eliminating borders still present in the original. As he says, it makes no difference whether you live in the mountains or in the palace: you can take refuge or face dangers in either. A famous dictum of his is, "While sitting quietly and silently, even in the midst of government, the sage's mind mysteriously identifies with all even beyond the four seas" (DZ 745, 1.30). That is to say, he can be at ease no matter what. Guo Xiang thus does away with the delimitation between wilderness and society, solitariness and involvement, moving significantly beyond Zhuangzi. So, how did he himself live? He was somewhere between the second and third type of recluse, solidly based in the division between body and mind. Serving as an official, his body was in one place; writing scholarly exegeses and liberating his thinking, his mind was in another. But he did not give expression to eccentricities like Dongfang Shuo or Ruan Ji.

We have thus three different models of the reclusive life that each come with particular motivations and worldviews. Why would one choose one over the other? They are different in how they evaluate the self and deal with body and mind. To some degree, they all begin with a feeling of isolation and social alienation, recognizing the fact that living in this body and in this world imposes clear limitations and requires major choices. One has to accept these limitations and work with them. For example, one is born male and can never at the same time be female. This is one way in which we are limited by the body. Another is that we are entirely unique in ourselves and can never be, or even fully feel like, anyone else. The mind is not subject to the same restrictions—we can overcome its distinctions and limitations.

Recluses in general criticize and reject the dominant cultural values of their time, its moral shortcomings, political power structure, and debased thinking. Aimed at a particular concrete situation or social pattern, this rejection can become the direct reason for going into seclusion. But this is fairly superficial. On a deeper level, the ultimate cause of the recluse phenomenon is an inner quest that comes from the very depth of the person, a profound desire for seclusion.

This urge toward seclusion does not mean one cannot have other goals, such as accomplishments and productivity in the world, acclaim and valor in the military, high rank and honor in civil society, excellence and recognition in academia, and so on. But beyond all these, and more than anything, these people have an urge toward seclusion—however differently they may express it. This urge we can all sympathize with to a certain degree: there are inevitably times when we all get tired of the busy life and want to retreat to a quiet place, times when we just want to be left alone, want to play Hide and Seek like little kids. To me, this urge is built fundamentally into the human being, a trait strongly activated as and when we pursue it.

Seen from this perspective, recluses are really not all that different from us—they just openly manifest a part we all share. In certain periods of history, many elected life in seclusion; in others, there were hardly any, and most people dedicated themselves to the public good or pursued artistic ideals. Even when most people stayed within society, the inner urge toward seclusion was still there and found some expression. Whenever the urge superseded all other desires in a significant number of people, a strong culture of seclusion arose.

Recluses of the second and third types are significantly different from those of the first in that they remain within society and can thus raise the awareness of the majority, opening up questions of how best to live. Boyi and Shuqi held on tight to their ideals and forfeited their life; later recluses held on to their lives and created new options of living. Thus Ruan Ji expanded much effort and strength in coming to terms with the world. He didn't really manage to do so and was often in agony, as can be seen from his poems. His primary goal was to keep himself alive, but within that framework he had the power to actively choose, and dedicate himself fully to, a recluse lifestyle while yet retaining office. Xi Kang, on the other hand, elected not to serve in office, drawing a very clear line between himself and political power; then, however, he ran into direct conflict with the establishment and lost his life.

For recluses after Zhuangzi, life and seclusion were equally important, forming central facets of their worldview. This is quite obvious in the poetry of Tao Yuanming. To alleviate his debilitating poverty and support his family, he agreed to serve in office, obviously feeling that he had no choice. He says that he didn't want to bow down for a measly five pecks of rice, but found himself caught between the need for the rice and the obligation to bow. In the end, he left officialdom again and, as is made clear in his *Guiqulai ci*, was split between his concern for personal survival and his desire for inner peace and freedom—once more exemplifying the conflict at the core of the recluse phenomenon.

Bibliography

Chang, Leo S., and Yu Feng. 1998. *The Four Political Treatises of the Yellow Emperor: Original Mawangdui Texts with Complete English Translation and an Introduction*. Honolulu: University of Hawaii Press.

Cui Dahua 崔大華. 1996. *Zhuangxue yanjiu* 莊學研究. Beijing: Renmin chubanshe.

Crump, James I. 1970. *Chan-Kuo Ts'e*. Oxford: Clarendon Press.

Dong Zhi'an 董治安. 1994. *Hanfu zhong suojian Lao Zhuang shiliao shulue* 汉赋中所见老庄史料述略. Shanghai: Shanghai Guji chubanshe

Fung Yulan 冯友兰. 1988. *Zhongguo zhexue shi* 中国哲学史. In *Sansong tang quanji* 三松堂全集, vol. 2. Zhengzhou: Henan renmin chubanshe.

_____. 1952. *A History of Chinese Philosophy*. Translated by Derk Bodde. 2 vols. Princeton, Princeton University Press.

Graham, A. C. 1981. *Chuang-tzu: The Seven Inner Chapters and Other Writings from the Book of Chuang-tzu*. London: Allan & Unwin.

Guo Qingfan 郭庆藩. 1982. *Zhuangzi jishi* 庄子集释. Beijing: Zhonghua shuju.

Hanshan Deqing 憨山德清. 1956. *Zhuangzi neipian Hanshan zhu* 莊子内篇憨山注. Taipei: Jiankang shuju.

Johnston, Ian. 2010. *The Mozi: A Complete Translation*. New York: Columbia University Press.

Knaul, Livia. 1982. "Lost *Chuang-tzu* Passages." *Journal of Chinese Religions* 10:53-79.

Knoblock, John. 1988a. *Xunzi: A Translation and Study of the Complete Works, Books 1-6*. Vol. 1. Stanford: Stanford University Press.

_____. 1988b. *Xunzi: A Translation and Study of the Complete Works, Books* 7-16. Vol. 2. Stanford: Stanford University Press.

_____. 1994. *Xunzi: A Translation and Study of the Complete Works, Books 17-32*. Vol. 3. Stanford: Stanford University Press.

_____, and Jeffrey Riegel. 2000. *The Annals of Lü Buwei*. Stanford: Stanford University Press.

Lau, D. C. 1984. *Mencius*. Hong Kong: Chinese University Press.

_____. 2003 [1979]. *The Analects by Confucius*. London: Penguin.

Legge, James. 1960. *The Ch'un ts'eu, with the Tso chue*. Hong Kong: Hong Kong University Press.

Liebenthal, Walter. 1948. *The Book of Chao*. Peking: The Catholic University Press.

Liu, Xiaogan 劉笑敢. 1987. *Zhuangzi zhexue ju qi yanbian* 莊子哲学及其演变. Beijing: Zhongguo shehui kexue chubanshe.

_____. 1994. *Classifying the Zhuangzi Chapters*. Translated by William E. Savage. Ann Arbor: University of Michigan, Center for Chinese Studies.

Mair, Victor H. 1994. *Wandering on the Way: Early Taoist Tales and Parables of Chuang Tzu*. New York: Bantam.

Major, John S., Sarah A. Queen, Andrew S. Meyer, and Harold D. Roth. 2010. *The Huainanzi: A Guide to the Theory and Practice of Government in Early Han China*. New York: Columbia University Press.

Mathieu, Remi. 1983. *Etude sur la mythologie et l'ethnologie de la Chine ancienne*. 2 vols. Paris: Collège du France.

Perkins, Franklin. 2010. "Recontextualizing *Xing*: Self-Cultivation and Human Nature in the Guodian Texts." *Journal of Chinese Philosophy* 37.1:16-32.

Pound, Ezra. 1954. *The Confucian Odes*. Cambridge, Mass: Harvard University Press.

Rickett, W. Allyn. 1985. *Kuan-tzu: Political, Economic, and Philosophical Essays from China*. Vol. 1. Princeton: Princeton University Press.

_____. 1998. *Guanzi: Political, Economic, and Philosophical Essays from Early China*. Vol. 2. Princeton: Princeton University Press.

Ryden, Edmund. 1997. *The Yellow Emperor's Four Classics: A Literary Study and Edition of the Texts from Mawangdui*. Shanghai: Guangqi chubanshe.

Tang, Yijie. 2003. "Emotion in Pre-Qin Ruist Moral Theory: Dao Begins in *Qing*." Translated by Brian Bruya and Wen Haiming. *Philosophy East & West* 53.2:271-81.

Thompson, Paul. 1979. *The Shen Tzu Fragments*. New York: Oxford University Press.

Wang, Bo 王博. 2001. "Lun 'Lunyu de bianzuan" 論論語的編纂. In *Jianbo sixiang wenxian lunji* 簡帛思想文獻論集, 299-337. Taipei: Taiwan guji chubanshe.

_____. 2007a. "Ch. 9: Zhuangzi and the Seven Inner Chapters." Translated by William Crawford. *Contemporary Chinese Thought* 38.2:9-18.

_____. 2007b. "Preface: The World of Zhuangzi's Thought." Translated by William Crawford. *Contemporary Chinese Thought* 38.2:19-36.

_____. 2007c. "Ch. 2: This Human World." Translated by William Crawford. *Contemporary Chinese Thought* 38.2:37-69.

_____. 2007d. "Ch. 5: A Discussion of the Equality of Things." Translated by William Crawford. *Contemporary Chinese Thought* 38.2:70-96.

Wang Fuzhi 王夫之. 1985. *Zhuangzi jie* 庄子解. Beijing: Zhonghua shuju.

Watson, Burton. 1968. *The Complete Works of Chuang-tzu*. New York: Columbia University Press.

Wilhelm, Richard. 1950. *The I Ching or Book of Changes*. Translated by Cary F. Baynes. Princeton: Princeton University Press, Bollingen Series XIX.

Xiong Tieji 熊鐵基, et al. 2003. *Zhongguo Zhuangxue shi* 中國莊學史. Changsha: Hunan renmin chubanshe.

Yan Lingfeng 嚴靈峰. 1972. *Wuqiu beizhai Zhuangzi jicheng chubian* 無求備齋莊子集成初編. Taipei: Yiwen chubanshe.

Yates, Robin. 1997. *Five Lost Classics: Tao, Huang-Lao, and Yin-Yang in Han China*. New York: Ballentine.

Zhang Dainian 张岱年. 1996. *Zhongguo gudian zhexue gainian fantao yaolun* 中国古典哲学概念范畴要论. In *Zhang Danian quanji* 张岱年全集, vol. 4. Shijiazhuang: Hebei renmin chubanshe.

_____. 2002. *Key Concepts in Chinese Philosophy*. New Haven, Conn.: Yale University Press.

Ziporyn, Brook. 2009. *Zhuangzi: The Essential Writings with Selections from Traditional Commentaries*. Indianapolis: Hackett Publishing.

Index